Guillotine E3 (page 91) - James McHaffie  Henry Iddon

FRCC CLIMBING GUIDES

# Borrowdale

FRCC
GUIDES

Seathwaite from Grains Gill  📷 Richard Tolley

# Contents

Borrowdale from Raven Crag  Richard Tolley

Raindrop E1 (page 116) Ron Kenyon  Richard Tolley

## FRCC GUIDES

The Fell & Rock Climbing Club is the premier rock climbing and mountaineering club in the English Lake District. The Club was formed in 1906 and now has over 1200 members worldwide, all of whom have an affinity with the fells and crags of the Lake District. The Club is open to any active climber, mountaineer or fell walker with a keen interest in its objects – climbing and walking in the mountains and enjoying the company of fellow members. Our members have the use of 7 huts and 3 cottages in the Lakes and Scotland and enjoy an interesting and varied meets programme.

The Club has been publishing climbing guides to the Lake District since 1922. These guides are written and published by a committed and enthusiastic team of volunteers. Information about the FRCC and FRCC Guides and an interactive route database can be found on the Club's website at www.frcc.co.uk

An award winning selective guide to the District, **LAKE DISTRICT ROCK**, is published by the FRCC and Wired Guides. www.wired-guides.com

Borrowdale is a beautiful and iconic valley drawing climbers to its crags from the ever popular and accessible Shepherd's Crag to the more remote crags such as Sergeant's Crag Slabs, Allen Crags and Lining Crag. It has a special charm and offers tremendously varied year round climbing, and with one of the best cafes in the Lakes - it has the lot!

Guides to the valley have developed over the years and the team, that have produced this guide, have meticulously visited every crag, checked and re-written text, painstakingly captured photos to illustrate the climbs and imaginatively created the page layouts. The outcome is a tribute to their commitment, energy and enthusiasm. The Club and the climbing community are indebted to them all.

Ron Kenyon
President FRCC May 2016

# Crag Guide

| | Routes | ← VD | S | VS | HVS | E1 | E2 | E3 | E4 | E5 → |
|---|---|---|---|---|---|---|---|---|---|---|
| **Derwentwater** | | | | | | | | | | |
| Lower Falcon Crag | 36 | | | 3 | 3 | 6 | 7 | 7 | 5 | 5 |
| Upper Falcon Crag | 5 | | | | | 1 | | 2 | 2 | |
| Gowder Crag | 4 | | | 2 | 1 | | | 1 | | |
| Shepherd's Crag | 114 | 6 | 8 | 25 | 14 | 21 | 13 | 16 | 2 | 9 |
| Upper Shepherd's Crag | 6 | 6 | | | | | | | | |
| **Watendlath** | | | | | | | | | | |
| Ashness Gill | 1 | 1 | | | | | | | | |
| Reecastle Crag | 30 | | | 1 | 2 | 3 | 4 | 5 | 2 | 13 |
| Reecastle South Crag | 4 | | 1 | | | | 2 | | 1 | |
| Goat Crags | 38 | 2 | 8 | 5 | 4 | 9 | 5 | 2 | 3 | |
| Garotte Buttress | 4 | | | | 2 | 1 | 1 | | | |
| **Grange** | | | | | | | | | | |
| Car Park Crag | 14 | | | 3 | 1 | 3 | 3 | 3 | | 1 |
| Black Crag | 28 | | 1 | 7 | 3 | 5 | 5 | 3 | 4 | |
| Christmas Crag | 26 | 1 | 8 | 9 | 6 | 2 | | | | |
| Greatend Crag | 4 | | | | | 2 | 1 | | 1 | |
| Quayfoot Buttress | 16 | 1 | | 3 | 5 | 3 | 2 | | 1 | 1 |
| Woden's Face | 11 | 1 | 5 | 3 | | | 2 | | | |
| Bowder Crag and Hell's Wall | 29 | 2 | 5 | 4 | 3 | 1 | 3 | 2 | 1 | 8 |
| Dalt Quarry | 26 | 1 | | 10 | 6 | 5 | 2 | | 2 | |
| Castle Crag | 12 | | 1 | 2 | 2 | 6 | | 1 | | |
| Lobstone Buttress | 1 | | 1 | | | | | | | |
| Perched Block Buttress | 6 | | | 1 | | 2 | 1 | 1 | 1 | |
| Steel Knotts Bluff | 5 | 2 | 3 | | | | | | | |
| Steel Knotts | 20 | | | 4 | 5 | 2 | 4 | 3 | 2 | |
| Goat Crag | 27 | | | | 2 | 4 | 4 | 6 | 4 | 7 |
| **Stonethwaite** | | | | | | | | | | |
| Long Band Crag | 10 | | | | | | 1 | | 2 | 7 |
| Lining Crag | 11 | 3 | 2 | 2 | 3 | 1 | | | | |
| Long Crag | 8 | | | 1 | 1 | | | 3 | | 3 |
| Eagle Crag - Lower and Main | 20 | | | | 1 | 3 | 4 | 2 | 4 | 6 |
| Bleak How | 25 | | | 3 | 5 | 7 | 4 | 3 | 1 | 2 |
| Fat Charlie's Buttress | 10 | | 1 | 4 | 1 | 2 | 2 | | | |
| Heron Crags | 18 | | 2 | 1 | 3 | 3 | 8 | | 1 | |
| Sergeant's Crag | 8 | 1 | 3 | | 2 | 2 | | | | |
| Sergeant's Crag Slabs | 14 | | | 1 | 4 | 5 | 2 | 1 | 1 | |
| Blackmoss Pot Slab | 5 | | 1 | | 2 | | 1 | | 1 | |
| Hooker Buttress | 5 | | 2 | 2 | 1 | | | | | |
| Black Wall | 7 | | | | 2 | | 1 | | 2 | 2 |
| Cam Crags | 16 | 1 | | 1 | 2 | | | 3 | 2 | 7 |
| White Crag - Ivy Knott | 3 | | | | 1 | 2 | | | | |
| **Combe Gill** | | | | | | | | | | |
| Glaciated Slab Area | 23 | 8 | 8 | 4 | | | 1 | 1 | | 1 |
| Twa Hummocks Area | 7 | 3 | 4 | | | | | | | |
| Dovenest Crag | 15 | 3 | | 7 | 3 | 2 | | | | |
| Dovenest Slabs | 23 | | 9 | 9 | 5 | | | | | |
| Raven Crag | 34 | 5 | 9 | 11 | 6 | 3 | | | | |
| **Seathwaite** | | | | | | | | | | |
| Hind Crag | 7 | | 3 | 4 | | | | | | |
| Allen Crags Area | 33 | 5 | 9 | 13 | 5 | 1 | | | | |
| Aaron Crags | 2 | | | 1 | 1 | | | | | |
| Taylor Gill Slab | 5 | 3 | 2 | | | | | | | |
| Gillercomb | 19 | 3 | 2 | 4 | 2 | 2 | 1 | 1 | 1 | 3 |
| Seathwaite Slabs | 18 | 16 | 2 | | | | | | | |
| | | ← F3 | F4 | F5 | F6a | F6b | F6c | F7a | F7b | F7c → |

| ⚲ min | 🧭 | ⛰ | | Page | |
|---|---|---|---|---|---|
| 5 | W | 145m | A serious crag peppered with natural features providing exhilarating climbing. | 36 | Derwentwater |
| 15 | W | 190m | Brilliant steep wall climbing: loose rock on lower section and to right. | 46 | Derwentwater |
| 10 | W | 200m | Steep imposing buttress with areas of clean rock but some vegetation and loose rock. | 48 | Derwentwater |
| 5-15 | W | 140m | Wide selection of routes at all grades. Not Shepherd's again - why not! | 50 | Derwentwater |
| 15 | S | 200m | Ideal location to introduce youngsters to climbing. | 83 | Derwentwater |
| 10 | NW | 390m | An interesting and usually wet expedition. | 86 | Watendlath |
| 5 | NW | 300m | One of the best crags for those who climb at E2 and above - immaculate edgy rock. | 87 | Watendlath |
| 10 | SW | 300m | Early sun, small selection of fine routes. | 93 | Watendlath |
| 20 | SW | 400m | Idyllic setting, splendid views to the central Lakes and a selection of good routes. | 94 | Watendlath |
| 10 | E | 260m | Small crag nearest to the hamlet of Watendlath. | 102 | Watendlath |
| 2 | NW | 90m | Very accessible - visible from car park. | 106 | Grange |
| 20 | W - N | 260m | One of the best and most impressive valley crags in the Lake District. | 108 | Grange |
| 30 | W | 340m | Quick drying and in an attractive setting. | 120 | Grange |
| 25 | NW | 225m | Imposing crag - unfortunately returning to nature. | 126 | Grange |
| 5 | WNW | 135m | Very accessible high quality climbing. | 128 | Grange |
| 5 | W | 110m | Very popular with some wear and tear but still quality routes. | 133 | Grange |
| 20 | SW | 220m | Routes of all grades but Hell's Wall is a must for the harder grades. | 136 | Grange |
| 20 | S & N | 120m | Borrowdale's own sports crag - don't get too excited - surprisingly pleasant. | 144 | Grange |
| 20 | W | 200m | On the "jaws" peak - some good interesting routes. | 150 | Grange |
| 40 | E | 280m | Good way to top of Maiden Moor. | 154 | Grange |
| 50 | E | 300m | Large detached slab on the fellside with steep routes. | 155 | Grange |
| 20 | SE | 160m | Delightful slab - great for youngsters. | 158 | Grange |
| 20 | S&E | 240m | Excellent clean rock, dries quickly and good quality climbing. | 159 | Grange |
| 50 | NE | 350m | Special and iconic crag - steep and uncompromising. | 165 | Grange |
| 60 | W | 430m | Impressive crag of superb rock with good sustained routes. | 178 | Stonethwaite |
| 70 | W | 460m | Beautiful setting - this crag deserves more attention. | 180 | Stonethwaite |
| 90 | NW | 600m | Wonderfully remote (and quiet) crag - on very good and compact rock. | 184 | Stonethwaite |
| 45 | ENE/N | 440m | Steep and imposing crags - solitude, adventure and memories guaranteed. | 186 | Stonethwaite |
| 40 | NW | 270m | Justifiably popular crag - beware midges can be a serious problem. | 193 | Stonethwaite |
| 20 | W | 160m | Though short - well worth a visit - excellent rock. | 199 | Stonethwaite |
| 60 | W | 360m | Group of varied crags in a stunning location. | 201 | Stonethwaite |
| 50 | N-W | 400m | Large crag overlooking Langstrath providing long mountaineering outings. | 207 | Stonethwaite |
| 45 | W | 360m | Suberb collection of routes on immaculate rock. | 209 | Stonethwaite |
| 45 | W | 310m | Excellent climbing on solid clean rock. | 214 | Stonethwaite |
| 60 | W | 410m | Small buttress of good rock. | 216 | Stonethwaite |
| 60 | E | 500m | A place for those wishing to escape the crowds. | 217 | Stonethwaite |
| 45 | E | 340m | Immaculate rock with a collection of superb routes and a long classic scramble. | 220 | Stonethwaite |
| 45 | SE | 300m | Some good climbing on west side of Langstrath. | 224 | Stonethwaite |
| 30 | W&SW | 300m | Collection of crags on east side of Combe Gill. | 228 | Combe Gill |
| 40 | W | 360m | Excellent rock in superb mountain setting. | 238 | Combe Gill |
| 50 | W | 475m | Very sunny with an interesting cavern system. | 240 | Combe Gill |
| 65 | SW | 550m | Short routes and excellent rock. | 246 | Combe Gill |
| 50 | NE | 360m | Atmospheric, long, mountaineering climbs with some shorter tasters. | 254 | Combe Gill |
| 45 | W&S | 350-475 | Long mountaineering routes; some recent additions on superb rock. | 269 | Seathwaite |
| 70 - 100 | W | 550-700 | Fair walk but rewarded with some good climbs, tremendous views and no crowds. | 276 | Seathwaite |
| 45 | N&NE | 500m | Accessible with remote feel. | 288 | Seathwaite |
| 45 | NW | 450m | Superb, easy angled climbing - great for beginners. | 289 | Seathwaite |
| 45 - 60 | SE | 480m | "Sunny" mountain crag - excellent climbing on marvellous rock. | 290 | Seathwaite |
| 5 - 30 | S | 150-375 | Delightful slabs and a classic scramble. | 301 | Seathwaite |

# Using this Guide

## Getting Here

Fly:      Liverpool, Manchester, Newcastle, Blackpool and Glasgow - all are about two hours drive.

Rail:      Penrith.

Bus:      Keswick, bus stops outside Booths supermarket.

Moving around: By car, or there is a regular bus.

www.visitcumbria.com/tourist-information-centres
www.lakedistrict.gov.uk/visiting/planyourvisit/

## When to Come

Borrowdale is sheltered and a suitable crag can usually be found, however, in winter it is best to come when it has been dry for a while and dry conditions with sunny afternoons are forecast. www.mwis.org.uk/english-welsh-forecast/LD/ The BBC rain radar is a great source if showers are expected www.bbc.co.uk/weather. Midges can be a nuisance, especially on sheltered crags, from late May to early September. Restrictions for nesting birds apply to some crags between early-February and the end of June; check www.frcc.co.uk/conservation_birdrestrictions.asp

## Maps

BMC/Harveys    1:40,000 Lake District – probably the most useful for climbers

OS Explorer    1:25,000 Sheets OL4 The English Lakes (North West Area)

OS Landranger    1:50,000 Sheet 89

## Accommodation

The valley is popular and Keswick is a tourist honeypot – campsites, B&Bs, hostels and hotels abound. A number of clubs have huts in and around Borrowdale that are available to groups and individual BMC members, check the BMC Hut directory at www.thebmc.co.uk/essential-club-know-how

## Character

Almost all of the routes in the valley are 'trad', with leader placed protection. Many styles of climbing can be found here with an immense variety of rock, steep and overhanging walls, megalithic boulders and long blank padding on immaculate slabs.

## Layout

The valley is divided into six geographical sections. See area map inside cover.

## The Crags

Crag location is indicated by OS grid reference together with aspect of the main faces, altitude and approach time.

**Wall of Cracks**
NY 237 092    🧭    ▲630m    🚶85 mins

## Directions

The terms 'true left' and 'true right' are used to describe the position of a crag in a valley or gill relative to the direction of flow of the stream. The terms 'left' and 'right', unless otherwise stated, mean as the climber faces the climb or the crag.

## Gear

Most of the climbs require the use of leader-placed protection, generally a pair of 50m half-ropes will be adequate and a full traditional rack. If pegs, sky-hooks, 60m ropes or crucial pieces of gear are needed this will normally be mentioned. For bolted climbs take quick-draws.

## Bouldering

A myriad of outcrops and boulders of superb volcanic rock creates numerous opportunities for bouldering enthusiasts, with both valley and mountain settings. Comprehensive information can be found in the Rockfax Lakes Bouldering Guide and on Greg Chapman's website www.lakesbloc.com

## Stars and Quality

The conventional star system indicating the quality of a climb has been adopted with a range extending up to 3 stars. Routes are given no stars if they have limited merit, a route with one star is considered worthwhile. Routes of 2 stars and above can be expected to have good continuously interesting climbing, strength of line, technical or historical merit and be clean. Hollow stars indicate that the route is thought to be of that quality but may be dirty or has had very few recent ascents.

## Aid, Bolts and Fixed Gear

Routes on Lake District mountain crags are bolt free and we should strive to keep it that way. Bolts are accepted on certain quarried crags and a few agreed outcrops. To preserve the crag and the mountain environment, and to maintain the tradition that British climbing in general should continue with the principle of leader-placed

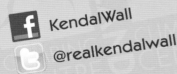

removable protection, the FRCC are in accord with the BMC policy on the use of drilled equipment.

Recent accidents confirm that you should not trust any fixed gear. Fixed gear, including pegs, threads and slings, bolts and wires, may date back to the first ascent. There can be no guarantee that the fixed gear mentioned in the text will still be in place or, more importantly, that it will be of any use. In-situ gear will deteriorate to a fraction of its original strength. This can occur in a matter of months rather than years, particularly wires or hard steel blade pegs. It is for you, the climber, to assess the reliability of any fixed gear you decide to use. Bolts are not infallible and have been known to fail.

Fixed abseil points are indicated and others may be found. If you intend to make use of them, they should be thoroughly inspected and if you are in any doubt you should replace them, or back them up, with new equipment. If you do use an abseil descent please be aware of other climbers below; they don't want your ropes or dislodged stones coming down on them!

The Cumbria Bolt Fund provides funding and training for the replacement of fixed gear. For more information and to support this ongoing work please make donations by visiting www.cumbriaboltfund.com

## Unrepeated Routes

'†' indicates climbs which have not been checked or where some aspect of the description is in doubt. As there will have been little or no comment any stars indicated will be hollow. Feedback on these routes would be appreciated at www.frcc. co.uk/rockclimbing.

## Mixed Climbing of Established Rock Routes

The Lakes has become an important centre for hard mixed climbing. Many fine summer rock climbs have been climbed or attempted in winter conditions. As the number participating is steadily increasing, it was felt that the growing level of activity was unsustainable. To preserve our heritage, leading climbers, both summer rock and winter mixed, have developed an accord that covers the climbing of rock climbs in winter and you should strive to follow the guidance that this gives. Drytooling should only be practised at agreed venues.

www.thebmc.co.uk/lake-district-winter-conditions-guide

## Routes Archive, New Routes and Corrections

Detailed information about the fascinating historical record of climbing in the area will often be available in the searchable detailed First Ascents database, enhanced by pictorial and archive information, which is being developed on the FRCC website. Post your comments, corrections and descriptions on the FRCC website. Several "New Routes books" exist in the area, including the Log Books in FRCC huts. As these may not be checked regularly, you are urged to use the website or your entries may be overlooked.

www.frcc.co.uk/rockclimbing.asp

In their research and checking the authors have encountered countless new routes that have probably received only one or two ascents. Unless they are regularly climbed most routes will revert to their natural pre-cleaned state in one or two seasons. Extensive gardening activity to produce or unearth a route that is unlikely to ever become popular, revert back to nature and remain no more than a record in the FRCC archive is now unacceptable. Rick Graham's maxim 'if it takes longer to clean it than to climb it, then it's not worth doing' is one to which new routers might sensibly adhere, and it is to be hoped they will consider the likely end result of their efforts a little more carefully before reaching for their brushes, saws and secateurs.

It seems that climbers in general are focusing their activities on a relatively small number of routes on the more accessible crags. As a result of this, excellent lines on less popular crags are becoming more vegetated and less attractive. Thanks to the efforts of some selfless individuals a few crags have experienced something of a spring clean recently. If more climbers were prepared to go a little further afield and, in the short term, put up with some less than perfectly clean rock, then maybe some of the classics of the past would regain their former status.

Another trend is for new routes to be squeezed onto already crowded buttresses and for short sections of existing routes to be linked up in new ways to be claimed as first ascents; an inevitable result of people wanting to create something new when there is only a finite amount of rock available. Some of these lines have no real merit as climbs. However, some imaginative, surprisingly good and independent lines have been created and are given deserved credit. Poor or overgrown routes and, in some cases, entire crags have been omitted from this guide and descriptions placed in the archive section of the FRCC website.

## Grades

Trad – The grade is for a ground-up and on-sight ascent with leader-placed protection. Adjectives describe overall difficulty; Difficult, Severe... combined with numbers to indicate the technical difficulty of the hardest sequence of moves, 4c 5a 5b... For the hardest routes >E5 a French grade may be given as well as a British grade, e.g. E6 6c F7c.

Sport - Equipped routes are given French grades.

Bouldering - Font grades.

Routes are generally described and graded with reference to the best style in which they are known to have been climbed.

| UK Adjectival and Technical Grade | French Grade |
|---|---|
| Moderate | 1 |
| Difficult | 2 |
| | 2+ |
| Very Difficult | 3- |
| | 3 |
| Mild Severe Hard | 3+ |
| 4a Mild Very Severe 4c | 4 |
| | 4+ |
| 4a Very Severe 4c | 5 |
| 4c Hard Very Severe 5b | 5+ |
| 5a E1 5c | 6a |
| | 6a+ |
| 5b E2 6a | 6b |
| 5c E3 6a | 6b+ |
| 6a E4 6b | 6c |
| | 6c+ |
| 6a E5 6c | 7a |
| | 7a+ |
| 6b E6 6c | 7b |
| | 7b+ |
| 6c E7 7a | 7c |
| | 7c+ |
| 6c E8 7a | 8a |
| | 8a+ |
| 7a E9 7b | 8b |
| | 8b+ |
| | 8c |
| | 8c+ |

# Access & Conservation

## Bird Restrictions

Bird restrictions are agreed each January with climbers represented by the FRCC and BMC. The agreements are published by late January with updates posted through the spring and early summer and can be found at www.thebmc.co.uk/modules/RAD/ or on the FRCC website www.frcc.co.uk. Many crags contain nesting sites and are protected by law. Crags where there are likely to be restrictions are indicated with this bird icon – 🦅 Not all of the crags are signed and restrictions will normally be lifted if birds are not nesting.

## Abseiling from Trees

Pulling your ropes after abseiling directly from trees damages the bark and eventually the tree will die. In Borrowdale several trees have been lost already from indiscriminate use. There are established abseil points which have fixed gear that protects the trees, please use them. If there is no fixed gear then you should place your own sling around the tree and be prepared to leave it in place.

## Site of Special Scientific Interest (SSSI)

When climbing in the valley you need to be aware that nearly every crag is in a designated SSSI. This means that plants or geology are protected by statute and, if damaged, some type of action may follow, this could take the form of a warning or, in serious or repeated cases, prosecution. Heavy gardening is now frowned upon, and usually illegal. The situation has become awkward with the amount of gardening required to unearth some existing routes raising environmental concerns.

SSSI designation is made by Natural England. Site management resides with the landowner, with DEFRA responsible for enforcement. The map of the sites can be found here – www.magic.gov.uk/MagicMap.aspx

Langstrath 📷 Richard Tolley

## Acknowledgements

To all of the writers and editors of earlier editions of Borrowdale guides, their work exploring and recording the routes in the valley has been the bedrock for this edition. As well as leading the team initially, Peter Latimer scrupulously carried out extensive checking and research for a number of crags. Personal circumstances forced him to reluctantly hand the baton over to me. I now understand what the cryptic smile was about!

One of the main aims of the authors was to produce a guidebook in which as many routes as possible had been checked and descriptions reviewed and rewritten. With so many routes recorded, and despite being rock super-athletes, clearly this task could not be completed by the authors alone! So, thank you to all the climbers who held ropes, led routes or just willingly shared their knowledge of climbs in Borrowdale. Apologies to anyone I have omitted: Dave Absalom, Martin Bennett, Dave Bodecott, Gerald Bonington, Duncan Booth, Geoff Brindle, John Byrne, Chris Campbell, Julie Carter, Barry Clarke, Paul Clarke, Adrian Clifford, Steve Crowe, Martin Dale, Mandy Glanvill, Rick Graham, Adam Hocking, Jonathan Hughes, Rob Matheson, James McHaffie, Mike Norbury, Stephen Reid, Ted Rogers, Paul Ross, Cath Sullivan, Glen Sutcliffe, Chris Thistlethwaite, Matt de Vaal, Caroline Webb and Al Wilson. Thanks also to those who contributed their 'Top 5' Borrowdale routes.

The majority of the base images for photo-diagrams were the work of Richard Tolley with contributions from the rest of the team. Many high quality action shots were submitted and thanks go to all of you for making the final selection so difficult.

Initial proof reading Al Davis and Chris Shiels. Final proof reading Trevor Langhorne, Al Davis and Ken Taylor.

The advertisers provide a valuable subsidy to production and printing costs, please thank them with your custom.

All the authors have other people in their lives who will have suffered some neglect while this guidebook was being produced - or perhaps they were just glad of the break. Their patience and support was crucial to the completion of the guide: Chris Shiels, Caroline Langhorne, Chris Kenyon, Belle Hepworth and Christine Barbier.

Justin Shiels
January 2016

Ron Kenyon, Justin Shiels, Andy Dunhill, Trevor Langhorne, Richard Tolley

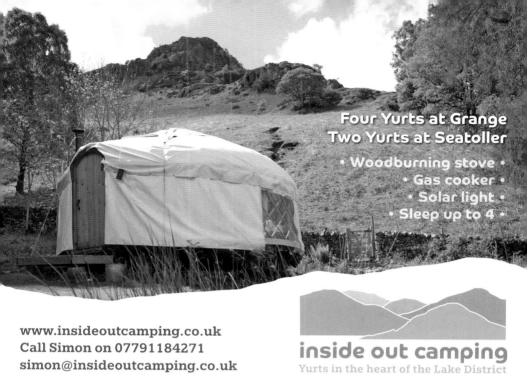

**Four Yurts at Grange**
**Two Yurts at Seatoller**

- Woodburning stove
- Gas cooker
- Solar light
- Sleep up to 4

www.insideoutcamping.co.uk
Call Simon on 07791184271
simon@insideoutcamping.co.uk

**inside out camping**
Yurts in the heart of the Lake District

# Editorial

Borrowdale is arguably the most popular valley in the district. There is a massive amount of rock and the climbing is varied, absorbing and likely to be in the most beautiful setting, high above the valley or lost in the woods.

The well-received FRCC Guides ninth series, begun in 2007, has already seen huge content revisions to the popular titles – Lake District Winter Climbs (FRCC Cicerone) and Lake District Rock (FRCC Wired), three significant presentation changes and two format changes; the pace of development is breathtaking. We trust that we are managing to meet your expectations  and now only one area of the District remains to be covered - the South Lakes: Dow, Coppermines, Slate, Eskdale & Duddon.

A new guide is always keenly anticipated and this edition of the Borrowdale guide has been wanted more than most. This guide was originally scheduled to be last in the current series. Under Peter Latimer's guidance the 'Blue Valley' team had been methodically working towards a 2018 publication date. After seven years engaged with the project, Peter handed the reins to Justin Shiels. The realisation that a 'modern' guide to such a popular area was overdue, coupled with the demands to produce a Borrowdale 'set' for Lake District Rock and the inevitable dynamism of a new lead-author have all contributed to the decision to publish this summer. Justin, Peter and all of the members of the Borrowdale 'team' are to be congratulated. Yet, without a slick and skilful technical team this demanding schedule could not have been met and we have leaned heavily on the industrious input from Don Sargeant and Peter Sterling producing the photo-diagrams, maps and setting the pages.

In his editorial to the 2000 edition Stephen Reid commented upon the difficulty of locating and checking all of the recorded climbs. This can be even more of a problem if you are not researching a guidebook and have only limited time to climb! An early decision was made to visit all of the crags in the valley and check as many of the routes as possible. If the crag was found to be overgrown with vegetation or offered only a poor selection of routes it would be archived. On other crags, like Shepherd's, the same criteria has been applied to the routes and many, considered to be of little merit, no longer appear. The Borrowdale archive can be found on the FRCC website: www.frcc.co.uk/archived-routes/ Do take a look as some of the comments are humorous and interesting and you'll find information and topos for many of these archived crags.

Another decision that we took was to print in the currently popular A5 format. This is appropriate for Borrowdale as many of the crags are 'outcrop' style and only a short walk from your base. It also gives us a much bigger canvas for presenting the material. The Crag Guide contains really useful information to help you decide where to climb. To sort out how to get there and the line of the route all of the crags now have a clear approach map and photodiagram set. We also felt that less was more when it comes to action shots and we hope that the selection ignites your enthusiasm.

Whether a Borrowdale tyro or veteran, our vision is that this guide will inspire you to search out the places in the valley you haven't yet visited and better enjoy those that you know well.

We do value your feedback, please let us know what you think of our guides and how we can do better – www.frcc.co.uk/contact-us/

Steve Scott
May 2016

This guide is dedicated to Martin Weir    1939 - 2012
Proprietor of Shepherd's Café, he made all welcome, especially the climbers.

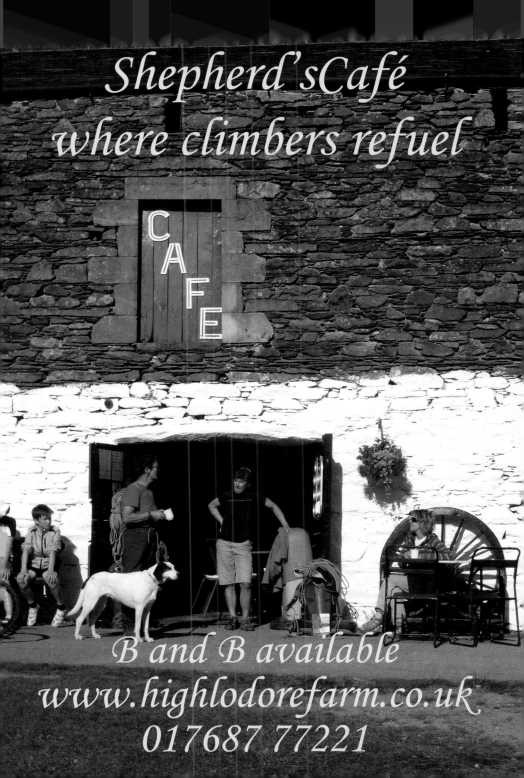

# Climbing Walls

There is a good range of climbing walls available to those living in or visiting the Lake District. Listed for use on those occasional rainy days and dank evenings:

### Ambleside: Adventure Peaks
Climbing wall and bouldering area available to anyone. Location 101 Lake Road, Ambleside.

Tel: 015394 33794                    LA22 0DB
www.adventurepeaks.com
Distance from Keswick 30 miles

### Ambleside: University of Cumbria
Low cost revamped wall at the college, with good bouldering but no leading. At the time of publication of this guide the Wall was open only to students at the College.

Tel: 015394 30274                    LA22 9DB
Distance from Keswick: 29 miles

### Barrow in Furness: Park Leisure Centre
Good access and low cost, but very limited lead climbing and a cramped bouldering area. Excellent other facilities.

Tel: 01229 871146                    LA13 9DT
www.theparkleisurecentre.com/indoor-sports/
climbing/
Distance from Keswick: 56 miles

### Carlisle: Eden Rock
With over 800sqm of climbing surface this is one of the largest dedicated bouldering walls in the UK. Excellent facility for all abilities and ages. (See advert on page 15)

Tel: 01228 522127                    CA1 3NQ
www.edenrockclimbing.com
Distance from Keswick: 35 miles

### Carlisle: The Sands Centre
Reasonable, low cost, climbing facility in a large sports centre. Good bouldering and leading. Very good access and excellent general facilities.

Tel: 01228 633766                    CA1 1JQ
www.better.org.uk/leisure/the-sands-leisure-
centre/
Distance from Keswick: 37 miles

### Cockermouth: Leisure Centre
Varied bouldering with natural stonework and Bendcrete. Low cost and good access in the town's leisure centre.

Tel: 01900 823596                    CA13 9JR
www.allerdale.gov.uk
Distance from Keswick: 14 miles

### Egremont: Wyndham Sports Centre
A good facility located in the centre of Egremont on the west coast, only half an hour from Wasdale Head. There are practice areas, bouldering, leading walls and a huge roof. Unfortunately no longer open to the public except on a club booking basis.

Tel: 01946 820356                    CA22 2DQ
Distance from Keswick: 29 miles

### Kendal: The Lakeland Climbing Centre
A magnificent indoor climbing facility with excellent bouldering and leading. Includes a very impressive 23 metre main wall and a huge roof. Located on the Lake District Business Park, across the A6 from Morrison's supermarket. Changing and shower facilities. (See advert on page 13)

Tel: 01539 721766                    LA9 6NH
www.kendalwall.co.uk
Distance from Keswick: 45 miles

### Keswick: Climbing Wall & Activity Centre
Located to the east of Keswick near the Castlerigg Stone Circle. Bright, airy climbing wall and boul-dering wall with a stunning view of Helvellyn out of the main barn doors - feeling like the Outdoors "Indoors".

Tel: 017687 72000                    CA12 4RN
www.keswickclimbingwall.co.uk
Distance from Keswick 2 miles

### Keswick: King Kong Climbing Centre
Various lead walls, large bouldering area, training room, real ice wall, cave experience, kids adventure play area and cafe. In central Keswick, opened 2014. (See advert on page 21)

Tel:  017687 79959                    CA12 5EZ
www.kingkongclimbingcentre.co.uk
Distance from Keswick: 0 miles

### Penrith: Leisure Centre – Eden Climbing Wall
An excellent leading wall adjoining the town's swimming pool and leisure centre.

Tel: 01768 863450                    CA11 8JH
www.northcountryleisure.org.uk/eden/penrith-
leisure-centre
Distance from Keswick: 18 miles

Troutdale Pinnacle S (page 115) Richard Tolley  Justin Shiels

# BORROWDALE

To climb in Borrowdale is an absolute joy. The rock is generally good quality, featured volcanic ash and the situations are amazingly varied and, with few exceptions, exquisite. Borrowdale's crags stand serenely above the steep tree lined valley sides, they hide away to be discovered amongst the arborial ferns or imperiously dominate the bare fellside of the higher combes.

Arguably the most beautiful Lakeland valley, Borrowdale is understandably popular, not just with climbers. The valley is well endowed with quaint hamlets, country pubs, welcoming cafes and sylvan campsites all linked by a network of good paths. Most of the crags are reached by a lovely walk and, once there, the situations and views are stunning. The downside is the difficulty you may have parking your car, especially on fine summer days. Don't be put off by this popularity, if you venture a little further there are many attractive sunny crags where you can find solitude, your only companions being the ewes, the ravens and the wind in your hair.

Rack Direct E2 (page 91) Chris Shiels  📷 Justin Shiels

# Map of Guidebook Areas

Thirlmere

Penrith 24km

A66

A591

SHOULTHWAITE VALLEY

High Seat ▲

High Tov

Bleaberry Fell ▲

Rakefoot Farm

**Watendlath** page 85

Castlerigg

ASHNESS GILL

GOAT CRAGS

Keswick

REECASTLE SOUTH CRAG

Watendla

UPPER FALCON CRAG

Ashness Bridge

REECASTLE CRAG

GARR BUTT

B5289

P

P

Grange

LOWER FALCON CRAG

GOWDER CRAG

BLACK CRA

CAR PARK CRAG

CHRIS CR

SHEPHERD'S CRAG

GREAT END CRAG

**Derwentwater** page 35

BOWDER CR & HELL'S WA

P

Derwentwater

River Derwent

P

Grange

STEEL KN

▲ Cat Bells

Nitting Haws

**Grange** page 105

NEWLANDS VALLEY

A66

0        mile                    1

0    kilometres     1              2

North

WYTHBURN VALLEY

EASEDALE

to
Grasmere

*Easedale Tarn*

▲ Ullscarf

*Blea Tarn*

Low
Saddle ▲

▲ High Saddle

▲ Ullscarf

**Stonethwaite** page 177

*Bleatarn Gill*

*tendlath
n*

**LONG BAND CRAG**

**EAGLE CRAG**

**LINING CRAG**

**LONG CRAG**

High Raise ▲

**BLEAK HOW**

**HERON
CRAGS**

**SERGEANT'S CRAG**

**SERGEANT'S CRAG SLABS**

**HOOKER BUTTRESS**

**BLACKMOSS POT SLAB**

to Langdale

**FAT CHARLIE'S
BUTTRESS**

*Langstrath Beck*

**WHITE CRAG - IVY KNOTT**

**CAM CRAGS**

L A N G S T R A T H

Rosthwaite

Stonethwaite

**BLACK WALL**

B O R R O W D A L E

**TWA HUMMOCKS AREA**

▲ Rosthwaite Fell

**GLACIATED SLAB AREA**

**DOVENEST SLABS AREA**

**DOVENEST CRAG**

*Combe Gill*

Combe Head

to Hanging Knotts
& Angle Tarn 1km

ASTLE
CRAG

**RAVEN
CRAG**

Glaramara ▲

**Combe Gill** page 227

**GRAINS GILL &
ALLEN CRAGS**

**HIND CRAG**

Allen
Crags ▲

P Seathwaite

Stockley Bridge

**AARON CRAG**

*Grains Gill*

**SEATHWAITE
SLABS**

Seathwaite
Fell

*Sprinkling
Tarn*

**TAYLOR GILL
SLAB**

Great
End ▲

Honister
Pass

*Styhead Gill*

Base
Brown ▲

*Styhead
Tarn*

Dale Head ▲

**GILLERCOMB**

*Sour Milk Gill*

B5289

B U T T E R M E R E

Grey Knotts

Green
Gable ▲

*CORRIDOR ROUTE*

to Buttermere

**Seathwaite** page 267

to Wasdale

▲ Brandreth

Great
Gable ▲

# Derwentwater

Usurper E1 Lower Falcon Crag (page 42) - Jonathan Hughes    Justin Shiels

# Lower Falcon Crag
NY 270 204          ⊖ West              ▲ 145m          ⋇ 5 mins

Lower Falcon Crag is peppered with natural features: corners, cracks and grooves linking slabs between roofs, which provide exhilarating climbing sometimes in unlikely situations.

Imagine how Paul Ross, as he stood on the ferry tingling with excitement, was drawn to this 'unclimbable' crag rising invitingly above Derwentwater. Most of the routes were originally climbed with the aid of, or with protection from, pegs. Many of these have now gone or are useless and all have been dispensed with for direct aid. Treat all pegs and any reference to a peg with suspicion. Many routes weave around and there is a need for good rope management with long extenders and slings being useful. On some climbs there is loose rock, route-finding can be tricky and the gear can be elusive or sparse. All in all, the crag offers great adventurous climbing but is not for the inexperienced.

**Descent:** Abseil or follow the path to the left. The abseil points are particularly useful if there is a bird ban on the descent path. Please check the signs. The middle abseil is easily accessible.

### 1   Spinup              50m   VS 4c   ★★
P Ross, D Sewel - 1957

A popular route with exciting situations. Start at the back left corner of the grassy bay.
1    20m 4c   Follow a small slab leftwards and step left around a rib to a ledge. Climb straight up from its left end to a gangway leading left for 3m, then climb up right to a stance just left of a black groove. Bold yet straightforward climbing.
2    30m 4c   Move up for 2m, step right and climb the black groove for about 5m. Step right and down to gain an exposed traverse line above the overhangs. Follow this to its end, either continue diagonally up and right to finish up a short groove above a pedestal, or directly straight up at the same grade. Belay well back.

### 2   Alternator           35m   VS 4c   ★
T Martin, D Mills - 1967

Reasonable climbing at an amenable grade.
1    18m 4c   Climb the open groove, stepping left over a bulge and move up to a slab and belay on *Spinup*.
2    17m 4c   Move right and climb the black groove of *Spinup*, then straight to the top.

### Map labels
P Great Wood Car Park 400m
limited roadside parking (2-3 cars)
B5289
Cat Gill
Derwent Water
UPPER FALCON CRAG
LOWER FALCON CRAG
Watendlath turn off
metres   North
0   100   200   300
Barrow House
Strutta Wood
Ashness Bridge

Hedera Grooves VS (page 39) - Trevor Suddaby  📷 David Simmonite

**3   The Raging Bull**   36m   E4 6b
J Lamb, P Botterill – 1 Feb 1981

Tackles the hanging groove right of *Alternator* with some hard moves. Climb easily up the back left-hand corner of the bay to a ledge. Climb the groove (old bolt) to the traverse of *Wuthering Heights*. A fierce pull despatches the bulge above, step right and finish up the rib.

**4   Wuthering Heights**   48m   E2 5c   ★
A Hyslop, R McHaffie, R Graham - 9 Apr 1978

Pleasant climbing with an airy traverse between the overhangs.
1   10m 5a   P1 of *The Dangler*.
2   38m 5c   Climb the groove and pull out left to a ledge (peg), as for *The Dangler*. Traverse horizontally left for 6m to gain a short crack and climb it to a resting place. Move right, then up left onto a steep wall which is climbed on good small holds to the top. Extend your runners.

## Lower Falcon Crag - Left

| | | | | | | | | |
|---|---|---|---|---|---|---|---|---|
| 1 | Spinup | VS 4c | ★★ | 11 | Stretch | HVS 5a | ★ |
| 2 | Alternator | VS 4c | ★ | 12 | Funeral Way | E1 5a | ★ |
| 3 | The Raging Bull | E4 6b | | 13 | Masquerade | E2 5c | ★★ |
| 4 | Wuthering Heights | E2 5c | ★ | 14 | Close Encounters | E3 5c | ★★ |
| 5 | The Dangler | E2 5c | ★★ | 15 | Vicky | E5 6b | ★ |
| 6 | Nothing by Chance | E5 6b | | 16 | The Niche | E2 5c | ★★★ |
| 7 | Hedera Grooves | VS 4c | ★★ | 17 | The Left Exit | E4 6a | ★ |
| 8 | Inarticulate Speech | E4 6a | ★ | 35 | Girdle Traverse | E1 5b | ★★ |
| 9 | Cyclotron | E4 6a | ★ | | | | |
| 10 | Atomiser | E3 6a | | | | | |

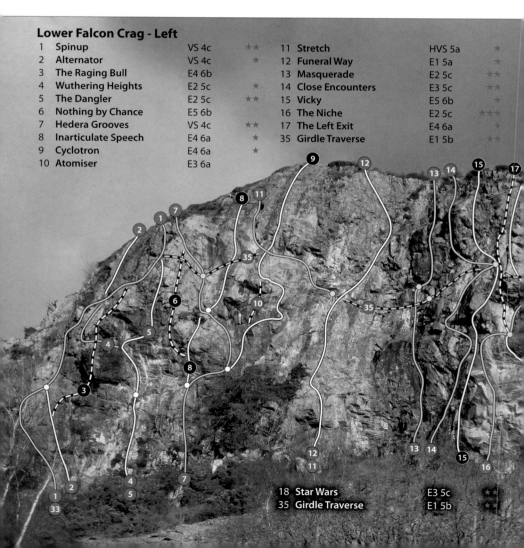

| | | | |
|---|---|---|---|
| 18 | Star Wars | E3 5c | ★★ |
| 35 | Girdle Traverse | E1 5b | ★ |

## 5   The Dangler        40m   E2 5c   ★★ ✿
S Clark, T Martin – May 1963; FFA R Fawcett, C Gibb – 1976

A very good route giving steep and exciting climbing. Start 2m left of the back right-hand corner of a grassy bay.
1   10m 5a   Climb a wall and small bulge. Move diagonally right past a small rose bush then straight up to a block belay.
2   30m 5c   Climb a steep groove on the left (ancient and useless bolt) and pull out left onto a ledge (peg). Pull up right (peg) and traverse right on large flat holds. Move up and right into a groove-line, climb this and continue direct to the top.

## 6   Nothing by Chance    47m   E5 6b
K Telfer, J Gilhespy – 1989

A good line with some steep hard climbing.
1   10m 4a   P1 of *Hedera Grooves* to the niche.
2   37m 6b   Step left and climb the cracked overhanging groove to the large overhang. Using a large undercut, reach out left and climb the overhang and wall to a ledge. Move left onto the steep black wall and climb this to easier ground and the top.

## 7   Hedera Grooves      42m   VS 4c   ★★
P Ross, P Lockey – 10 Aug 1956

The best easier route at Falcon giving a good introduction to the crag and a great second pitch.
1   24m 4b   Gain a grass ledge and climb the short groove above. Traverse boldly right to a groove and climb this to the holly tree.
2   18m 4c   Make an awkward start to climb the groove above the holly then the ramp leftwards.
It is also possible to step left onto the arête and climb straight up to the top. Photo page 37.

## 8   Inarticulate Speech   42m   E4 6a   ★
C Dale – Nov 1983

This eliminate line, based on *Hedera Grooves*, offers steep climbing on good holds but is extremely bold and serious.
1   10m 4a   P1 of *Hedera Grooves* to the niche.
2   32m 6a   Climb the cracked overhanging groove on the left of the niche or the wall on the right to the same point. Move up to the holly belay at the top of p1 of *Hedera Grooves*. Follow the easier crackline on the right.

## 9   Cyclotron        51m   E4 6a   ★
K Forsythe, TW Birkett – 26 Apr 1978

A steep and sustained route with a bold, poorly protected crux up the black wall right of *Hedera Grooves*. Take a good selection of microwires.
1   16m 4a   P1 of *Hedera Grooves* to a belay in the groove after the traverse right.
2   35m 6a   Climb the steep groove until it is possible to pull up right to a small ledge on the black wall. Traverse right to a niche in the arête, pull up and left, then move back right to better holds in a slim groove. Follow this and go left above the overhang for 5m then straight up to a ledge. Climb directly up the bulging wall above.

## 10   Atomiser        30m   E3 6a
R Fawcett, B Swales, I Dobson - 1979

Ron's variation leaves the original route at the small ledge to rejoin below the top bulges.

## 11   Stretch         54m   HVS 5a   ★
MA Toole, J Cook – 19 Sep 1965

A good climb starting up the clean corner immediately right of the ivy.
1   20m 5a   Bridge up the corner and make a hard move left. Move up the wall and belay.
2   34m 4c   Climb up and left and continue left across a slab until a broken crack above provides the exit.

## 12   Funeral Way      45m   E1 5a   ★ ✿
P Ross, PJ Greenwood – 29 May 1956
Direct start P Allison, JJS Allison - 1963

Good climbing and a direct line. It has a serious feel due to limited protection and some loose rock. Top end of the grade. Follow *Stretch* and continue up to the groove above. Climb it carefully to an exit ramp on the left.

## 13   Masquerade       44m   E2 5c   ★★
W Freelands, R McHaffie – 24 Jul 1969
P2 as described J Taylor, C Downer - 26 Apr 1978

A good route with a strenuous start up a rust-coloured groove, just left of the tree.
1   22m 5b   Climb the groove direct, moving left at the top. Move up and left to some large blocks and saplings.
2   22m 5c   Step down and traverse right for 3m to a steep crack. Climb this to a ledge. Ascend a steep crack in the bulge above and continue direct to the top.

Derwentwater · Watendlath · Grange · Stonethwaite · Combe Gill · Seathwaite

### 14  Close Encounters  53m  E3 5c  ★★
R Graham, TW Birkett, R McHaffie - 15/16 Apr 1978

Interesting with some very good climbing.
1   30m 5c   Climb the groove to an overhang then move right and up to a junction with *The Niche*. Traverse left to a groove and climb this over a bulge to belay on the right.
2   23m 5c   Move left for 6m and enter the obvious steep groove using a magnificent jug. Commit upwards and exit left to easier ground and the top.

### 15  Vicky  48m  E5 6b  ★
A Jones, R Graham - 1990

Exciting athletic fingery climbing.
1   28m 6b   Pull over the overhang and move up to the wall and short crack (peg). Desperate climbing first left, then back right leads to a runner on the lip of the overhanging nose above. Move up and left to belay.
2   20m 6a   Climb up to the overhang on the left and go over it with difficulty via a groove on the right. Finish more easily.

### ⑤ 16  The Niche  59m  E2 5c  ★★★
A Liddell, R McHaffie - 20 Aug 1962

The classic of the crag at the top of the grade, giving good sustained climbing in excellent positions. Many people find p2 the hardest.
1   25m 5c   Climb the bulging wall for 10m, step left onto a rib and climb to 3m left of the niche. Traverse right with difficulty and pull up to belay in the niche.
2   34m 5b   Climb the back of the niche and exit on the right. Traverse right to a break in the overhang. Pull through this to gain and climb a leftward-leaning groove. Pull over a slight bulge on the right and finish up the slabby wall.

### 17  The Left Exit  32m  E4 6a  ★
B Robertson, P Ross - 24 Sep 1966; FFA C & T Dale - 1984

Climb the left wall of the niche and up to a small ledge; move left to a groove which is followed to the top.

### 18  Star Wars  50m  E3 5c  ★★
TW Birkett, R Graham - 8 Apr 1978

Steep bold climbing providing an alternative entry and exit to the niche. Tough for the grade.
1   22m 5c   Climb straight up to a bulge. Step left and climb into the right side of the niche using a hollow flake.
2   28m 5b   Climb the back of the niche. Traverse right to a nose, as for *The Niche*, then pull directly over to a groove. Climb the groove slightly leftwards to finish up a short crack/slab.

### 19  Terrierman  42m  E5 6a  ★
P Rigby, J Williams - 26 Sep 1999

A seriously loose but exciting route taking the large open corner immediately right of *The Niche*. Climb straight up the broken groove to a narrow ledge below the green coloured corner. Move left with care past a small spike to bold moves up the wall. Enter the fine V-groove above and follow it to a finish up the slabby wall on the right.

### 20  Interloper  50m  E1 5c  ★★
A Liddell, R McHaffie - 8 Jul 1962
FFA C Read, J Adams - 12 Jun 1971

An enjoyable route which takes the steep and well-protected groove line 6m right of *The Niche*.
1   29m 5c   Climb to the large ledge. After an awkward start, climb the steep groove on the left on good holds to a belay on the left.
2   21m 4c   Climb up and follow the gangway leftwards to a bulge. Move right and up the slabby wall to the top.

### 21  Premonition  45m  E4 6a  ★★
P Botterill, J Lamb – 14 Feb 1981

Bold and exciting climbing up the wall and overhang linking *Interloper* to *Dedication*. From the large ledge of *Interloper* pull onto the wall above, just right of a slim green groove. Boldly climb the wall to the roof (peg). Pull over (thread) and continue to join *Dedication*. Move 2m left and climb the right-hand groove above to finish.

### 22  Dedication  48m  E1 5a  ★★★
P Ross, E Metcalf – May 1957

A very popular engaging climb. Climb to the large ledge then move up and right via ledges. Pull over a small overhang into an open groove. Climb this to gain a fine slanting corner. Follow this until a traverse left leads to the finishing groove.

### 23  Dedication Direct  48m  E1 5b  ★★★
P Ross, E Metcalf – May 1957;  Direct start C Bacon, J Cook - 1965

A technical groove reaches the original route creating a great way up the crag. Climb the groove and continue to reach a steep traverse left into a fine slanting corner which is followed until moves left lead to the finishing groove.

### ⑤ 24  Kidnapped  42m  E2 5c  ★★★
P Botterill, J Lamb – 25 Apr 1978

Tremendous and sustained climbing in the upper part. Climb the groove and continue in the same line. Climb up right into the overhung niche and move up to the roof (peg). Traverse left to the arête and follow the groove above to the top.

Derwentwater  Watendlath  Grange  Stonethwaite  Combe Gill  Seathwaite

Borrowdale has been my back yard since I was a kid bunking off school, hoping not to get seen in my uniform. A truly beautiful valley with magic everywhere. Here are some routes that I remember with a smile.

**Guillotine** (E3) As the sunlight starts to ebb away on a summer's evening, the crag becomes basked in a glorious burnt orange. Perfect rock and keep moving to escape the pump.

**Prana** (E3) One of the greats, truly magnificent. Dick Pattey, who lived below the crag, used to spend his summer evenings watching climbers plummeting down the crag.

**Mirage** (E5) Best done as a mighty single pitch, be careful with the rope drag. Wild moves help you reach the relative sanctuary of the oasis.

**Kidnapped** (E2) A great route on an unjustifiably neglected crag. Awkward with plenty of interest.

**The Torture Board** (E7) Slightly spicy low down heading into gear and bouldery moves. A classic of it's style, if the spanner doesn't fit the nut!

FAVOURITE ROUTES ⑤
Adam Hocking

Derwentwater

Watendlath

## Lower Falcon Crag - Right

| 16 | The Niche | E2 5c | ★★★ |
| 17 | The Left Exit | E4 6a | ★ |
| 18 | Star Wars | E3 5c | ★★ |
| 19 | Terrierman | E5 6a | ★ |
| 20 | Interloper | E1 5c | ★★ |
| 21 | Premonition | E4 6a | ★★ |
| 22 | Dedication | E1 5a | |
| 23 | Dedication Direct | E1 5b | ★★★ |
| 24 | Kidnapped | E2 5c | ★★★ |
| 25 | Canna Do It | E5 6a | ★★ |
| 26 | Plagiarism | E2 5c | ★★ |
| 27 | Plagiarism Direct Finish | E3 5c | ★★ |
| 28 | Usurper | E1 5a | ★★ |

| 29 | Vanishing Act | E3 5c | ★★ |
| 30 | Illusion | HVS 5a | ★★★ |
| 31 | Joke | E3 6a | ★★ |
| 32 | Lamplighter Eliminate | E5 6b | |
| 33 | Lamplighter | HVS 4c | ★★ |
| 34 | Extrapolation | E2 5c | |
| 35 | Girdle Traverse | E1 5b | ★★ |

### 25 Canna Do It     45m   E5 6a    ★★ ⚑
A Jones, T Daley, W Hannah – 6 Sep 1986

The climb requires confidence and has a tremendous second pitch.
1.   30m 5c   Climb the overhanging rib to a ledge. Move up for runners on *Plagiarism* then swing left and over an overhang into a scoop between *Kidnapped* and *Plagiarism* - bold and thin. Climb up and left to a yellow slab and go up to join *Plagiarism*. Continue up this and traverse right under the overhang (old ring peg) and belay.
2.   15m 6a   Climb up to the roof, traverse left (nuts on *Plagiarism*) and climb straight up the black wall. Move right on jugs to the middle of a green wall. Move up to a horizontal crack and then make a hard finishing move to a rest. Climb the slab leftwards to the tree.

### 26 Plagiarism     48m   E2 5c    ★★
P Nunn, O Woolcock – Aug 1962

A justifiably popular route up the rust-coloured groove just left of *Illusion*, at the right end of the grade – a good E2 to start on. Climb straight up then move left and climb the slanting groove, finishing up its left rib to gain a small ledge. Traverse left across a steep wall (peg) to a shallow groove which is followed up to a roof (peg). Surmount this on the right to reach the groove above which is followed to the top.

### 27 Plagiarism Direct     E3 5c    ★★
### Finish
R Graham, P Ingham – 2 Jun 1986.

Climb straight up then move left and climb the slanting groove, finishing up its left rib to gain a small ledge. Make bold moves rightwards to gain the hanging flake and continue up steeply to the tree.

### 28 Usurper     43m   E1 5a    ★★ ⚑
P Gomersall, N Bulmer – 20 Jun 1975

Enjoyable steep open climbing with great moves through the bulge. Climb straight up to the obvious groove which is followed to a huge flake on the right. Move up left to a ledge. The overhang up and right is overcome strenuously on good holds. The groove is followed to the tree.
Photo page 35 and opposite.

### 29 Vanishing Act     42m   E3 5c    ★★ ⚑
K Telfer, J Gilhespy - 5 May 1991

A good direct and strenuous route at the top end of the grade. It takes the hanging groove/crack left of *Joke* in a spectacular position but has some worrying rock. Climb *Illusion* to the top of the large flake. Continue up the wall to the overhang and bottomless crack/groove on the left. Climb this and the short wall above to the tree.

### ⑤ 30 Illusion     47m   HVS 5a ★★★ ♂
P Lockey, P Ross – 10 Jun 1956

Exhilarating and exposed climbing with a big feel crossing the wall below the large overhang. Climb straight up to the steep groove. Continue up then traverse right via a large flake crossing several grooves into the corner. Climb up this until forced right round the arête. Continue to the tree. Extend your runners.

### 31 Joke     42m   E3 6a    ★★
P Ross, W White – 6 Oct 1965; FFA R Fawcett, C Gibb - 1976

An impressive route which breaches the huge overhang on its left side with reachy moves. The rib leads up to an obvious groove which is followed to its top. Climb up leftwards to the roof, then left to the corner and up (peg). A long move left and back right gains the hanging groove above the roof; follow this to the tree.

### 32 Lamplighter     42m   E5 6b    ★
### Eliminate
J Lamb, P Botterill – 8 Feb 1981

Thin and serious, if the peg is absent, until you reach *Lamplighter*, then hard and fingery. Climb a blunt rib for 5m then step right and pull over a bulge at a hairline crack. Traverse right then up into the groove of *Lamplighter*. Climb this until a pull up the bulging wall above reaches a ledge. Step right and use a high side hold next to a thin crack to reach tiny holds above. Climb up the short wall to a ledge and on to the holly.

### 33 Lamplighter     40m   HVS 4c    ★★
L Hewitt, S Glass – 29 May 1964

An interesting and popular route up the obvious slanting groove. Ascend the short steep crack with a hard move, then up left to the groove. Follow this up through a bulge and continue up to join *Illusion*.

### 34 Extrapolation     42m   E2 5c    ★★
D Nicol, I Conway, R Wilson – Jul 1975
FFA J Lamb, P Botterill – 29 Jul 1975

A good route with sound rock and an awkward crux bulge. From 7m up *Lamplighter* make a delicate step right, then follow steep slabs to below a red groove. Climb this and pull left onto a perch below a steep wall. This is climbed at its weakest point.

Usurper E1 - Adam Hocking 📷 David Simmonite

**35  Girdle Traverse**          132m  E1 5b     ★★
R McHaffie, L Kendall – 15 Sept 1962

Excellent positions and climbing make this very
worthwhile. Good ropework essential.
1    20m 4c    P1 of *Spinup*.
2    24m 4c    Follow p2 of *Spinup* to the end of
     the traverse right. Climb up until it is possible
     to move down a gangway on the right to a
     stance on *Hedera Grooves*.
3    22m 5a    Traverse to the right across a steep
     wall and follow the obvious traverse line to
     a small ledge. Continue the traverse across
     *Funeral Way* to a stance on a small vegetated
     ledge.
4    24m 4b    Traverse right and continue past
     the groove of *The Niche* to reach the belay on
     *Interloper*.
5    42m 5b    Climb up and right across a steep
     wall into the groove of *Dedication*. Downclimb
     this until just above the initial bulge. Move
     out right onto *Plagiarism* and descend a short
     way to a small ledge at the top of a groove.
     Move right (peg) round a steep rib to join the
     first groove of *Illusion* which is followed to the
     abseil point.

**Five Nations of the**      182m  E3 5c     ★★
**Iroquois**
R Graham, E Cleasby – 7 Oct 1978

Little new climbing but an enjoyable expedition.
To add to the adventure, it is not shown on the
photodiagram.
1    22m 4c    Follow p1 of *Lamplighter* to a belay in
     the groove below the bulge.
2    15m 5b    Step down and traverse leftwards,
     passing below the groove of *Joke*, to a stance
     at the base of the groove of *Illusion*.
3    24m 5b    Climb the groove of *Plagiarism* for
     5m, traverse leftwards and descend *Dedication*
     to a ledge and belay.
4    33m 5c    Traverse left for 10m (peg). Step
     down and then ascend into the niche as for
     *Star Wars*. Reverse *The Niche* traverse and
     continue leftwards to the corner on *Close
     Encounters*. Step left and across to a stance and
     belay beside a large flake.
5    24m 5a    Traverse leftwards, descend the
     corner and then move left and up to the holly
     belay on *Hedera Grooves*.
6    36m 5c    Step down and traverse left round
     the arête to a junction with *The Dangler*. De-
     scend this to the top of its initial groove (peg).
     Traverse left, as for *Wuthering Heights* and
     continue traversing to a belay on *Spinup*.
7    12m 4c    Move right and climb the black
     groove of *Spinup*, then straight to the top.

Falcon Crag Buttress Route 1 E3 (page 46) - Duncan Campbell ☐ Jonathan Hughes

# Upper Falcon Crag

NY 271 206          West          190m          15/20 mins

Dominated by a superb blank headwall composed of immaculate rock, Upper Falcon offers brilliant steep wall climbing. The rock on the lower section of the crag is easier angled and of variable quality. The crag offers climbers two very good but different experiences. The first is to climb the whole crag in three classic pitches. The second is to set up an abseil rope from the top and to climb a number of the single pitches on the headwall.

**Approach:** For the base of the crag; from the roadside layby follow the approach for Lower Falcon Crag. As soon as there is scree on your left, ascend it. When you reach a fence, follow it rightwards under the crag.

**For the headwall only:** Approach from Ashness Bridge and abseil from nuts and cams on the summit.

**Descent:** To the left; awkward.

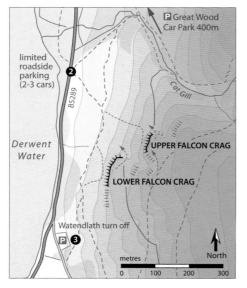

limited roadside parking (2-3 cars)

Great Wood Car Park 400m

B5289

Cat Gill

Derwent Water

UPPER FALCON CRAG

LOWER FALCON CRAG

Watendlath turn off

metres          North
0     100     200     300

### 1   Route 2          67m     E1 5b     ★★
JJ Allison, D Hadlum, A Liddell - 11 Jul 1963

The climb starts above an ash tree on a grassy hump below the centre of the crag and gives some pleasant climbing.
1   25m 4c   Climb the broken groove past an old oak tree until a short groove leads up left to some broken ledges.
2   20m 5b   Climb the rib on the left and move right into a groove. Climb this to belay below

the headwall. A steep and tricky pitch.
3   22m 5b   Climb to the top of the pinnacle on the left. Step up onto the wall and move left to a steep crack. Climb it and the groove above to the top.

### 2   Qantas          22m     E3 6a     ★
J Peel, G Peel - Sep 1979

A good pitch. Start at the base of the headwall and follow *Route 2* to the top of the pinnacle. Step up onto the wall and climb for 3m to a thin crack. Climb this to a good pocket; finish direct with a long reach or move right and climb to the top.

### ⑤ 3   Dry Gasp          60m     E4 6a     ★★★
P Livesey - 22 Jun 1974

Mistakenly called Dry Grasp for decades and one of the iconic Livesey Borrowdale quartet. Despite some loose rock, this is a brilliant and varied route.
1   22m 4a   Climb the broken groove past an old oak tree until a move right and a short right-slanting groove leads to a ledge. Belay below the groove on the left.
2   20m 5b   Climb the groove over two bulges. Continue up leftwards via an easy groove to a stance below the headwall.
3   18m 6a   Climb the crack diagonally left (peg) and then directly up (thread). Holds lead up leftwards then back rightwards to a crack, up which the route finishes.

### 4   Stumble Bum          30m     E4 6a     ★
R Graham, D Lyle - 6 Sep 1981

Climb the corner for 5m then diagonally left to a junction with *Dry Gasp*. Move straight up for 6m, step right to the small sentry box and climb the diagonal crack back left to the top.

### 5   Falcon Crag Buttress     60m     E3 5c     ★★
    Route 1
P Ross, P Lockey - 4 May 1958; FFA A Parkin, P Clarke - May 1975

A great route with a good second pitch, then finishing up the impressive corner on the headwall.
1   20m 4a   Climb the broken groove past an old oak tree and belay at the right-hand end of the ledge below a bristly short wall.
2   22m 5b   Climb the wall for 6m (peg) then move diagonally up left to climb an overhanging crack. Continue up via a groove to belay below the headwall.
3   18m 5c   Strenuously climb the corner to a tricky finish. Photo page 45.

### 6   Plastic Happiness        75 m    E1 5b
W Freelands R Allen - 13 Aug 1969

Joins *Dry Gasp* to reach a devious finish up the
loose headwall left of *Falcon Crag Buttress Route
1*. Start 12m down and to the right of *FCB Route 1*,
just right of a large ash tree, beside a hawthorn.

1    22m 4c    Climb a short corner to a gangway/
      slab which is ascended to a peg belay in a
      block niche (junction with *Dry Gasp*).
2    23m 5b    Climb the groove system to belay on *FCB
      Route 1* below the headwall; as for p2 of *Dry Gasp*.
3    30m 5b    Traverse right to reach a hold on
      the arête. Swing right into a corner and climb
      this (peg) to gain twin cracks. Climb these to
      a large pinnacle then finish up the shattered
      wall above.

### 7   The Walk on the       61m    HVS 5a
###     Wild Side
P Ross P Armstrong - 4 Aug 1995

An exposed and bold adventure, possibly still
awaiting a second ascent, taking a direct line up
the very centre of the crag and giving a taste of the
atmosphere. Start above a hawthorn.

1    31m 4c    Climb the bulges directly above the
      hawthorn, then follow the right facing groove.
      Climb slightly up left and back diagonally right
      then follow a broken seam to the foot of the
      conspicuous three step groove. Belay near its
      top on a small ledge. Large friend or Hex useful
      for belay.

2    30m 5a    From the top of the ramp climb
      straight up the very steep wall to a niche; here
      the difficulties ease and easier rock leads to
      the summit.

### Girdle Traverse        80 m    HVS 5a
R McHaffie A Liddell - 1963

From a grassy alcove near the left end of the crag,
12m of easy scrambling leads to a tree belay. Some
rather doubtful rock on p3 needs care.

1    30m 4c    Traverse to the right to below the
      base of a gangway. Pull over a bulge onto the
      gangway which trends to the right to a pin-
      nacle (junction with *Route 2*).
2    10m Traverse right to a peg belay below the
      corner of *FCB Route 1*.
3    18m 5a    Descend 5m until it is possible to
      traverse right across a brown slab (peg). Swing
      right and traverse loose rock to a groove.
      Climb the groove to a stance and peg belay.
4    22m 4c    Traverse right to reach easier ground
      and ascend to the top of the crag.

Derwentwater    Watendlath    Grange

### Upper Falcon Crag

| | | | |
|---|---|---|---|
| 1 | **Route 2** | E1 5b | ★★ |
| 2 | **Qantas** | E3 6a | ★ |
| 3 | **Dry Gasp** | E4 6a | ★★★ |
| 4 | **Stumble Bum** | E4 6a | ★ |
| 5 | **Falcon Crag Buttress** | E3 5c | ★★ |
|   | **Route 1** | | |
| 6 | **Plastic Happiness** | E1 5b | |
| 7 | **The Walk on the Wild Side** | HVS 5a | |

# Gowder Crag

**NY 266 187**        ⊖West        ⛰170m        🏃10mins

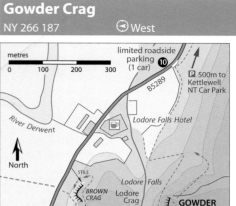

5m and traverse right to a small tree. Climb up and move right awkwardly to belay beside a large doubtful block (care).

4    22m 4b   Move left and climb the steep groove to a stance; tree belay.

5    20m 4b   Step left and climb a thin crack and the arête to finish.

## 2   Revenge of the Giant Climbing Ants        99m   VS 4c   ★

A good alternative start to *Fool's Paradise*.

1    15m        P1 of *Fool's Paradise*.

2    24m 4c   Climb the groove just right of the trees to a small ledge at a break. Either continue up the very steep crack above or, easier step left onto the arête and climb it to a ledge.

3    18m 4c   Climb broken cracks directly behind the belay until it is possible to traverse right on the slab below the overhangs to a belay beside a large doubtful block (care).

4    42m 4b   P4 and 5 *Fool's Paradise/Kaleidoscope*.

## 3   Kaleidoscope        74m   HVS 5a   ★★
R McHaffie, C McCormick - 23 Dec 1971

This enjoyable route starts about 10m up and right of the toe of the buttress at a narrow ridge.

1    12m        Ascend to a ledge and yew tree belay.

2    42m 5a   Move right, then climb up and pass to the left of a tree. Climb the wall above to a sloping ledge beneath the large overhang. Move left and climb the black groove to a large block on the left. Step right to the arête and climb the shallow groove and wall above to a ledge.

3    20m 4b   Traverse a few metres right and climb a thin crack and the arête to finish.

## 4   First Offence        77m   E3 6a   †
M Doyle, K Telfer D Barr - 19 Feb 1978

A problematic roof with mediocre protection. Start as for *Kaleidocope*.

1    12m        P1 of *Kaleidoscope*.

2    45m 6a   Move right then climb up to the small tree on *Fool's Paradise* p3. Go rightwards to a small ledge. Step left and climb the wall to a bulge. Step up left, climb the hanging groove at the right side of the overhang and gain a slab. Climb the crack on the left, step right and take the middle of the slab and short wall to a belay.

3    20m 4c   Traverse right under the arête then climb straight up broken cracks to climb a small overhang on the left.

The steep and imposing grey buttress rising out of the trees behind the Lodore Hotel has a well-deserved reputation for poor rock and vegetation; however, the main buttress of clean compact and quick-drying rock provides some excellent climbing above the initial short and unattractive pitches and is worth the short walk.

The crag is home to a large population of ants which have built some amazing anthills and there is a popular path below. The best time of year to climb here is on spring or autumn afternoons.

**Approach:** From Kettlewell NT car park.

**Descent:** A path behind the crag either to the left (shorter) or right (better).

## 1   Fool's Paradise/ Kaleidoscope        103m   VS 4c   ★★★
PW Vaughan, JDJ Wildridge - 13 Aug 1951; P2 R Kenyon – 1985;
P5 R McHaffie, C McCormick – 23 Dec 1971

A popular classic offering varied climbing.

1    15m        Climb the short buttress to a ledge; tree belay.

2    24m 4c   Gain the groove above the tree then make a surprising  move left onto the arête. Climb just left of the arête to a ledge; tree belay.

3    22m 4c   Descend the groove on the right for

**Gowder Crag**

West    ▲ 140m    🚶 5-15mins

The Belvedere

Jackdaw Terrace

*Shepherd's Delight*

**North Buttress**
Page 68

**Wild Sheep Area** Page 58
**Monolith Crack Area** Page 54

**Brown Crag**
Page 80

**Fisher's Folly Area**
Page 64

**Chamonix Area**
Page 62

**Jackdaw Ridge Area**
Page 51

B5289 to KESWICK

B5289 to GRANGE

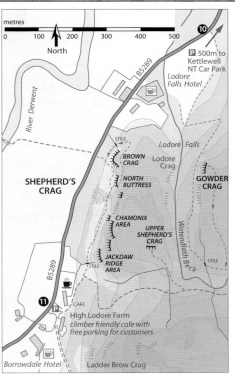

Described by Paul Ross as the "super-boulder," Shepherd's is with good reason the most popular crag in the valley, offering a wide selection of enjoyable routes across the grades. Quick and easy access, generally good, varied, quick-drying rock and a welcoming café at the bottom - what more could you want?

Climbers have traditionally used the parking at Shepherd's Café, High Lodore Farm. Parking here is for customers. If you do park here please spend freely at the café so that climbers can continue to enjoy the friendly relationship that has existed for a long time. Besides that, it is the best café in the world. The map indicates other parking but beware of restrictions especially between Good Friday and 31 October.

**Approach:** From behind the café.

## Jackdaw Ridge Area

The first part of Shepherd's offers, amongst other things, a number of long and relatively easy routes.

**Descent:** Walk south from The Belvedere, the flat area at the top of the crag, down to the top of a gully and up the other side to a good path that leads back down to the stile. Alternatively, descend the gully itself or head right (West) just before the gully and scramble down over blocks to Jackdaw Terrace.

### 1  Free 'n' Easy          15m   HS          ★
P Poole, K Telfer – 28 May 1980

A worthwhile but outlying route. Instead of bearing left to the stile, follow the path up for a couple of minutes and go left above a boulder field to an obvious clean steep slab right of a large yew tree. Hand traverse right up a diagonal crack to a block. Surmount the block, move right to a slab and continue up to a large spike belay.

### 2  Why Not          20m   VS 4b
FW Crosby, S Thompson – 18 Apr 1979

Start just left of the stile and follow the leftwards-slanting crack, finishing rightwards.

### 3  Plug          23m   E1 5b
A Cannon, N Gilbourne – 13 Jun 1993

Start 3m left of the stile and climb the overhanging wall.

### 4  Jackdaw Ridge          66m   D          ★
B Beetham – 27 Aug 1946

A route which has clearly given many people pleasure over the years. Start 7m left of the stile at the prominent well-worn rib.
1   26m     Climb the rib for 8m and continue directly above to a ledge with an oak. Continue up easier blocky rock to a good ledge with a large oak tree. An alternative start climbs the less pronounced rib 3m left of the ordinary start at VD.
2   23m     From just above the oak, climb the rightward-slanting V-groove to easier-angled rocks on the ridge line and a tree belay.
3   17m     Follow the line of the ridge, starting up an awkward V-groove and finishing up a rib to The Belvedere.

### 5  Jackdaw Ridge Direct          20m   MS          ★
B Beetham – 4 Sep 1946

Could more properly be called the Indirect Start; like the parent, somewhat polished. Start at the lowest point of the buttress at a rightward-slanting groove. Climb the groove and continue up and right to the first oak on *Jackdaw Ridge*.

### 6  Ethelred          24m   HVS 5a
T Dale, D Bowen – 15 May 1983

An easier variation on *Odds 'n' Sods*. Follow the groove of *Jackdaw Ridge Direct* for 5m to a leftward-slanting crack which leads to the large doubtful looking block on *Odds 'n' Sods*. Finish up that route.

### 7  Odds 'n' Sods          24m   E2 5c          ★
K Telfer, G Telfer – 7 Apr 1980

Takes the prominent nose at the lowest point of the crag. Start at a steep crack behind a large tree. Climb the tricky crack to a ledge and move right to a large doubtful-looking block. Surmount this and go up the wall onto the arête. Cross the easy slab of *Ant Highway* and climb the right side of the wall above direct.

### 8  Ant Highway          42m   MVS 4b          ★
B Beetham – 7 Sep 1947

Start 5m up and left of the toe of the buttress at the right-hand end of a ledge. An interesting start is followed by scrambling.
1   20m 4b   Climb the wall strenuously to gain a grassy slab on the right. Climb to the top of the slab then move leftwards up the wall to an oak tree belay.
2   22m     Climb easily up to a tree ledge, then move left to ascend the left-hand of two sharp ridges to a belay on *Jackdaw Ridge*. Either continue up *Jackdaw Ridge* or descend to the left, below *Monolith Crack*.

### 9  Human Racing          18m   E3 5c
R Curley, D Williamson, N Stansfield, C Thwaites – 23 Sep 1984

Climb *Ant Highway* until half way up the easy slab. Pull left onto the wall and climb up to and over the bulge using a hidden slot.

### 10  Bits 'n' Pieces          21m   VS 4c          ★★
D Armstrong - 1976.

Start one metre left of *Human Racing*. Climb straight up the wall on mainly good holds to a ledge. Step up left from the ledge to climb the short groove and wall directly to the top.

### 11  Mule Train          18m   E2 5c          ★
D Armstrong – Jul 1976

The wall 2m right of the chimney start to *Donkey's Ears*. Make hard unprotected moves up the wall to a shallow niche. Follow the small grooveline on the left to a tree belay on the ledge above.

Derwentwater

Watendlath

Grange

Stonethwaite

Combe Gill

Seathwaite

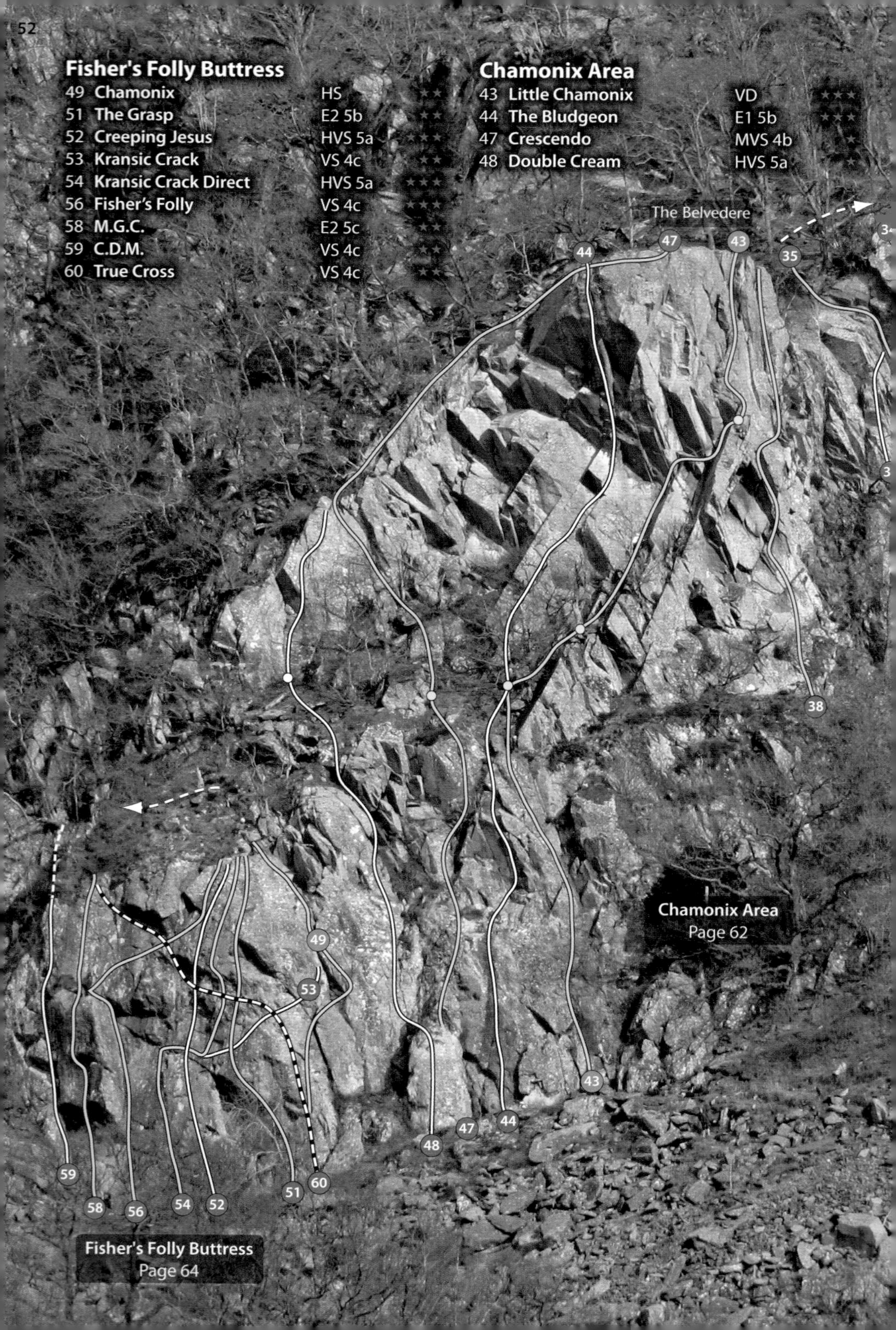

## Fisher's Folly Buttress

| 49 | Chamonix | HS | ★★★ |
| 51 | The Grasp | E2 5b | |
| 52 | Creeping Jesus | HVS 5a | |
| 53 | Kransic Crack | VS 4c | |
| 54 | Kransic Crack Direct | HVS 5a | |
| 56 | Fisher's Folly | VS 4c | |
| 58 | M.G.C. | E2 5c | |
| 59 | C.D.M. | VS 4c | |
| 60 | True Cross | VS 4c | |

## Chamonix Area

| 43 | Little Chamonix | VD | ★★★ |
| 44 | The Bludgeon | E1 5b | |
| 47 | Crescendo | MVS 4b | |
| 48 | Double Cream | HVS 5a | |

The Belvedere

Chamonix Area
Page 62

Fisher's Folly Buttress
Page 64

53

Jackdaw Terrace

Wild Sheep Area
Page 58

Monolith Crack Area
Page 54

## Wild Sheep Area

| 26 | Bob's Exasperation | E3 6a | ★★ |
| 28 | Shepherd's Chimney | VS 5a | ★★ |
| 30 | Inclination | E5 6b | ★★ |
| 31 | Exclamation | E6 6b F7b+ | |
| 33 | Wild Sheep | E2 5b | ★★★ |
| 34 | Wild Side | E3 6a | ★ |
| 35 | Derision Groove | MVS 4b | ★ |
| 36 | Thin Air Variation | VS 4c | |
| 38 | Battering Ram | E3 6a | |

Jackdaw Ridge Area
Page 51

## Monolith Crack Area

| 17 | Monolith Crack | HVS 4c | ★★ |
| 19 | Porcupine | E3 6a | ★★ |
| 20 | The Black Icicle | E1 5b | ★★★ |
| 25 | The Devil's Alternative | E6 6b F7a+ | ★★ |

## Jackdaw Ridge Area

| 4 | Jackdaw Ridge | D | ★ |
| 5 | Jackdaw Ridge Direct | MS | |
| 8 | Ant Highway | MVS 4b | |
| 12 | Donkey's Ears - Chimney Start | VS 4c | |
| 13 | Donkey's Ears | HS | |

Derwentwater
Watendlath
Grange
Stonethwaite
Combe Gill
Seathwaite

### 12 Donkey's Ears - Chimney Start    12m    VS 4c

The obvious chimney up and left of *Bits 'n' Pieces* is smooth and strenuous requiring traditional technique!

### 13 Donkey's Ears    67m    HS    ★★
B Beetham – 1 Apr 1947

A classic climb with a decisive final pitch. Start 5m left of the obvious chimney where an ash tree is guarded by a slim flake.

1    26m    Climb the easy wall then follow the well scratched line into a wide grassy trough. Scramble up to belay by a small cave below the huge projecting block.
2    20m    From outside or inside the cave, climb up onto an outward-pointing spike. Either hand-traverse left and up to a ledge or fight up between the 'two ears' to the ledge. Ascend the pile of blocks above trending right, to belay at a tree on *Jackdaw Ridge*.
3    21m    Traverse left into a corner and then delicately continue left along an obvious traverse line to V-cracks. Climb these precariously and continue up to The Belvedere.

## Monolith Crack Area

A large variety of middle-grade and hard routes of one or two pitches makes this area worth seeking out.

**Approach:** Follow the base of the crag up and left to a large yew tree. Then scramble up and right to a broken terrace beneath a steep smooth orange/brown wall. Continue scrambling up right over large blocks to Jackdaw Terrace. At the upper right-hand end of the terrace is an open corner. The routes are described from right to left.

**Descent:** Via Jackdaw Terrace or further south – see *Jackdaw Ridge* descent and overview diagram.

### 14 Hee-Haw    16m    VS 5a    ★
R Kenyon, C Eckersall - 1983.

Short, pleasant and high in the grade. Start 2m left of a conspicuous large rusty streak. Climb a faint cracked groove to gain the traverse of *Donkey's Ears*. Above are two cracks - an obvious crack slanting left, with a faint crack on its right. Climb the right-hand crack to gain a ledge and continue to The Belvedere.

### 15 Straight and Narrow    16m    E3 5c    ★
TW Birkett, D Lyle – 20 Aug 1983

An escapable eliminate with a poorly protected crux pulling through the overlap. Follow *Hippos Might Fly* for 4m to a small triangular niche. Step right and pull directly over an overlap on small holds to gain a small pocket in the slab above. Go straight up to the horizontal break and finish up a triangular wall on the left.

### 16 Hippos Might Fly    26m    E1 5a    ★
A Brown, J Geeson – 16 Jul 1983

Another poorly protected offering. Climb precariously up the leftwards-sloping fault to the stunted oak. Move right and climb the crack rightwards to join and climb *Donkey's Ears*.

### 17 Monolith Crack    32m    HVS 4c    ★★
B Beetham – 28 Jul 1947

A varied and popular route up the centre of the wall sporting a classic finishing crack. Start below the stunted oak.

1    12m 4c    Climb the leftward-slanting break for 3m to a small niche. Move up using a small slanting foot-ledge on the left. Pass the oak and gain the ledge above. Ascend a short chimney to a tree belay.
2    20m 4c    To the left is the Monolith. Climb the off-width crack just to its right, then ascend a short corner and finish up the wall above.

### 18 Monolith Chimney    34m    S
B Beetham – 30 Jul 1948

An alternative for those unwilling or unable to tackle the parent route. From the tree belay, move left of the Monolith and ascend the chimney. Finish up the short corner and wall above.

### 19 Porcupine    28m    E3 6a    ★★
P Ross, E Ray – 2 Jul 1955; FFA P Whillance - Feb 1977

A pleasant first pitch leads to a short sharp corner. Start at the jumble of large spikes just to the right of the obvious left-slanting V-groove.

1    18m 5a    From the spikes, carefully pull directly up the overhanging rib on the right then follow the groove and wide crack above to the large ledge and tree belay of *Monolith Crack*.
2    10m 6a    Ascend the prominent short corner pulling up rightwards to finish. Intense but well-protected.

### Porcupine/Devil's Wedge    40m    E1 5a    ★★

Combining p1 of *Porcupine* with p2 of *Devil's Wedge* makes a good outing at a more consistent grade.

20  **The Black Icicle**       30m   E1 5b   ★★★
D Fielding - 1958

An excellent route with a bold second pitch. The 'Midterm Exam' in Shepherd's E1s. Care needed to protect the start; on p2 the protection is good but spaced.

1    14m 5b   Climb the thin black quartz crack running up the steep wall then move up to a yew tree belay.

2    16m 5a   With or without the use of the tree, gain and climb the blunt arête. Move up and right to finish airily up the wall.

21  **Devil's Wedge**       34m   E1 5a   ★
B Beetham – 30 Jul 1948

The glaringly obvious smooth left-slanting V-groove. A fearsome traditional climb which reportedly gave Don Whillans a run for his money. Harder for the tall!

1    12m 5a   Climb the groove to a belay on the right, below *Monolith Chimney*.

2    22m 5a   Step up onto a rib and traverse left into a V-groove which is ascended directly to the top.

The next four routes tackle the steep smooth orange-brown wall.

22  **The Witness**       12m   E6 6b F7b   ♂
K Telfer, J Telfer – 11 Apr 1987

A serious boulder problem solo above a poor landing. Start below the right-hand arête and climb its overhanging left side.

23  **Geronimo**       12m   E7 6c F7c+ ★   ♂
P Ingham, R Parker - 2 Jun 1986

A technical and very serious problem starting one metre left of the right arête. Climb small pockets leading up left and then go straight up (peg) to a good hold. Pull left to an obvious layaway and climb straight up the wall above on small holds to the trees at the top of *The Devil's Alternative*. A pre-placed sling on the peg reduces the grade to E6.

### 33 Wild Sheep          33m   E2 5b      ★★★
K Wilkinson, D Booth, A Morris - 31 Mar 1989.

Absolutely brilliant. Takes the arête of *Black Sheep* on the left in its entirety. Similar to but more sustained than the original. Gain the pedestal as for *Black Sheep* and continue up steeply, just left of the arête, on superb incut holds. Photo page 57.

### 34 Wild Side          35m   E3 6a      ★★
J Dunne, D Savage - 15 Apr1985

A worthwhile variation at the lower end of the grade. From the top of the flake left of the bush move left across the steep wall (peg) to finish up a short corner.

### 35 Derision Groove      34m   MVS 4b    ★★
P Ross, JA Wood – 27 Feb 1955

A popular route with some interesting moves. Climb the steep stepped groove on good holds to a ledge. Climb the gangway until a traverse left can be made to The Belvedere.

### 36 Thin Air Variation    28m   VS 4c      ★
R McHaffie, N Robinson - 14 Sep 1978

Climb directly up the rib to a ledge and small oak tree. Climb the rib above until a move right leads to a finish up *Derision Groove*.

### 37 Shepherd's Gully      26m   MVS 4b    ★★
Variation
R Wilkinson, D Wilkinson - 2003.

Climb the right wall of the vegetated gully to the small oak. The shallow groove behind the tree and the left-slanting ramp-line above leads to the finishing move of *Derision Groove*.

### 38 Battering Ram         33m   E3 6a      ★★
R Smith, J Earl – 27 May 1984

A great route taking the steep wall. From a large flake, climb the wall first left, then right to gain the right-hand end of the overhang. Follow the diagonal groove above the overhang to a ledge and move right to an oak tree. Climb the thin right-hand crack directly behind the oak to a groove which is followed to the top. Photo opposite.

### 39 Stone Tape           34m   E3 6a      ★★
P1 J Lamb, R Cowells – 17 Aug 1978; P2 L Ainsworth - 1964

Good steep climbing and an airy finish on the upper buttress.
1   12m 6a   Follow the right-slanting break across the wall to a spike below the right side of the overhang. Step left and up to below the top of the overhang. Swing out left and up to belay on the saddle of *Little Chamonix*.
2   22m 5b   Descend a slab on the left and stand on a large block below an overhanging groove. Climb this, past a large dubious spike, to a ledge. Continue up the groove above to a sloping ledge and finish up the short wall.

### 40 Entertainment        18m   E2 5c       ★
Traverse
P Ross, P Lockey - 10 Jun 1958

An alternative p2 to *Stone Tape*. Move up leftwards to a junction with *Stone Tape*, just right of an overhanging rib. Swing left and descend a steep groove to an overhanging niche, just right of the pinnacle of *The Bludgeon*. Finish up the pinnacle and crack above, as for *The Bludgeon*.

### 41 Edge of Trust        20m   E7 6b F7b    †
M Przygrodzki, C Swanepoel - 10 Aug 2012;
all gear was pre-placed.

An impressive line; a blinkered approach and practice will be required to achieve the grade. It takes the overhanging arête right of *The Bludgeon*. From directly below, climb first on the left then the right of the arête. At the top of the pillar continue in the same line through the overhang to finish. Awaits an on-sight flash.

Derwentwater
Watendlath
Grange
Stonethwaite
Combe Gill
Seathwaite

## Chamonix Area

This very popular area holds a number of classic multi-pitch routes, including possibly the most famous climb in the Lake District.

**Approach:** From the stile follow paths leftwards across the scree.

**Descent:** Go rightwards across The Belvedere and down via Jackdaw Terrace or continue further southwards - see *Jackdaw Ridge* descent and overview diagram page 52.

### 42  Scorpion          50m    VS 5a          ★
G Fisher, R Richardson - 22 May 1952

This variation on the original route allows good climbing on moss-free rock at the same grade. P2 requires careful ropework.
1    30m 4c   Climb the black slab to a ledge and go straight up the wall above, just left of a large spike on *Little Chamonix*. Scramble up to belay at a 3-stemmed oak tree on the right-hand side of the large tree-covered terrace.
2    20m 5a   Ascend the left-hand groove of *Little Chamonix* for 3m, then move left with difficulty to below a projecting rock and up into a V-scoop. Head diagonally left to a platform below a groove. Awkward moves up this gain good holds and the top. It is also possible to climb diagonally leftwards from the platform to gain the spiky arête on the left - 5b but possibly easier!

### ⑤ 43  Little Chamonix     71m    VD    9/6/20  L    ★★★
B Beetham - 26 May 1946

Originally named Chamonix by Bentley Beetham, subsequent editors have transposed the names of this and its 'Little' neighbour. To avoid confusing everyone the error will remain uncorrected.

Varied climbing, good positions and a spectacular final pitch have made this a hugely popular route. Having been the stage for a folk-band gig and suffering the indignity of an ascent in roller-skates and boxing-gloves has enhanced its classic status. Deservedly polished.
1    30m      Climb up to a groove at 15m and follow this finishing up the flake-crack on the left to gain a tree belay.
2    12m      Scramble up rightwards through a wood to below the left-hand of two conspicuous V-corners.
3    29m      Ascend the left-hand corner to an overhang. Use the block under the overhang to gain and cross the slab on the right. Climb its right arête to the saddle.
4    13m      Up to the base of the pinnacle above;

step right and up to gain its top. Make a couple of very steep and sensationally exposed moves up and left to gain The Belvedere. A superb pitch.

### ⑤ 44  The Bludgeon        54m    E1 5b          ★★★
P Ross, P Lockey - 14 Apr 1957

A magnificent, well-named climb, with a strenuous and spectacular final pitch up the steep wall below the left side of The Belvedere. Start at the base of a black slab and to the right of the chimney forming the right-hand side of the prominent pinnacle. The 'Final Exam' in Shepherd's E1s.
1    30m 4c   P1 of *Scorpion*.
2    24m 5b   Move left and climb the left side of the easy-angled rib up the right side of the large dirty central groove. Step right around the rib and go up a short groove to a niche below and right of a large overhanging pinnacle. Climb the crack on the right of the pinnacle and manoeuvre onto its top. Finish directly using the crack above and flake holds on the right wall. Photo cover.

### 45  Missing Link       24m    E3 5c          ★
A Jones, D Hellier – Feb 1982

An exciting climb. Follow p2 of *The Bludgeon* to the overhung niche right of the large pinnacle. Climb the groove on the right and pull round a corner to a junction with *Stone Tape*. From the ledge, move left and climb a crack in the wall to The Belvedere.

### 46  Shepherd's Pie Finish   24m    E3 6a
R Curley, D Williamson, N Stansfield, C Thwaites - 9 Sep 1984

A very contrived set of boulder problems up the overlaps to the left of the normal finish. Follow *The Bludgeon* p2 to the top of the rib. Climb the overhanging scoop on the left and pull up right onto a slab. Climb straight over the bulge above onto another slab, step left and climb the final bulge, at twin thin cracks, passing a sapling.

| 38 | **Battering Ram** | E3 6a |
| 39 | **Stone Tape** | E3 6a |
| 40 | **Entertainment Traverse** | E2 5c |
| 41 | **Edge of Trust** | E7 6b F7b |
| 42 | **Scorpion** | VS 5a |
| 43 | **Little Chamonix** | VD |
| 44 | **The Bludgeon** | E1 5b |
| 45 | **Missing Link** | E3 5c |
| 46 | **Shepherd's Pie Finish** | E3 6a |
| 47 | **Crescendo** | MVS 4b |

| 48 | **Double Cream** | HVS 5a |
| 49 | **Chamonix** | HS |

The Belvedere

**Fisher's Folly Buttress**
Page 64

**47 Crescendo** 68m MVS 4b ★
B Beetham – 14 Aug 1948

A challenging route starting at the chimney just right of the large pinnacle.

1 35m 4b Climb the chimney past the chock-stone to a platform. Climb boldly up the polished wall, trending first left, then right, to reach an easier line of grooves leading to a ledge. Move left and climb over blocks, then scramble through trees to belay on a large oak tree below a triangular block with a steep wall behind.

2 33m 4a Move up past the triangular block to reach a steepening in the wall. Move left for 3m on good holds to reach another tree-covered ledge. Now climb the ridge on the right to reach The Belvedere.

Original finish: Just before reaching The Belvedere, traverse slightly down and right across a wall to gain and climb the obvious groove above a sapling – rather contrived but good climbing.

**48 Double Cream** 66m HVS 5a ★
SJH Reid, C Dale - 10 Jun 2008. R Graham (Cream) – 1997
M Przygrodzki, F Przygrodzki (Milk) - 26 Jun 2011

A homogenised version of Milk and Cream making the best of the rock left of *Crescendo*. Take care with the ropes on p1 to avoid lifting out the runners. Start under the left of the pinnacle.

1 30m 5a Climb the arête until a traverse left behind the pinnacle leads onto a ledge. Climb the wall immediately left of a wide vegetated crack to a ledge and brown niche/chimney on the right. Exit spectacularly rightwards through huge blocks to reach a scramble up leftwards through scrub and trees to belay near the left-hand end of the wall, at the base of a groove.

2 36m 5a Twin cracks snake up the wall to the right. Step into the groove and cross to the cracks and a hollow jug. Follow the left-hand crack steeply for 2m, then step rightwards to the right-hand crack and climb straight up to the top of wall. Continue up the easy rib of *Crescendo* to the top.

**49 Chamonix** 25m HS ★★
B Beetham - 10 Apr 1946

A rather devious route, nevertheless it's often occupied. Climb the wall rightwards to gain the arête. Climb this then go rightwards to a pinnacle (possible belay). Step rightwards from the pinnacle onto the wall up and climb up and left into a wide crack, or climb the crack direct (harder). Continue more easily to a tree belay.

## Fisher's Folly Buttress

Just down and left of the Chamonix area is a small steep compact buttress offering enjoyable routes with the prominent wide *Kransic Crack* in its centre.

**Descent:** Carefully follow a clear path leftwards. Please do not abseil off or top rope directly from the trees or they won't be there in the future!

**50 Poop and Clutch** 23 m E2 5c
S Ringrose, A Cannon – 31 Jul 1998

Contrived. Start up *The Grasp* and continue up the corner where it moves left. Move right and head for the shallow scoop above; climb this direct using high holds on the right.

**51 The Grasp** 24m E2 5b ★★
D McDonald, R McHaffie, N Robinson – 5 Oct 1978

Good but bold climbing with ground fall potential! Climb the left-hand side of the large flake and move up to the scoop, right of the black overhang. Move left to a good hold then make committing moves over the overhang onto the wall. Continue up, moving ever further from your gear and with a possible ground fall. Cross *Kransic Crack* to gain a leftwards-slanting gangway which is followed to the top.

**52 Creeping Jesus** 24m HVS 5a ★★★
J Healy, A Mitchell – 22 Jul 1978

A quality direct pitch of continuous interest, at the upper end of the grade. Start below the middle of the flake. Using positive holds climb the front of the flake to its top; move up the scoop above then go right to finish up the wall.

**53 Kransic Crack** 22m VS 4c ★★
GB Fisher, D Oliver, F Bantock - 6 Jul 1952

A very good route, although the starting crack sorts out a few climbers. Climb the crack to the top of the flake, traverse to the right along the flake and make an awkward move onto the wall. Traverse rightwards to reach the wide crack of *Chamonix* and finish up this. For those searching for variety, an alternative start struggles up the unprotected off-width right-hand crack of the enormous flake.

**54 Kransic Crack Direct** 20m HVS 5a ★★★
D Peel - 1956

Excellent, well-protected and varied climbing. Climb *Kransic Crack* then traverse the top of the flake to its right-hand end below a bulge. Climb up then right, over the bulge and take the crack on the left, on excellent holds, to the top.

**55 Twittering Heights**    25m    E4 6a    ★
C Bainbridge, PJ Kane – 27 Apr 1993

Struggling for independence, but a direct line. Climb the wall to the centre of the bulge. Surmount the overhang using a hidden slot for the left hand. Climb directly up on good holds to the next overhang then climb this on the left.

**56 Fisher's Folly**    25m    VS 4c    ★★★
M Thompson, P Nicol – Apr 1955

A fine climb starting at the well-defined right-facing corner. The 'Entrance Exam' in Shepherd's VSs. Pass the stubborn first few moves and climb the corner to a ledge on the left. Step right onto the wall and move delicately rightwards for 5m. Climb up to the overhang, pass it on the right, and continue to the top. At HVS 5a it is possible to climb directly over the overhang to the top from the delicate traverse.

**57 Shanna**    22m    E4 6a
M Wilford, K Lindhorne, C Downer – 13 Jul 1981

A tough route taking the arête just left of *Fisher's Folly*. Starting on its left, climb the arête to gain the halfway ledge of *Fisher's Folly*. Climb the wall above direct.

**58 M.G.C.**    20m    E2 5c    ★★
B Roberts, G West - 1958

This extremely well-protected Shepherd's test piece, which is always amply chalked, tackles the steep wall split by a thin peg-scarred crack.

**Derwentwater**

**Watendlath**

**Grange**

**Stonethwaite**

**Combe Gill**

**Seathwaite**

**59 C.D.M.** 18m VS 4c ★★
D Armstrong – Jun 1975

The steep and safe little crack sporting a horizontal oak tree is good fun. Climb the crack past the oak and finish directly up the blunt juggy arête, just right of another tree.

There are two girdle traverse lines which start on Fisher's Folly Buttress. Both will make you very unpopular on a busy day.

⑤ **60 True Cross** 30m VS 4c ★★
SJH Reid, W Phipps – 3 Apr 1996

A rising traverse across Fisher's Folly Buttress giving steep, sustained but well-protected climbing along a natural break. Start on the very large boulder on the right-hand side of the buttress. Climb the blunt arête for 10m to gain the almost horizontal juggy break that cuts across the crag. Make a rising traverse leftwards passing above the roof to join *Fisher's Folly* followed by a tricky step down left. Move up to the roof and traverse left under it to its left-hand end. Keep moving diagonally leftwards to finish at the top of *M.G.C.*

**61 Chamonix Girdle** 101m HVS 4c ★
T Dale, R Kenyon – 14 Oct 1972

This expedition traverses the crag from left to right giving an even more complete girdle than *Rogues' Gallery*.
1   20m 4c   Climb *Kransic Crack* to the flake. Continue right to belay beside the pinnacle on *Chamonix*.
2   18m 4b   Traverse right, cross *Crescendo* to join and follow *The Bludgeon* p1 and belay on *Little Chamonix*.
3   28m   Scramble up right to below p3 of *Little Chamonix*. Gain and climb the arête on the extreme right to belay on the saddle.
4   20m 4b   Move right over suspect rock into *Shepherd's Gully*; then continue right across a wall and round a corner, into *Shepherd's Chimney*.
5   15m 4a   Finish up p2 of *Shepherd's Chimney*.

**62 Shepherd's Delight** 81m S ★
B Beetham – 29 Jul 1946

A route that may appeal to mountaineers. Despite appearances there is a surprising amount of interesting climbing on mostly good rock. To enhance the experience it is excluded from all of the diagrams.

Ascend the path on the right of North Buttress to the point where North Gully (the gully bounding the upper half of North Buttress), swings up more steeply leftwards. Start 5m to the right.

1    17m  Climb the buttress for 6m moving slightly left then make a rising traverse right which leads to a many-stemmed oak.

2    24m    Turn the overhanging flake above on the right and climb the arête of the buttress above to a grass ledge at the foot of a steep wall. Huge hanging oak branch belay.

3    25m    Go rightwards down the grass ledge for 4m to a rock slab. Traverse right and up this, then back left and pull steeply up to ledges. Continue up, going left of a pillar to an oak belay on a good ledge.

4    15m    Scramble up 10m to below a ridge with a groove in it. Climb the ridge to the top.

**Descent:** Scramble 20m higher to level ground then walk left about 200m to an easy grassy gully. Half-way down this, pick up a trail leading left (facing out) to the top of North Buttress, or continue down to join the Brown Slabs descent path.

Inclination E5 (page 58) - Ben Scraggs    Stuart Wood

## North Buttress

This tall buttress offers a wide selection of fine long pitches. It is split down the middle by a steep corner/slab, the classic *Ardus*.

**Approach:** Follow paths leftwards across the scree.

**Descent:** Walk up the hill behind the crag a few metres to a path that leads north to the top of Brown Slabs from where an easy descent can be made to the left. More popular, but initially requiring VD down-climbing, is to descend to the right.

### 1   Turning the North     70m   VD
B Beetham - 1 Aug 1946

Start below the prominent left-facing corner at the upper right-hand side of the buttress. The route crosses the descent path and can be abandoned at this point if you've persevered this far.

1   18m      Start up the corner then make an awkward move up and right onto a small ledge below a smooth grey wall. Traverse right to an oak and climb the ridge right of the yew tree to a good ledge and tree belay. Rather vegetated.

2   19m      Step left and climb to the edge and follow this in a fine position. The descent gully to the right is spanned at the top by a block.

3   33m      Pass under the block and climb the wall, just to the left on good holds. Now climb the steep wall on the left, with interest, to the ridge above.

| 1 | Turning the North | VD |
| 2 | Gemma | HVS 5b |
| 3 | Warsaw | E3 5c |
| 4 | P.P.S. | E2 5c |
| 5 | P.S. | E1 5b |
| 7 | North Buttress | E1 5b |
| 9 | True North | E2 5b |
| 11 | Adam | VS 5a |

**2  Gemma**          40m    HVS 5b    ★★
PJ Kane, C Bainbridge – 18 May 1993

A pleasant, clean and direct climb up this part of the crag. Excellent protection and a bit of a soft touch. Start as for *Turning the North*. Climb the crack in the corner to a resting place and make delicate moves up and left to a horizontal oak. Climb the groove above and, at a small tree, swing left onto the arête and climb it on good holds to the top.

**3  Warsaw**         38m    E3 5c
M Przygrodzki, H McGhie – 26 Sep 2010

The wall between *Gemma* and *P.P.S.* Stay in lane without straying onto either of the neighbouring routes. Blinkers obligatory. Finish as for *Gemma*.

**4  P.P.S.**         38m    E2 5c     ★
K Forsythe, TW Birkett, R McHaffie, R Graham – 22 Oct 1978

A bold and direct route up the right-hand side of the buttress with a short steep difficult section. Start at the blunt arête, 3m left of *Turning the North*. Ascend thin cracks to a slab below an overhang. Move right and gain a short hanging arête. Go up this to a junction with *P.S.* and climb easily up the arête above to the top.

**5  P.S.**           38m    E1 5b     ★★★
P Ross, B Aughton – 19 Apr 1959

An exhilarating climb, starting at the obvious broken groove 8m up and right from the foot of the buttress. The 'Entrance Exam' in Shepherd's E1s. Climb the groove to a ledge. Continue up the fault above to a wedged block, then swing right using good technique or a long reach to side pulls and follow the arête to the top.

**6  P.S. -**         36m    E3 6a     ★
    **The Direct Finish**
J Lamb, P Botterill – 28 Jun 1981

Follow the original to below the wedged block, then step left onto the wall and climb straight up past a short crack, finishing directly up the easier rock above.

**7  North Buttress** 45m    E1 5b     ★★
PJ Greenwood, D Whillans, P Whitwell - 1954

A long and exciting pitch. Climb the flake and the bulge above. Continue up until a short traverse left gives access to a gangway trending back right. Immediately step left to the obvious overhanging groove. Ascend this with difficulty then easier climbing leads to the top.

**8  North Buttress -**  48m  HVS 4c
    **Slab Finish**
PJ Greenwood, E Mallinson - 6 Jun 1954

1  30m 4c  Follow the original route to the gangway trending back right and belay on the right.
2  18m 4a  Move right to below the overhang then make a long reach to gain a ledge. Easier climbing leads to the top.

**9  True North**     40m    E2 5b     ★★★
J Lamb, R Allen –1981

An excellent direct pitch with thin fingery climbing up the hanging slab and a magnificent finish; just warranting the grade. Start at the blunt arête just left of the flake-crack of *North Buttress*. Climb the blunt arête and groove above to a broken ledge. Continue straight up the ragged crack in the black wall above to a ledge, just right of a hanging slab. Step left onto the slab and climb it to a ledge. Swing up and right to finish up the steep rib in a fantastic position.

**10  Crunchy Frog**  40m    E1 5b     ★★
TW Birkett, R McHaffie – 28 Aug 1975

An exciting and challenging climb taking a direct line up the buttress. Climb the blunt arête (or the crack) and the groove above to a broken ledge. Move slightly left and ascend the tricky groove above to gain holds at its top. Move steeply up and right on magnificent holds to reach a ledge and continue direct to the top.

**11  Adam**          40m    VS 5a     ★★★
P Ross, B Wilkinson - 30 Aug 1955

A superb, better-protected companion to *Eve*. Start in the corner immediately right of the lowest point of the crag. The 'Final Exam' in Shepherd's VSs, but only if the original way is followed! Ascend the corner to the belay on *Eve*. Climb up right then back left and up a short crack to a holly tree. Climb straight up above the holly and continue slightly leftwards up the wall above. The original way is equally good but a tougher proposition. From the holly tree move right to boldly climb the overhanging arête then straight up the steep juggy wall above.

| 1 | Turning the North | VD | |
|---|---|---|---|
| 2 | Gemma | HVS 5b | ★ |
| 3 | Warsaw | E3 5c | |
| 4 | P.P.S. | E2 5c | ★ |
| 5 | P.S. | E1 5b | |
| 6 | P.S. - The Direct Finish | E3 6a | |
| 7 | North Buttress | E1 5b | ★ |
| 8 | North Buttress - Slab Finish | HVS 4c | ★ |
| 24 | Aaros | E1 5b | ★★★ |

**12 Magnetic North**     42m   E1 5b     ★
D Bodecott, D Absalom – 9 Apr 1995

An imaginative diagonal line providing a good way up the crag.

1   12m      P1 of *Eve*.
2   30m 5b   Climb up *Adam* and into the corner of *Crunchy Frog*. Climb this until 3m above the holly tree of *Adam* and, at the obvious break, pull right on flat hand and foot holds onto the hanging slab on *True North*. Go up the hanging slab and traverse right under a nose into the groove of *North Buttress* which is climbed to the top.

**13 Katherine**     45m   E1 5a     ★
A Lywood, R Patey – 17 Aug 1999

Little new climbing but takes a fairly direct right to left line up the buttress. Start at the lowest point of the buttress, left of *Adam*.

1   12m 4c   Climb straight up the centre of the buttress to belay on the ledge.
2   33m 5a   Climb the groove to its top and exit onto the wall above *Eve* on the left. Climb boldly straight up for 5m to a ledge 3m left of the holly tree. Move up and left along grassy parallel cracks to an obvious depression. Climb the crack in the wall above (crux) leading to *Eve*. Finish up *Eve* or the groove of *Delight Maker* above.

| | | |
|---|---|---|
| 7   **North Buttress** | E1 5b | |
| 9   **True North** | E2 5b | |
| 10  **Crunchy Frog** | E1 5b | |
| 11  **Adam** | VS 5a | |

| | | |
|---|---|---|
| 13  **Katherine** | E1 5a | |
| 14  **Eve** | VS 4c | |
| 15  **Delight Maker** | HVS 5a | |
| 16  **Golden Delicious** | E2 5c | |
| 17  **Islands in a Deep Blue Ocean** | E5 6a | |
| 18  **Sin** | HVS 5a | |

Justin Shiels – **Grand Alliance** (E4) Friday 3.40, the school bell rings and we dash for the car. Chris drives to Scotch Corner as I sleep (normal). Extreme Rock Route, first E4, fear of failure contrasts with the tranquillity of Troutdale. P1 and 2 straightforward but jittery. P3. I hate mantelshelves (long levers) but it succumbs. The rest is sublime: delicate, technical, thought provoking. I'm so psyched that it ends abruptly. Surprisingly the ropework turns out fine. The ab, beers in The Salutation, R's stag weekend - cloud 9.

Steve Scott - **The Voyage** (E3). A testing start up and across the crux of Tumbleweed teases the team onto a serious, exposed and technical traverse which unfolds its secrets only through persistence and guile. The final wall retains the bold theme yet with strenuous replacing delicate… whether a stately cruise or a gripping trip it will reside long in your memory.

Trevor Langhorne - **Eve** (VS). The most elegant and exposed of Peascod's ladies finds an intricate way up a fine buttress. Never dull there is a bit of everything, groove, slab, wall, traverse and even a helpful tree root; this route never fails to both delight and thrill. In my formative years Eve was seen as low in its grade and an ascent was an obligatory right of passage into the Mild VS grade, changes in attitudes to spaced protection have turned it into a VS which is serious for leader and second – how things change!

Richard Tolley - **Gillercombe Buttress** (S) is one of the few true mountaineering routes in Borrowdale and one of the best in the Lake District. Taking a long, direct line up the centre of the crag on immaculate rock, it holds the sun for much of the day. All the pitches are very good, but the best is held to the last. A steep crack and groove leads to delicate work on a rib followed by the final sweep of slabs giving some of the best severe climbing in the valley. Its mountain setting with tremendous views across Lakeland is hard to beat.

Andy Dunhill - **The Question** (E2). It's a long walk but more than worth the effort. The line is obvious and compelling; the central grooved arête. An awkward start gives access to the groove & protection. Then it's simply a matter of climbing the steep and constrained groove ... to belay at the top in the afternoon sunshine. The terraces below the wall offer fantastic views making it a wonderful and relaxing place to be in the early evening.

Eve VS (page 75) - Trevor Langhorne · Richard Tolley

74

| 7 | North Buttress | E1 5b |
| 8 | North Buttress - Slab Finish | HVS 4c |
| 9 | True North | E2 5b |
| 10 | Crunchy Frog | E1 5b |
| 11 | Adam | VS 5a |

| 13 | Katherine | E1 5a |
| 14 | Eve | VS 4c |
| 15 | Delight Maker | HVS 5a |
| 17 | Islands in a Deep Blue Ocean | E5 6a |

| 18 | Sin | HVS 5a | |
| 19 | Savage Messiah | E3 6a | |
| 20 | Ardus | MVS 4b | *** |
| 24 | Aaros | E1 5b | *** |
| 30 | Finale | HVS 5a | *** |

⑤ **14  Eve**          50m   VS 4c   ★★★
W Peascod, B Blake – 11 Aug 1951

A popular and memorable route weaving up the buttress. The 'Mid-term Exam' in Shepherd's VSs. P2 is quite serious and demands competence from both leader and second.
1    13m 4b   Climb the short slab and steep crack to a ledge.
2    22m 4c   Ascend the groove for 2m and step left to gain the arête and slab. Arrange the best runners you can and boldly climb the slab diagonally leftwards to reach a stance.
3    15m 4b   Climb the short rib above until it abuts the overhang. Move diagonally right onto the face and continue to the top using a good crack. Photo page 73.

**15  Delight Maker**    40m   HVS 5a   ★★
R McHaffie, B Johnson – May 1982

An excellent direct line up the buttress with a bold middle section, starting just left of *Eve*. Climb the shallow groove then move left onto the arête and follow this in an improbable position to a junction with *Eve* at the start of its traverse. Climb the overlap at a thin crack then the slab to an obvious depression above grassy cracks. Climb its right-hand side and continue up and left to cross *Eve* and finish up the groove above.

**16  Golden Delicious**    40m   E2 5c
M Duff, C Bolton – 17 Sep 1983

An eliminate up the steep wall between *Sin* and *Eve*. Start behind the split block at a pointed flake. Climb up the right side of the wall above, passing a thin crack. Go diagonally left into the centre of the wall and up to a junction with *Eve*. From here you can finish up *Eve* or *Delight Maker*.

**17  Islands in a Deep**    40m   E5 6a   ★
     **Blue Ocean**
M Przygrodzki, D Sperry - 2011

An unbalanced line that is rather squeezed in combines the lower wall with a good finish up the prow. The wall between *Sin* and *Golden Delicious* is bold; avoid using holds on either of them. Continue up to the obvious prow. Climb the overhanging groove in its right side to the top. The prow can be taken on its left at a similar grade.

**18  Sin**          40m   HVS 5a
R McHaffie, P Tinning, J Glen – 27 Nov 1971

Start at the wide dirty left-slanting crack left of the split block at the start of *Eve*.
1    10m      Climb up to a tree.
2    30m 5a   Move awkwardly right to the arête

and follow this to a small ledge and junction with *Eve*. Move right over the overlap and climb the slab to the obvious depression above grassy cracks. Finish up *Eve* or *Delight Maker*.

10m to the left, a line of four large trees marks the foot of the slabby ramp start of *Ardus*, which leads up right into the obvious big corner. Several other routes share this start.

**19  Savage Messiah**    42m   E3 6a   ★
TW Birkett, R McHaffie – 7 Sep 1975

A strenuous and intimidating route which takes the hanging gangway in the overhangs right of *Ardus*.
1    28m 4a   Follow p1 of *Ardus* to the main corner. Climb this then move right slightly to belay as for *Eve*.
2    14m 6a   Climb the rib above to the overhang, pull up left, and follow the steep left-slanting gangway to gain the slab above with difficulty. Continue more easily to the top.

**20  Ardus** ∠ 9/6/20    42m   MVS 4b   ★★★
V Veevers, H Westmorland, P Holt – 15 May 1946

Another editorial anomaly; originally named Andus by the first ascent team.
A wonderful and very popular climb up the large corner. Start at the foot of the slabby ramp-line leading right to the corner.
1    18m 4a   Climb the ramp-line and go up to a block belay at the foot of the main corner.
2    24m 4b   Ascend the block and the corner above to a ledge. With difficulty, traverse left across the exposed slab for 5m and climb a crack to the top. Photo page 76.

**21  Ardus - Direct Finish**    39m   VS 4c   ★★
PJ Greenwood, F Travis - 1956

Instead of making the traverse left continue up the corner/chimney to the top.

**22  Ardus Right -**    40m   VS 4c   ★★
     **Hand Start/Short Notice**
P1 M Przygrodzki – 2 Jul 2010
P2 DW English, W O'Hare - 11 Aug 1960

A direct start followed by a good bold pitch up the wall left of the corner of *Ardus*.
1    18m 4b   Follow *Sin* to the tree and then continue up slabby ramps to join *Ardus* at its belay.
2    22m 4c   Ascend the block above then move leftwards across the wall in an exposed position, to finish up the final crack of *Ardus*.

Ardus MVS (page 75) - Rachel Somerville 📷 Keith Sanders

| 23 | **Saturday Night Beaver** | 40m | E3 6a | ★ |

C Downer, R McHaffie – Nov 1997

Follow *Ardus* to the foot of the corner, move left onto the wall and arrange a clutch of runners. Hard moves on crimps and layaways lead to a standing position on a good hold above. Continue straight up to a bulge and pull over to join the traverse of *Ardus*. Climb the wall between *Aaros* and *Ardus* on small but good holds.

| 24 | **Aaros** | 40m | E1 5b | ★★★ |

R Graham, R McHaffie, TW Birkett, K Forsythe - 22 Oct 1978

An outstanding pitch of fine fingery climbing up the steep wall with the crux saved until the end. Move up the ramp for 4m then follow the narrow right-slanting gangway, just left of *Ardus*, for another 4m. Gain a shallow V-shaped sentry box in the wall on the left and follow the groove above for 3m. Move right and climb straight up the steep wall. Continue in the same line leading to the traverse of *Ardus*. Follow this right then move up to reach and finish up a thin slanting crack in the headwall, just left of the corner.

| 25 | **Ovation** | 40m | E1 5b | ★★ |

D Bodecott, D Absalom, P Arkle – 18 Aug 1992

Good climbing. Step from *Ardus* onto the narrow gangway of *Aaros*. Step left and boldly climb the left side of a rib up to the cracked wall between *Evil Kneivel* and *Aaros*. Climb the wall to a blunt pinnacle and finish up the overhanging wall on the left or the rib.

| 26 | **Evil Kneivel** | 43m | HVS 5a | ★★ ♂ |

R McHaffe, H Rainer – Jun 1975

Another good gap filler.
1    30m 5a    Follow *Aaros* to its groove. Traverse left to below the cracked groove and ascend this to a tree belay.
2    13m 4a    Finish up p3 of *Slings* or abseil off.

| 27 | **Encore** | 23m | E1 5b | ★ |

I Dunn, C Dunn – 1983

Not much original climbing but a direct line up the crag. Follow *Slings* for a short way until below a small black roof. Pull over this and climb up to the groove of *Evil Kneivel* then follow this to the tree.

| 18 | Sin | | HVS 5a | | 25 | Ovation | | E1 5b |
| 20 | Ardus | | MVS 4b | | 26 | Evil Kneivel | | HVS 5a |
| 21 | Ardus - Direct Finish | | VS 4c | | 27 | Encore | | E1 5b |
| 22 | Ardus Right - Hand Start/Short Notice | | VS 4c | | 28 | Slings | | HVS 4c |
| | | | | | 29 | Jaws | | E1 5b |
| 24 | Aaros | | E1 5b | | 30 | Finale | | HVS 5a |
| | | | | | 31 | Imago | | E1 5c |

### 28  Slings                    44m    HVS 4c
G Fisher, R Richardson – 24 Oct 1948

The highlight, if it can be called that, of this route
is the first pitch which requires competence from
leader and second. Start as for *Ardus*.
1    14m 4c   Climb the ramp of *Ardus* for a short
distance to where a gangway-ramp leads left.
Make a difficult pull onto this, from where
better holds lead across and up to a junction
with *Finale*. Move left to the top of its initial
groove and step down to a hidden foothold
which facilitates an awkward move left round
a bulging rib and up to a tree belay.
2    17m 4a   Climb the steep wall behind the
belay, starting up the crack on its right and
finishing carefully with some rounded hollow-
sounding blocks. Traverse the ledge rightwards to a tree belay.
3    13m 4a   Move right and finish up the open
groove and crack in the slab on the right.

### 29  Jaws                      24m    E1 5b    ★★♂
M Lynch, E Cleasby – 20 Sep 1975

A good pitch with some strenuous climbing. Start
below the blunt steep arête above the start of
*Ardus*. Climb the blunt arête on its right side to join
*Finale*. Go up this for a metre or so and follow a line
of stepped grooves on the left to a small overhang.
Climb this, using a thin crack on its right, and continue up the wall to a tree belay.

⑤ ### 30  Finale                  21m    HVS 5a   ★★★♂
T Savage, P Ross 16 Jul 1965

A great test piece giving sustained climbing - was
HVS++. Protection is excellent, assuming you can
hang around to place it, although conoisseurs will
demonstrate that it's not at all strenuous! Start at a
short steep corner just left of the blunt arête. Climb
the corner for 6m, step right and climb the bulge,
groove and crack above to a tree.

### 31  Imago                     26m    E1 5c              ♂
R McHaffie, C Gibson, N Robinson - 1974

A short steep problem starting just left of *Finale*.
Climb up the thin overhanging groove with difficulty to a tree. Continue up the open corner to a
tree belay.

### 32  A Fistful of Dollars     40m    VS 4c      ★
R McHaffie, T Richardson – 1 Jan 1992

Start at a cleaned slab just left of a the large tree.
It supersedes earlier routes and makes the best of
the rock hereabouts.
1    25m 4c   Climb the slab to the base of a left-
facing black corner. Move left and up a steep
crack/fault until it is possible to step left to a
ledge on the arête. Pull up to a tree belay on
the ledge above.
2    15m 4c   Move 5m right along the ledge to
between two trees, climb black rock to below a
small overhang and pull right up a crack.

For those who prefer horizontal movement to vertical, here are two girdle traverses. Both link some
good pitches but are only suitable for a quiet day.
They are not shown on the photodiagrams.

### 33  Central Girdle           70m    VS 4c      ★
T Marsden, J Dowsett - 23 Aug 1955

Begin at the same point as *North Buttress*.
1    20m 4c   Ascend the flake and the bulge
above. Continue until a traverse left and down
leads to a belay on *Eve*.
2    22m 4c   P2 of *Eve*.
3    28m 4b   Move left into the groove of *Ardus*
and follow this to its top.

### 34  North Buttress           82m    E1 5b      ★
### Girdle
R McHaffie, P Phillips, G Barton – Jun 1971

Start 5m left of the corner of *Finale* behind a large
tree.
1    12m 4a   Climb up and then right to belay on a
tree.
2    20m 5a   Traverse right and move down to join
*Finale* and then climb its crack to a tree belay.
3    15m 4b   Go along the ledge to the right and
reverse *Short Notice* into the groove of *Ardus*.
Continue right and belay at the end of p2 of
*Eve*.
4    35m 5b   From the belay, descend slightly
then traverse right to the tree on *Adam*. Move
rightwards, with difficulty, to cross *Crunchy
Frog*, *True North* and finish up *North Buttress* or
*P.S.*

## Brown Slabs

Brown Slabs, composed of immaculate rock, is the home of a number of excellent single pitches where many a climber has been introduced to the sport.

**Approach:** This crag can be easily reached through the trees from the road 200m north of the Shepherd's Café, High Lodore Farm. Alternatively, walk along the base of the crag.

**Descent:** Looking down, take the right hand side of the easy sloping ground behind the slabs. Cross a stile over the northern bounding wall and walk back under *Brown Crag Wall*. If you abseil off the trees, please use a sling.

| 1 | **Gibbon Variation** | 13m | HVS 5b | ★ ♂ |

R Kenyon – Nov 1983.

25m before reaching Brown Slabs is an obvious overhanging layback crack up on the right. Climb it and abseil off. Small, perfectly formed and appropriately named.

| 2 | **Shadow Wall** | 30m | E2 5c | ★ ♂ |

H McGhie - 2010

Some good moves but very artificial. Climb *Brown Slabs Crack* for 5m until a wall is reached on the right. Establish yourself on the wall and follow a series of small ledges up and right to reach the top of the wall at a crack. Climb the blunt rib and slab to a steep groove and wall. Climb the groove to finish at a stance on the left.

| 3 | **Dark Side** | 30m | E3 6a | ★ ♂ |

M Pryzgrodzki, S Metcalf - 4 Sep 2010

A contrived boulder problem. Climb *Shadow Wall* but climb the arête direct. Traverse the flat top of the ridge and finish as for *Shadow Wall*.

| 4 | **Brown Slabs Crack** | 30m | VS 4c | ★★ |

B Beetham - 19 Apr 1947

A popular well-protected route that climbs the obvious corner/groove. Climb the easy corner for 10m to a tree stump. Ascend the slippery corner above with difficulty, passing a tree, to reach the top.

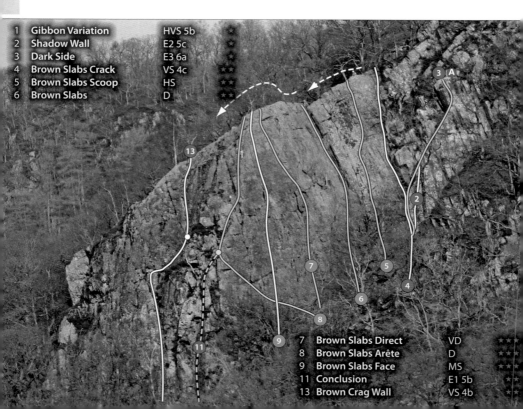

| 1 | Gibbon Variation | HVS 5b | ☆ |
| 2 | Shadow Wall | E2 5c | ☆ |
| 3 | Dark Side | E3 6a | ☆ |
| 4 | Brown Slabs Crack | VS 4c | ★★ |
| 5 | Brown Slabs Scoop | HS | ★★★ |
| 6 | Brown Slabs | D | ★★★ |

| 7 | Brown Slabs Direct | VD | ★★★ |
| 8 | Brown Slabs Arête | D | ★★★ |
| 9 | Brown Slabs Face | MS | ★★★ |
| 11 | Conclusion | E1 5b | ★★★ |
| 13 | Brown Crag Wall | VS 4b | ★★★ |

Widowmaker E2 (page 93) - Martin Dale  📷 Richard Tolley

Derwentwater

Watendlath

## Ashness Gill
NY 278 193                🌐 North West                ⛰ 360m                🚶 10 mins

| **Ashness Gill** | 100m  VD | ★★ |
| --- | --- | --- |
| A Dibona, AR Thomson - 1924 | | |

Approximately 100m of steeper climbing.

This is an interesting and usually wet expedition, which takes the right branch of the gill. It is easily accessible from Ashness Bridge where there is ample parking. From the bridge follow the path on the south side of the gill to the second stile then head down into the gill and continue for approximately 200m, until it splits and becomes much steeper. The real climbing starts here and should provide two or three pitches of enjoyment. The start is an excellent place for a picnic and perhaps a dip in the pool on a warm day.

Some sections have poor protection. The gill may be crossed and re-crossed several times. The way is reasonably obvious but the exact line is left to the adventurous. The difficulty will depend on the volume of water and the gill is not recommended in very wet conditions. It is a historical curiosity, to be enjoyed by everyone; a classic.

**Descent:** Walk right, where the watercourse levels off, to the descent path or continue up High Seat.

# Reecastle Crag

NY 273 176      ⊙ North West      ⚠ 300m      🚶 5 mins

One of the best crags in Borrowdale for those who climb at E2 and upwards and a great venue for headpointing hard routes. Immaculate edgy rock provides strenuous fingery climbing in a beautiful setting. It gets the sun from late afternoon in the summer and, when there are no midges, it makes a superb evening venue. It may take a couple of days to dry after heavy rain.

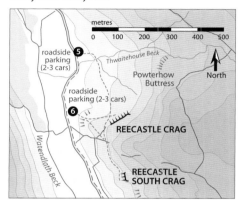

**1   Ador**       25m   VS 4c    ★
R McHaffie, M Wingrove – 27 Apr 1979

A useful route at the grade giving some steep juggy climbing. Climb the block, step across to the slab and cross this leftwards to a ledge. Continue straight up the steep wall above on long reaches, finishing up a short groove.

**2   Bold Warrior**       25m   E1 5b    ★
R McHaffie, M Wingrove – 27 Apr 1979

A good steep route with an awkward start. Climb the short square-cut groove to a foothold on the left. Move up to gain a spike on the left and then go straight up to a shallow V-chimney which leads to the top.

**3   The Executioner**       25m   E4 6a    ★★
P Whillance, D Armstrong – 28 Apr 1979

Short, bold and technical climbing up the left side of the bulging wall. Steep moves lead up and left to reach a shallow green scoop. Move rightwards and climb the easier wall above.

**④ 4   The Torture Board**       25m   E7 6c F7c    ★★
P Cornforth - 24 May 1987

A popular testpiece which climbs the obvious twin cracks. Climb steep rock to gain the base of the twin cracks (peg). Make hard moves up the cracks to the horizontal break. Continue directly up the steep wall with less difficulty.

**5   Grievous Bodily Arm**       25m   E7 6c F8a    ★★
P Ingham - 18 Jun 1987

Considered by some the hardest route on the crag, it takes the right-hand of the two crack systems. Start up the wall passing a small spike to gain the crack. Climb the crack to a good fingerlock then straight up (crux) to a good jug on the right. Move diagonally right to a good spike and continue up to the top.

**6   Last Request**       30m   E6 6c F7c    ★★
A Hocking, W Hunter - 22 May 1998

Finger-searing climbing providing an alternative exit to *Daylight Robbery*. From the top of the crack on *Daylight Robbery*, (peg) make desperate moves left and up on very small holds to a large spike. Climb the easy slab above.

**7   Daylight Robbery**       30m   E6 6c F7b+    ★★★
C Sowden, M Berzins – 6 May 1984

Steep crimpy climbing up the left-hand side of the red streak near the middle of the bulging wall. The crack is followed to its top (peg). Move right and make desperate moves up to a good hold. Continue up the easy crack/groove then slabs above to the top.

**8   Disorderly Conduct**       30m   E7 6c F7b    ★★
A Hocking - 8 July 1997

A good route with very technical climbing which is also bolder than most on this wall. Climb up to a small break and roof (wire). Pull up right and make some hard and bold moves until a move up left gains a large hold and good gear. Follow the red wall to the top.

**9   Burn at the Stake**       30m   E7 7a F8a    ★★
P Cornforth – 1992

The central crackline right of *Daylight Robbery* is bold, powerful and technical. Climb a pale green streak to reach and climb the crack (peg).

## Reecastle Crag

| | | | |
|---|---|---|---|
| 1 | Ador | VS 4c | ★ |
| 2 | Bold Warrior | E1 5b | ★ |
| 3 | The Executioner | E4 6a | ★★ |
| 4 | The Torture Board | E7 6c F7c | ★★ |
| 5 | Grievous Bodily Arm | E7 6c F8a | ★★ |
| 6 | Last Request | E6 6c F7c | ★★ |
| 7 | Daylight Robbery | E6 6c F7b+ | ★★★ |

| | | | |
|---|---|---|---|
| 8 | Disorderly Conduct | E7 6c F7b | ★★ |
| 9 | Burn at the Stake | E7 7a F8a | ★★ |
| 10 | The Whipping Post | E7 7a F8a | ★★ |
| 11 | Remission | E7 6c F8a | ★★ |
| 12 | Penal Servitude | E5 6b | ★★★ |

| 13 | Sentenced to Hang | E5 6b | ★ |
| 14 | White Noise | E3 5c | ★★★ |
| 15 | Rack Direct | E2 5c | ★★★ |
| 16 | Squashed Racquet | E6 6a F7a+ | ★★ |
| 17 | The Rack | HVS 5a | ★★ |
| 18 | Finger Flake Finish | E2 5c | ★★★ |
| 19 | Guillotine | E3 5c | ★★★ |
| 20 | Inquisition | E4 6a | ★★★ |
| 21 | Thumbscrew | E3 5c | ★★★ |

| 22 | The Gibbet Direct | E2 5c | ★★ |
| 23 | The Gibbet | E1 5c | ★ |
| 24 | The Gauntlet | E1 5b | ★ |
| 25 | Off the Cuff and in the Neck | E3 5c | ★ |
| 26 | The Noose | HVS 4c | ★★ |
| 27 | Breach of the Peace | E7 6b F7b+ | ★ |
| 28 | Short Sharp Shock | E6 6c F7b+ | ★ |
| 29 | Water Torture | E2 5c | |

Guillotine E3 - Justin Shiels ◎ Andy Birtwistle

**10  The Whipping Post**    25m    E7 7a F8a    ★★
D Birkett – 14 Apr 1992

Incredibly fingery climbing - the blinding white heat! Climb directly to the thin crack (peg) on *Remission* with the hardest moves past the break.

**11  Remission**    25m    E7 6c F8a    ★★
P Ingham – 31 May 1987

Wandering at the start but offering some of the best climbing on the wall – the slow burner! Gain the obvious quartz break and follow it left to below a thin crack. Technical moves, crux, (peg) lead up using a hidden edge. Step up right to finish up *Penal Servitude*.

**12  Penal Servitude**    30m    E5 6b    ★★★
D Armstrong, P Whillance – 12 May 1981

Brilliant climbing up the bulging wall. Hard for the grade. Climb up rightwards past quartz breaks (peg; RP2 higher). Pull up then leftwards on tiny finger pockets and up to a resting place. Step left into a slight groove and follow it more easily to the top. It is also possible to climb directly from the peg to the shallow groove at E5 6c.

**13  Sentenced to Hang**    30m    E5 6b    ★
P Cornforth – 1 May 1990

Probably the easiest of the E5s. Place gear in the crack of *White Noise* then move left up an obvious flaky rising traverse (RP2). From here go directly and boldly up the wall for about 6m (crux) until it is possible, and advisable, to move back right to rejoin *White Noise*.

⑤ **14  White Noise**    30m    E3 5c    ★★★
J Lamb, R McHaffie – 8 Aug 1978

Brilliant pumpy but well-protected climbing up the left-slanting crack. Climb up to a small overhang; pull up left to gain the crack and follow this up the wall.

**15  Rack Direct**    30m    E2 5c    ★★★
S Miller, R Parker – 19 Sep 1977

A good introduction to the crag up the obvious faultline; a bit of a soft touch. Strenuously climb up the steep wall to a break in the bulges. Pull over and climb the crack to the top with a short deviation out right. Photo page 30.

**16  Squashed Racquet**    30m    E6 6a F7a+    ★★
C Sowden, M Berzins – 23 June 1984

An eliminate, squashed between neighbouring routes but quite independent. Boldly climb the smooth scoop and then pull over the overlap and up to the traverse of *The Rack*. Continue up the wall above moving rightwards to the top.

**17  The Rack**    35m    HVS 5a    ★★
R McHaffie, B Mallaghan – 7 Oct 1973

A good route which packs a lot into its length. Tackle the short crack then cross ledges and continue up left. A bold leftwards traverse gains the obvious crack. Climb this then up right to the tree.

**18  The Rack -**    30m    E2 5c    ★★★
**Finger Flake Finish**
P Whillance, D Armstrong – 9 Jul 1981

Fine steep climbing, well-protected with a short sharp section. From where *The Rack* traverses left go up right into a white scoop and follow a thin flake/crack. At its top move left onto a wall, up to a large sloping ledge and then the tree.

⑤ **19  Guillotine**    30m    E3 5c    ★★★
J Lamb – 5 Sep 1978

A superb route giving sustained and varied climbing which is well-protected. Never desperate but plenty of it. Climb to the ledge then continue up via a thin groove and rib to a bulge. Pull over this strenuously and up to a second bulge. Surmount this and continue up to the top. Photo page 3 and opposite.

**20  Inquisition**    30m    E4 6a    ★★★
C Downer, R McHaffie – 5 Aug 1984

An excellent route with independent climbing at a useful grade. From the ledge, bold layaway moves up a slight rib lead to a good hold on the left and the niche above. Move right then steeply up to gain a rightwards-sloping ramp. Follow this to *Thumbscrew* and the top.

**21  Thumbscrew**    30m    E3 5c    ★★★
J Lamb, D Cherry – 24 Aug 1978

A fine steep route, fingery and sustained, up the bubbly wall. Take the easy wall slightly leftwards to a ledge. Go up the steep wall to a flat hold between two parallel cracks. Climb the left-hand crack and groove above direct.

Derwentwater

Watendlath

Grange

Stonethwaite

Combe Gill

Seathwaite

**22 The Gibbet Direct** 30m E2 5c ★★
C Downer, R McHaffie – 24 Jul 1984

Fine fingery climbing and sustained for the grade. Start directly behind the silver birch. Climb up left, then right, to below the short wall at the foot of an obvious gangway. Gain the gangway with a hard move and immediately pull out steeply left onto the wall. Climb this and the central crack above to the top.

**23 The Gibbet** 32m E1 5c ★
P Ross, AN Boydell – 13 Aug 1964;
FFA D Armstrong, R Parker – 29 Aug 1978

Somewhat unbalanced but worthwhile. Climb *The Gibbet Direct* to its gangway and follow this rightwards to the steep groove. Climb this until it is possible to move out right and up to the top.

**24 The Gauntlet** 30m E1 5b ★
C Downer, R McHaffie – 5 Aug 1984

An eliminate but worth doing. Follow *The Noose* to a block 3m up in the corner/crack. Finger traverse left across the steep wall to gain the gangway. Climb straight up the wall above on improving holds.

**25 Off the Cuff and** 35m E3 5c ★
**in the Neck**
S Crowe, K Magog – 26 Jun 1995

A combination of two routes based around the gangway of *The Gibbet*. From directly below climb to the centre of the gangway. Move to the top of the gangway then out right to a good hold on the arête. Continue up the wall just right of the arête to the top.

**26 The Noose** 25m HVS 4c ★★
R McHaffie and party – Apr 1972

Strenuously follows the prominent crack and corner. Easy slabs lead up rightwards to a short corner. Climb the corner/crack above to a junction with *The Gibbet* at the top of the gangway. Follow this to the top.

**27 Breach of the Peace** 20m E7 6b F7b+ ★
P Ingham, P Cornforth, P McVey – 16 May 1987

Steep. Climb up to a spike runner followed by moves up left then right. Make crux moves up and continue to the top.

**28 Short Sharp Shock** 15m E6 6c F7b+ ★
P Ingham – 24 May 1987

The name says it all. Climb the obvious crack right of *Breach of the Peace* with the crux passing the peg.

**29 Water Torture** 20m E2 5c
P Botterill, P Whillance – 10 April 1981

Short but very fingery. Scramble up to spikes below thin twin cracks in a bulging wall. Climb the cracks then continue more easily up slabs trending leftwards to the top. It might need a bit of a clean.

**30 Crime and** 62m E3 6a ★★★
**Punishment**
C Downer, R McHaffie, S Howe – 29 Jul 1984

A left-to-right girdle giving excellent pumpy climbing throughout. Start from the ledge 10m up the slab of *Ador*.

1 36m 6a Follow the obvious break right to *Bold Warrior*. Descend a little and cross into the shallow green niche on *The Executioner*. Hand-traverse strenuously right to a rest on *Daylight Robbery*. Large flakes lead horizontally to a shallow groove on *Penal Servitude*. Descend slightly to a line of holds leading to *White Noise* then continue to the crack of *The Rack* and arrange a hanging belay; knee pads optional.

2 26m 5c Reverse the traverse of *The Rack* to a tiny ledge on the rib. Move across, past the groove of *Guillotine*, then up rightwards to *Thumbscrew* arriving at foot level on the 'flat hold'. Move right to a thin crack on *The Gibbet Direct* then cross the wall on the right on small holds into the corner of *The Noose* which provides the finish.

# Reecastle South Crag

**NY 273 174**          ⊘ South West          ▲ 300m          ⚹ 10 mins

A useful crag with a small selection of good routes, especially if E2 is your grade. It has the advantage of getting the sun earlier in the day than most crags in Borrowdale.

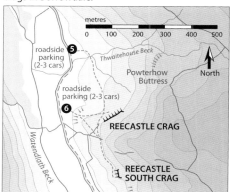

**Approach:** From the right hand end of Reecastle Crag, traverse southwards 150m, passing the top end of a fence.

| 1 | **Ricochet** | 35m | E2 5c | ★★ |
J Lamb, R Parker – Mar 1979

A steep route which takes the upper bulge at its left end. Climb through the block overhangs leftwards into a curving groove which is followed to the steep, blank bulge. Step left to climb a crack through this.

| 2 | **Scratch** | 45m | HS 4a | ★★ |
W Barnes, P Ross - 16 Aug 1964

A pleasant route taking in some good territory. Boldly climb the rib to the bulge and traverse leftwards below this to its end. Step left again and finish up the slabs on the right.

| 3 | **Blonde Ambition** | 30m | E4 6a |
K Wilkinson, D Booth – Sep 1990

Climb *Scratch* or *Ricochet* to the traverse. From a broken spike, climb up and right through the bulge.

| 4 | **Widowmaker** | 28m | E2 5b | ★★ |
D Mullen, H Walmsley – Nov 1978

A good, direct route taking the old aided finish to *Scratch*. Aiding it must have been interesting as there is limited protection. Climb *Scratch* to the bulge. Step up right and boldly follow the rounded arête to the top. Photo page 85.

## Goat Crags Upper

NY 277 170          ⊘ South West          ▲ 400m          🏃 25 mins

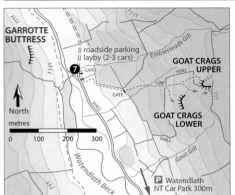

Goat Crags are in an idyllic setting affording splendid views of the central Lakes. The upper crag is quick drying and both offer a selection of very good routes. Well worth a visit, the crags are the last buttresses on the east side of the valley before the hamlet of Watendlath.

**Approach:** Park on the right immediately before the point where the walls begin on both sides of the road. The crags can be seen above the trees. Go through the gate opposite the lay-by, then another gate, just to the right. Take the left side of the field, crossing the fence at a gate, and then continue up the fell side keeping left of a dry-stone wall leading to the base of the lower crag. Follow the higher dry-stone wall to reach the upper crag. Please do not damage the dry-stone walls.

**Descent:** To the right or left.

| 1 | **Goat's Gangway** | 25m | MS 4a |
|---|---|---|---|

D Heard, RA Smithson –3 Aug 2006

Makes the most of the mossy rock on the left flank of the crag. Start beneath the left hand of two right-sloping gangways. Climb the stepped gangway to its apex, move up and step right, then continue straight up the slab.

| 2 | **Kid Gloves** | 25m | HS 4c |
|---|---|---|---|

Eden Valley MC Assault - 1996

The obvious slanting corner.

| 3 | **Littlejohn** | 25m | VS 5a |
|---|---|---|---|

A Hocking - 1996

To the right of *Kid Gloves* there is a short overhanging wall. Climb this to a ledge and the crack and wall above.

| 4 | **Mort** | 15m | E1 5b | ★ |
|---|---|---|---|---|

R Davies – 3 Sept 1989

Start at the lowest point of the crag to the left of the dry-stone wall. Climb up easy rocks to a small triangular overhang. Pass this on the right, with difficulty, to gain a small ledge and finish up the easier shallow groove above.

| 5 | **Balancing Act** | 14m | E1 5b |
|---|---|---|---|

M Turner, A Blyth – 29 May 1996

Climb up easy rock right of *Mort* to a small flake and follow incuts left of this to a good hold. Move right to a short crack and use this to reach the top.

| 6 | **Light Fantastic** | 14m | E2 6a |
|---|---|---|---|

R Davies, K Telfer – 3 Sept 1989

Up easy rocks to an obvious horizontal break offering protection. Pull over the bulge to some flake holds then move up slightly right, awkwardly, to easy climbing direct to the top.

| 7 | **Pussy Galore** | 13m | E2 5c | ★★ |
|---|---|---|---|---|

K Wilkinson, P Hirst – May 1989

The obvious leftward-slanting crack. Moving left to leave the niche is the crux but the upper crack maintains one's interest.

| 8 | **Lucky Luke** | 14m | E4 6a |
|---|---|---|---|

T Ralph, M Charlton – Summer 1993

The leaning wall to the right of *Pussy Galore*. Step off the block to climb the steep blunt rib on side pulls and make a long reach to gain better holds then up to the traverse line of *The Green*. Make a steep move up right to reach good holds leading to the top (side runner in *Munich Agreement*). High in the grade.

| 9 | **Munich Agreement** | 15m | E1 5b | ★★ |
|---|---|---|---|---|

N Brunger, J Gilhespy – 3 Sept 1989

A good route with a sting in its tail. Start at the foot of a large slanting block. Climb the steep wall up and leftwards to the traverse line of *The Green*. Move left to climb a rightward-slanting crack with a difficult finish.

| 10 | **The Green** | 18m | HS 4b | ★ |
|---|---|---|---|---|

RA Smithson, D Heard – 4 May 2004

Move up left to stand on an obvious spike then up left again onto a ledge and follow the obvious leftwards-rising traverse line (decorated with green lichen) to finish up a short corner.

Derwentwater · Watendlath · Grange · Stonethwaite · Combe Gill · Seathwaite

| 1 | Goat's Gangway | MS 4a |
| 2 | Kid Gloves | HS 4c |
| 3 | Littlejohn | VS 5a |
| 4 | Mort | E1 5b |

| 5 | Balancing Act | E1 5b | |
| 6 | Light Fantastic | E2 6a | |
| 7 | Pussy Galore | E2 5c | ★★ |
| 8 | Lucky Luke | E4 6a | |
| 9 | Munich Agreement | E1 5b | ★★ |
| 10 | The Green | HS 4b | ★ |
| 11 | Optional Omission | E2 5b | ★ |

| 12 | Inner Limits | HVS 5a | |
| 13 | The Slab | D | |
| 14 | Nightmare Zone | HVS 5b | |
| 15 | Poland | VS 4b | |
| 16 | Everybody's Dream | S 4a | |
| 17 | Berlin Wall | E2 5b | |
| 18 | Emma Line | HVS 5a | |
| 19 | Low End in sight | E1 5b | |
| 20 | Son of Oz | HS 4b | |
| 21 | Rogue Herries | E4 6a | ★ |
| 22 | The Colour of Magic | E4 6a | |
| 23 | Stranger to the Ground | E3 5c | ★★ |

| 24 | Mull Wait | HS 4c |
| 25 | Route 8 | E1 5b |
| 26 | Route 8.5 | VS 4c |
| 27 | Route 9 | HVS 5b |
| 28 | Scoopy Death | E1 5c |

Inner Limits HVS - Peter Sterling 📷 Laetitia Sterling

**11  Optional Omission**    14m    E2 5b    ★
J Gilhespy, N Brunger – 3 Sept 1989

Follow *The Green* to the ledge then climb the steep wall direct.

**12  Inner Limits**    14m    HVS 5a    ★
R Kenyon, C Kenyon – 30 Sept 1989

Climb the steep corner, step slightly left then move right onto a slab. Continue up the left edge of the slab in a fine position. Photo opposite.

**13  The Slab**    13m    D
R Davies – 3 Sept 1989

The obvious slab just right of the blunt arête.

**14  Nightmare Zone**    14m    HVS 5b    ★
R McHaffie, J Bosher – 1 Oct 1989

Gain and climb the overhanging groove avoided by *Poland* to finish up the arête on the left.

**15  Poland**    15m    VS 4b    ★
N Brunger, K Telfer – 3 Sept 1989

Start as for *The Slab* then go right to a corner. Move up right to pull onto a slab using an obvious clean hold on the arête. Ascend the left side of the slab to the top.

**16  Everybody's Dream**    15m    S 4a
J Bosher – 1 Oct 1989

The centre of the slab right of *Poland* starting just to the right of an obvious tree

**17  Berlin Wall**    15m    E2 5b    ★
1989

Follow *Everybody's Dream* to below the steep right wall. Climb this wall awkwardly, with a small spike runner on the right arête.

**18  Emma Line**    16m    HVS 5a    ★★
J Gilhespy, N Brunger, R Davies, K Telfer – 3 Sept1989

Start up *Son of Oz* then move left and climb the sharp arête in a fine position.

**19  Low End in Sight**    15m    E1 5b
M Dunne, J Timney, A Desmond – 15 Sept 2012

The wall, using neither the arête on the left nor the crack to the right, on surprisingly good holds and with reasonable gear.

**20  Son of Oz**    15m    HS 4b    ★
S Telfer, R Sharpe – 3 September 1989

Climb up to the obvious corner/crack and follow this steeply to the top. Large gear.

**21  Rogue Herries**    15m    E4 6a    ★
K Telfer, R Davies, N Brunger, J Gilhespy – 3 Sept 1989

A poorly protected route with some dubious holds. Climb the steep wall right of *Son of Oz*, which thankfully relents towards the top.

**22  The Colour of Magic**    15m    E4 6a    ★
R Davies, K Telfer, N Brunger, J Gilhespy – 3 Sept 1989

Start below the arête. Climb direct to undercuts below the overhang, span right and move up the shallow corner. Place some protection, move back left to the arête and follow this directly to the top.

**23  Stranger to the Ground**    12m    E3 5c    ★★
K Telfer, R Davies, N Brunger – 3 Sept 1989

Climb a short groove to a sloping ledge, just above a small tree. Step left and climb the wall directly and boldly on holds which never seem to go in the right direction.

**24  Mull Wait**    12m    HS 4c
G Baum, J Meeks – 8 July 1999

Climb the leftward-rising wide crack.

**25  Route 8**    10m    E1 5b
A Hocking – 1996

The short leftward-slanting arête, not using the slab. Contrived.

**26  Route 8.5**    10m    VS 4c
BJ Clarke – 8 Oct 2004

The left side of the slab using the arête.

**27  Route 9**    8m    HVS 5b    ★
B Larkin, D Musgrove - 22 Apr 2015

The centre of the slab with a bold but excellent finish.

**28  Scoopy Death**    8m    E1 5c
M Dale, A Dunhill – 13 Oct 2015

The final yellow slab. Climb the centre of the slab via a thin crack finishing up the scoop.

Derwentwater

Watendlath

Grange

Stonethwaite

Combe Gill

Seathwaite

## Goat Crags Lower

NY 276 169  ⊘ South West  ⚠ 375m  🚶 20 mins

**Descent:** Either down the open grassy gully on the right (take care in the wet) or to the left.

| 1 | **Copperhead** | 40m | D |

SJH Reid – 7 May 1991

Start at the lowest point of the crag 4m left of the shallow cave at a blunt rib. Climb a right-slanting groove, then a left-slanting one, then move up right and back left to a terrace. Follow the short crack and continue direct to the top

| 2 | **Silence of the Goats** | 45m | HS 4c |

A Clifford - 2002

Start just right of the shallow cave. Climb up dirty rock to easy ground (or traverse in easily from the right to this point) then up to a crack in a shallow groove above a vegetated shelf. Layback or finger-jam this (awkward) then climb easier rock to the strenuous wide crack/chimney above. Above this and to the right an easy shelf leads to the top.

| 3 | **Gone for a Pizza** | 25m | VS 4c |

SJH Reid, A Slattery – 7 May 1991

Start below the obvious chimney to the right. Go boldly up to the chimney on improving holds and climb it then easier ground more or less direct to the top.

| 4 | **Left-Hand Route** | 25m | S | ★ |

R McHaffie, J Bosher – 20 Jun 1990

Start on the left side of the bay at a slab. Climb the slab and vague groove moving right near the top.

| 5 | **High Pressure from the West** | 25m | E1 5b |

C Pickles, I Denton – 23 Sep 2001

The wall right of *Left-Hand Route*. Climb to a spike at the base of a steep wall (protection high on the left) and continue boldly up the wall to vague cracks. Pass these to reach good but hidden holds. Finish up the slab above.

The following four climbs are squeezed onto the steep rock to the right and offer good climbing

| 6  **The Niche** | 25m | E1 5b | ★★ |
|---|---|---|---|

R McHaffie, J Bosher – 20 Jun 1990

Start under the lowest overhang just left of the large block. Climb up into a corner/groove on the left of the overhang. At its top, swing right onto a narrow slab. Move up this until it is possible to traverse left on good holds and finish up a groove. Photo page 100.

| 7  **Mackanory** | 25m | E1 5b | ★ |
|---|---|---|---|

A Slattery, H Henderson - 12 May 1993

Follow *The Niche* to the top of the narrow slab. Move right into the overhung corner. Swing right round the overhang and continue direct to the top.

| 8  **The Witch** | 25m | E3 6a | ★ |
|---|---|---|---|

K Telfer, J Gilhespy – 31 Oct 1993

Step off the large block left of *Black Moss Groove* and climb the wall into a groove. Reach left from the overhang and climb the steep groove to the top.

| 9  **The Trick** | 25m | E2 5c | ★ |
|---|---|---|---|

K Telfer, J Gilhespy – 31 Oct 1993

Follow *Black Moss Groove* to the overhang and arrange protection (small cams useful). Make difficult and committing moves left crossing *The Witch* to gain the overhung corner of *Mackanory* which is followed to the top.

| 10  **Black Moss Groove** | 25m | VS 5a | ★ |
|---|---|---|---|

R McHaffie, J Bosher – 20 June 1990

The mossy corner on the right of the crag is better than it looks. Climb the corner, move boldly right under the overhang and finish up the obvious V-groove on the right. Take care to avoid rope drag.

**FAVOURITE ROUTES** ⑤
*Mandy Glanvill*

Living and working in Borrowdale is an incredible privilege and, although it's true there are times you need a waterproof, the variety of routes and crags is fantastic. There really is something for everyone. Favourite routes are never the same twice over whether I am out with Womenrock clients or with friends there's always something special about them, which never wears off.

**Brown Slab Arête** (D) - Teaching people to climb, everyone enjoys this as the view, when you come onto the arête, is of the whole of Borrowdale and makes people smile.

**Corvus** (D) - Everyone's favourite and, without fail, all are surprised when they look left along the traverse line thinking "is this really Diff?"

**Falconer's Crack** (VS) - Just an all round brilliant climb in a wonderful position away from the crowds and hopefully the Falcon.

**Troutdale Pinnacle Superdirect** (HVS) - I would recommend this as a first HVS if you have got slim fingers. I do it once a year with my partner as a treat, it's a family tradition.

**Banzai Pipeline** (E1) - Great memories of doing this with Kit Stuart in my 20s. Greatend is very underrated and deserves more attention.

**Irony** (HVS) - A lot of great climbing in a short route always good fun.

Derwentwater | Watendlath | Grange | Stonethwaite | Combe Gill | Seathwaite

The Niche E1 (page 99) - Martin Dale   Richard Tolley

# Garrotte Buttress

NY 271 171        ⊕ East        ⛰ 260m        🚶 10 mins

This is the small crag on the west side of the valley, nearest to the hamlet of Watendlath. The climbs are worthwhile but the crag does tend to be vegetated.

**Approach:** Park as for Goat Crags. Follow the farm track to the stream, cross it with interest and then strike up towards the crag. See map page 94.

**Descent:** Down the steep grassy slope to the left.

### 1    Supercrack        30m    E2 5c        ★
D Bodecott, P Buntin – 10 Aug 1999

A worthwhile route with a well-protected but tough crux. Climb the scoop, crack and wall above to the base of the right-slanting upper crack. Follow the crack rightwards making a series of awkward/sustained jamming moves where it flares and pull up to the terrace.

### 2    Fleet Street Hackers        30m    E1 5b
A Dunhill, H Rzadkiewicz, D Wood – 10 Jul 2011

A bold climb. Start in the bay 8m right of *Supercrack*. Scramble rightwards up steep grass then back left to reach the base of a steep open groove.

Climb this and pull out left. Move up right then left to a rest below a dubious block. Pull up to this then move out right into a chimney/groove which is followed to a tree at its top. Belay on a ledge on the left.

### 3    The Garrotte        42m    HVS 5a
R McHaffie, M Wingrove – 8 May 1975
FFA S Clark, B Wilson – 8 May 1975

1    20m 4c    Boldly up the impending wall to a ledge on the left. Go up left onto a grass ledge, move onto the rock rib then go up to a good crack above the detached block. Make an awkward traverse right to a small ledge on the arête. Traverse diagonally right under a bulge and climb the arête on the right to a block belay.

2    22m 5a    From the block, step onto the steep wall. Climb round the corner to the right and up the obvious left-slanting groove which forms the right side of the fin. Climb the crack to the top.

### 4    A Local Route        38m    HVS 5a
### (for Local People)
A Clifford, P Newton – 23 Aug 2002

1    16m 5a    Traverse left for a few moves into the open groove with a small tree. Climb the groove, step left onto the slab then move right to the arête. Go up to the foot of a steep wall and belay on a ledge by a large block

2    22m 5a    Follow p2 of *The Garrotte*, then up to a crack in a groove just right of a blunt rib and follow this to the top.

Borrowdale will always hold a special place in my heart as it's where I first started climbing with my Dad and his friends. My first ever climb was *Donkey's Ears* (HS) on Shepherd's Crag. This valley became my playground for trad climbing with amazing friends and mentors. I was truly lucky to grow up in such a beautiful area with amazing role models, going back I never tire of the view sitting atop Shepherd's and looking over Derwentwater. There are so many wonderful routes to pick from that choosing is virtually impossible and I'm certain I've not climbed all the gems in the valley.

**Raindrop** (E1) has to be one of my favourite multipitch routes in the Lakes, it really does have it all. Enough tricky climbing to keep you involved, some great exposure finishing up the last pitch of Troutdale Pinnacle and beautiful rock. I never get tired of re-climbing this route and having a fun day of adventure.

**Hell's Wall** (E6) was my first break into this grade so it holds a special place for me as this crag has a reputation for being hard and intimidating. I always hoped I would be good enough to climb here and it didn't disappoint when I finally was. The climbing is intense with really cool moves, but so safe that you can enjoy the feeling of having to try hard on a trad route without getting scared.

**Prana** (E3) was my first E3 as a teenager, what a line! Up immaculate rock it was hard not to look longingly at this route and be inspired. It's exhilarating to be on the sun kissed rock on the run out at the top with tiny gear testing your mental capacity of committing to maybe taking a big fall.

**FAVOURITE ROUTES** ⑤
*Emma Twyford*

**The Niche** (E2) holds some great memories and was another learning curve in my trad climbing. The great thing about Falcon Crag is that you have amazing views but this crag is exceptionally intimidating and not always solid so be prepared to have your best head screwed on.

**Guillotine** (E3) is such a beautiful route when its dappled in sunlight. A great day is going along the crag and climbing all the classic E3s, it's not the biggest crag but it packs a punch with short quality lines. The climbing is immaculate and so much fun. The first time I climbed this route I had fun unlocking it's secrets in the evening light and enjoying such a beautiful climb.

**Eve** (VS) is such a beautiful multipitch climb, truly stunning and one of my favourite climbs to do time and time again with my Dad. It's popular for a reason but it deserves the great reputation it has with a bold second pitch and safe, but fun, third pitch.

Derwentwater

Watendlath

Grange

Watendlath  📷 Laetitia Sterling

# Grange

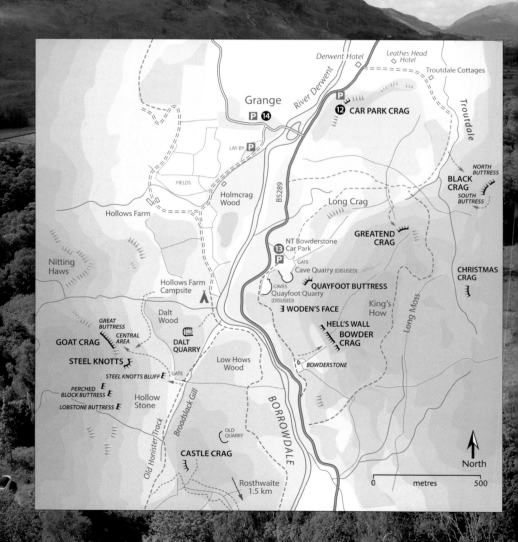

Mandrake HVS (page 129) - Peter Sterling · Richard Tolley

## Car Park Crag

NY 258 177    ⊕ North West    ▲ 90m    🏃 2 mins

A steep buttress with some good routes on sound rock immediately behind the parking area. The closest crag to the road in Borrowdale! Unearthed by some enthusiastic members of the Keswick Horticultural Society during the early 80s, this small crag has a northerly tree-shrouded aspect. Across to the left, the land is private: there is no access for climbing.

**Descent:** Either with care down the left side, or by abseil.

| 1    **Desmond Decker** | 18m   E2 5c | ☆ |

C Downer, C Bacon, R McHaffie, P Taylor - 10 Mar 1984

Good climbing up the open bottomless groove. Boulder the overhang and climb the groove above, mainly on its right side.

| 2    **Double Decker** | 18m   E3 6a |

A Hocking, A Wilde - Sep 1995

Bridge up the corner to the roof. Using small edges, lean out to reach a hold over the lip. Make a strenuous swing to reach/jump for two separate ledges and pull over. Reach *Desmond Decker* in a few moves.

| 3    **Fender Bender** | 20m   E3 5c | ★★ |

C Downer, R McHaffie - 1 Apr 1984

Interesting climbing up the grooved arête. Climb a short wall and grooves finishing directly over the top overhang.

| 4    **Lead Free** | 22m   E3 6a |

T Mawer, D Absalom - 29 Mar 1989

Move up *Mercedes* for a metre or so then awkwardly left round the arête. Climb up then right to the pinnacle. Continue directly up then step right onto *Mercedes* just below the top to finish.

| 5    **Mercedes** | 24m   VS 4c | ★★ |

R McHaffie, C Downer, P Taylor - 10 Mar 1984

The conspicuous slanting groove and chimney.

| 6    **Rush Hour** | 20m   E2 5c |

M Taylor, P Lince - 24 Jun1984

Climb the wall until forced onto *Mercedes* at the roof. Follow this to an overhang, step right and up the gangway then swing out boldly rightwards and climb the wall.

### 7    The Bodycount        24m    E6 6b F7b+
D Booth - 20 Jun 1991

A serious lead. Climb the 'awkward slab' of *Fuel Economy* to the obvious break in the roof above. Climb this and go directly up the steep wall on sidepulls and small holds.

### 8    Fuel Economy        24m    HVS 5a    ★★
C Downer, R McHaffie - 3 Apr 1984

Start at a large flake and climb the overhung corner or the wall just to the right. Move right and pull over bulges to a large spike. Finish up the groove on its right.

### 9    Fuel Crisis        18m    E2 5c    ★★
C Downer, R McHaffie - 3 Apr 1984

Thin climbing in good positions on the obvious upper white wall. Climb the cracked arête to a large spike. Step off this and move up left across the wall to finish up a short crack.

The next two routes start from a large ledge above split blocks.

### 10    Driving Ambition        12m    El 5b    ★
C Downer, C Bacon - 26 Feb 1984

The steep wall on good incuts.

### 11    The Crack        12m    MVS 4b
R McHaffie, P Hirst - 8 Sep 1984

Climb the wide crack in the back corner.

### 12    Hatchback        18m    El 5a    ★ ♂
C Downer, C Bacon, R McHaffie - 1 Apr 1984

Climb the scoop on the left side of the slab, pull over a bulge and continue up a groove above.

### 13    Plastic Pig        18m    E2 5b    ♂
R Curley, A Jack - 7 Aug 1984

A bold eliminate up the centre of the slab.

### 14    Cavalier        18m    VS 4c    ★ ♂
C Downer, C Bacon, R McHaffie, P Taylor - 1 Apr 1984

Enjoyable climbing up the right-hand side of the slab.

# Black Crag

**NY 263 172**    🧭 West through North    🔺 260m    🚶 20 mins

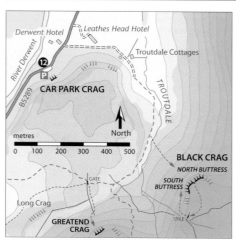

Indisputably one of the best and most impressive valley crags in the Lake District with a fabulous collection of high quality routes across the grades. A large gully splits the crag into two soaring buttresses, each of which has its own distinctive character. To the left, North Buttress provides atmospheric and intricate lines up walls and around overhangs, whilst South Buttress has a friendlier atmosphere and the climbs tend to follow strong natural lines.

The base of the crag is partly obscured by trees. The normal point of arrival is beside a fallen tree at the lowest point of the South Buttress. *Troutdale Pinnacle* starts left of this at a short and well-worn wide crack. The large gully, splitting the crag, is further to the left. About 50m left of this gully there is a prominent symmetrically split oak tree, below a 15m right angle corner marking the start of *The Shroud*.

**Descent:** Well to the South (right) to a path beside the stream that drains the valley behind the crag. ⚠ Attempting a descent before entering the stream valley will lead onto steep and dangerous ground.

| 1 | **The Coffin** | VS 4c | ★★ |
| 9 | **Prana** | E3 5c | ★★★ |
| 19 | **Troutdale Pinnacle** | S | ★★★ |

North Buttress
Page 109

South Buttress
Page 112

## North Buttress

The first two routes start a few metres left of the corner of *The Shroud*.

### 1    The Coffin            70m    VS 4c    ★★
R McHaffie, D Brownlee - 12 Feb 1967

An exhilarating route with steep and bold climbing on good holds. Start at an easy slab just left of *The Shroud*.
1    15m        Climb the slab leftwards, then a corner sprouting a tree, to a ledge; belay on the right.
2    33m 4c    Climb a steep wall behind, passing a bulge. Avoid the overhang by moving left along a gangway before pulling into a steep groove on the right. Climb this on good holds to a niche and step left to a short groove which leads to a ledge.
3    22m 4a    Move right and up for 3m then go left past ledges to below a steep wall which is avoided by a short groove round the arête to the left.

### ★ 2    Jubilee Grooves        114m    E1 5b    ★★
W Freelands, R McHaffie – 7 Jun 1977

Enjoyable climbing; p1 is bold and serious.
1    21m 5a    Climb straight up a scoop in the wall to a ledge, step right and climb up to a heather ledge (no belay). Traverse 5m right to belay on *The Shroud*.
2    33m 4c    Move back left for 5m, ascend a short wall and continue up a groove on the left. At its top, climb back right and down the slab, to belay below the big overhang.
3    36m 5b    Climb left for 3m to a reach and climb a groove at the end of the overhang, moving out right at the top. Continue up the slabby groove to a heather ledge. Walk right to a large block belay.
4    24m 4a    Go back left to the top of the groove. Climb a rib and continue to a tree belay.

### ⑤ 3    The Shroud            72m    VS 4c    ★★★
P Ross, P Lockey – 1 Jun 1958

A varied route of great interest, starting up the obvious corner.
1    12m 4b    The corner to a stance on the right.
2    15m 4c    Climb the groove behind the belay to an overhang (peg). A couple of precarious moves right lead to glorious jug pulling. Belay below the big overhang.
3    21m 4c    Cross the slab on the left for about 7m and then climb up left and up a short groove on the left of a nose. Continue up to the right to another small overhang which

is passed on its left. Go up the short groove above and step left to a ledge.
4    24m 4b    Move right onto a rib then climb a series of mossy slabs and grooves towards bulging rock up on the right. Move left at the bulge then up easily to the top.

### Shroud/Jubilee/Coffin    67m    VS 4c    ★★

This combination of pitches makes a very direct way up the crag avoiding the hollow jugs on p2 of *The Shroud*.
1    12m 4b    P1 of *The Shroud*.
2    33m 4c    P2 of *Jubilee Grooves* to the top of the groove then continue up *The Shroud* to a ledge and belay.
3    22m 4a/4b    P3 of *The Coffin* or p4 of *The Shroud*.

### ⑤ 4    Grand Alliance        57m    E4 6a    ★★★ ♂
R Matheson, E Cleasby – 28 Jul 1976

A thrilling route following an intricate line; the climbing is technical and delicate and requires competence and confidence from both the leader and second. Start at the arête on the right of the corner of *The Shroud*.
1    10m 4c    Climb the blunt arête to a ledge.
2    15m 5b    Traverse right to twin blocks on the ledge. Climb into the overhung corner above. Pull out right and climb the wall above to a slab and belay on *Vertigo*.
3    32m 6a    Traverse right across the slab to the left end of a long overhang, mantelshelf onto a ledge on the wall on the left and traverse delicately right between the overhangs. Climb with less difficulty to foot ledges then trend left to reach small undercuts. Step right and make difficult moves up the wall to better holds. Easier climbing leads to a large ledge.

### 5    Up for Grabs        60m    E4 6b    ★★
J Lee, S Clark - 13 Oct 1965; FFA K Wilkinson, S Miller - 4 Aug 1988

The large roof above the second belay of *The Shroud* gives sensational climbing. Start at the arête of *Grand Alliance*.
1    25m 5b    Climb the wall just to the right of the blunt arête and continue to belay below the roof.
2    35m 6b    Climb the roof at its widest point (peg) and finish up easy rock.

| | | | |
|---|---|---|---|
| 1 | The Coffin | VS 4c | ★★ |
| 2 | Jubilee Grooves | E1 5b | ★★ |
| 3 | The Shroud | VS 4c | ★★ |
| 4 | Grand Alliance | E4 6a | ★★ |
| 5 | Up for Grabs | E4 6b | ★ |
| 6 | Tristar | E4 6a | ★★ |
| 7 | Vertigo | E3 5c | ★★ |
| 8 | Astral Weeks | E3 6a | ★★ |
| 9 | Prana | E3 5c | ★★ |
| 10 | Prana Right Hand | E2 5b | ★★ |
| 11 | High Plains Drifter | E2 5c | ★ |

### 6  Tristar    63m   E4 6a    ★
P1 J Lee, S Clark - 13 Oct 1965
FFA P Livesey, R Fawcett, P Gomersall - Sep 1977

Good but contrived climbing with a serious second pitch. Start 2m right of the blunt arête, on a right-slanting gangway.
1    21m 5b   Climb the wall 2m right of the arête to a ledge. Climb straight up to a small overhang, above the overhang on *Grand Alliance*. Pull round right (peg) onto the face and go up to a slab and belay on *Vertigo*.
2    30m 6a   Climb the wall, just right of the cut-away roof on the left, to a small overhang. Traverse left above the lip of the roof to a resting ledge; a runner on *Vertigo* protects the traverse. Step up and back right on a narrow slab between the overhangs. Pull up into a groove above and climb it and the easier wall above to the large ledge.
3    12m       Easy scrambling leads up the rib above to the top.

### 7  Vertigo    80m   E3 5c    ★★
P Ross, W Aughton - 18 Oct 1958
FFA P Whillance, D Armstrong - 12 Jun 1977

A memorable and thuggy route taking a direct line through the mid-height overhangs. Start on a right-slanting gangway above a large holly.
1    12m       Walk up the gangway, climb a short corner and step right to a yew tree.
2    14m 4c   Step off a block into a corner on the left and climb it to a large slab. Move left for 5m to a block belay.
3    24m 5c   Traverse right across the slab to the left end of a long overhang and mantelshelf onto a ledge on the wall on the left. Climb a series of short left-trending corners, pull over the final roof and move right to gain a small ledge. Climb up left for 2m then up the wall above to a small ledge on the left.
4    30m       Climb the rib on the right and the groove above to a hanging block. Go over this and follow easy slabs above to the top.

The next three routes start at the easy-angled damp black slab left of the gully.

### 8  Astral Weeks    56m   E3 6a    ★ ♂
C Downer, S Kysow – 19 Sep 1982

An eliminate squeezed between *Grand Alliance* and *Vertigo*.
1    12m 4b   The fault leftwards, to a tree belay below the wall.
2    23m 6a   Climb the wall, just right of the tree, direct to the large slab. A desperate mantelshelf over the weakness in the overhang, 3m

right of *Vertigo*, leads to the traverse of *Grand Alliance*; follow this rightwards to a good block. Step up and traverse left along a narrow slab between the overhangs until a pull up left can be made onto a small stance above the overhangs on p3 of *Vertigo*.
3    21m 5b   Climb the wall behind to a bulge. Continue over this onto a steep wall which leads to easier climbing and a large ledge.

### ⑤ 9  Prana    54m   E3 5c   ★★★ ♂
P Gomersall – 4 Sep 1977

A thrilling absorbing wall climb with good holds and reasonable protection; a classic product of the 70s.
1    12m 4b   The fault leftwards to a tree belay below the wall.
2    42m 5c   Move right and climb up the wall, 3m left of the gully, pulling up left onto the slab below the mid-height overhangs. Pull over on small holds or use an easier alternative 2m right. Climb the wall until a step left can be made to a ledge. Climb the bulging wall above to where the angle eases and continue to a large ledge. Photo page 119.

### 10  Prana Right Hand    51m   E2 5b    ★★ ♂
R Graham, P Graham - Apr 2007

A big pitch taking a direct line up the clean rock right of *Prana*. Start up *Prana* to the tree, then climb the right side of the wall direct on excellent holds to the right end of the overhangs. Pull over as for *Prana*, then move up right to climb an open groove to a block (bold); step left and up to a small spike then continue to trees.

### 11  High Plains Drifter    88m   E2 5c    ★
P1 R Graham, P Graham - Apr 2007;
p2&3 W Freelands, J lamb, S Clark - 26 Jun 1977;
p4 W Freelands, R McHaffie - 7 Jun 1977

Originally a left-to-right traverse of the whole crag, the best section across the impressive *Grand Alliance* wall is very worthwhile and is now described in reverse starting up *Prana Right Hand* and finishing up *Jubilee Grooves*.
1    28m 5b   Follow *Prana Right Hand* to the end of the overhangs, then step right to belay in the gully.
2    18m 5b   Swing up and left onto the rib and traverse left, then climb up and left to the ledges on *Grand Alliance*. Traverse left to belay above the overhangs of *Vertigo*.
3    10m 5c   Step up and left, then traverse the narrow slab between overhangs; step up again to a block belay.
4    32m 4a   Finish up *Jubilee Grooves*.

## South Buttress

### 12 **Obituary Grooves**      100m  HVS  5a      ★★
PJ Greenwood, P Ross – 30 Jul 1955

Interesting sustained climbing. Start at the steep slab behind the old fallen tree.
1   30m 4b   Climb the steep slab to a ledge below a flake corner/crack then move left and climb the wall and crack, just right of a dirty corner, to a ledge. Move left and up a short corner then left again to a birch tree.
2   34m 5a   Climb a groove to a yew tree below an overhang. Move out to the right and up to the top of a groove, where an awkward 'swing-layback' move leads left. Climb a short way up the groove above and then move left. Go up and out to the right to a tree belay.
3   36m 4c   Easier rock leads to a large flake. Go up leftwards and make an awkward move into a leftward-slanting corner, from which an exit is eventually made on the right. Gain the groove above, move left to a holly tree and back right via twin cracks to the top.

### 13 **Tumbling Dice**      97m   E2 5c      ★
C Downer, A Brown - 8 Apr 1981

More direct than *Obituary Grooves* with good climbing but no real line.
1   30m 4b   P1 of *Obituary Grooves* to a tree belay.
2   15m 5b   A committing pitch. Go up a groove, past a yew tree, to a crack splitting an overhang. Pull up and swing right to gain a groove, then traverse left to the arête which leads to a ledge and junction with *Obituary Grooves*.
3   14m 5c   Move up below the roof and step round right onto the front face. Trend left to belay on *Obituary Grooves*.
4   26m 5a   Above and left is a wall with an undercut groove. Bridge up to reach an obvious foothold on the lip, continue up to a groove and follow this to a pull out right. Follow *Obituary Grooves* to a holly tree.
5   12m 4c   Move back right and climb a steep wall to the top.

### 14 **The Mortician**      93m   HVS 5a      ★★★
B Thompson, WA Barnes – 7 Aug 1969

A superb challenging cruxy route taking a direct line up the prominent steep groove and crack.
1   30m 4b   P1 of *Obituary Grooves*.
2   40m 5a   Step up right and make an enigmatic and committing pull to get established in the clean-cut groove; sustained climbing up this and the wide crack above lead to a belay below the finger-traverse of *Troutdale Pinnacle*

*Superdirect.*
3   10m 4c   Move into a broken groove and continue directly to the top of the pinnacle, or take the finger traverse; a better alternative unless you have fat fingers!
4   13m      The final pitch of *Troutdale Pinnacle*.

### 15 **Black Crag Eliminate**      110m  El 5b      ★★
R McHaffie, J Eastwood – May 1964

A meandering route offering two good pitches and an exciting finish.
1   21m 4b   Climb *Obituary Grooves* to a good ledge situated several metres below the corner of *The Mortician*.
2   31m 5b   Climb the groove just right of *The Mortician* to an overhang and step right to the arête. Climb the slab rightwards until it is possible to step right to another slab which leads to a crack. Move right to a small ledge.
3   22m 4a   Go up right and traverse the overhung slab to belay at its right hand end.
4   36m 5b   Move up left to the big black corner, step off a pointed block and climb the corner and overhang into a groove trending to the right. Follow this and the face above to the top.

### 16 **The Mortuary**      89m   E2 5b      ★
MG Mortimer, MG Allen - 23 Sep 1978;
Lower part of p2 C Read, GL Swainbank - 22 Jul 2000

Takes a line based on the arête right of *The Mortician*; contrived, but the climbing is worthwhile.
1   21m 4b   Climb p1 of *Obituary Grooves* to a good ledge several metres below the corner of *The Mortician*.
2   45m 5b   Climb the short clean wall on the right to beneath a hanging groove. Enter this with difficulty and continue up to an overlap. Step right and pull back left into the upper groove. Follow the groove until it is possible to enter a hanging groove in the arête on the left; climb this for 6m (serious) to below the jamming crack of *The Mortician*. Climb cracks in the right wall until forced left at 6m onto *The Mortician*.
3   23m 4c   Finish up *The Mortician*.

North
Buttress

| 9 | Prana | E3 5c | ★★★ |
| 12 | Obituary Grooves | HVS 5a | ★★ |
| 13 | Tumbling Dice | E2 5c | |
| 14 | The Mortician | HVS 5a | ★★★ |
| 15 | Black Crag Eliminate | El 5b | ★★★ |
| 16 | The Mortuary | E2 5b | |
| 17 | Troutdale Pinnacle Direct | VS 4c | ★★★ |
| 18 | Troutdale Pinnacle Superdirect | HVS 5a | ★★★ |
| 19 | Troutdale Pinnacle | S | ★★★ |
| 20 | Wasp | E1 5b | |
| 21 | Wack | E4 6b | |
| 22 | Raindrop | El 5b | ★★★ |
| 23 | Holly Tree Corner | VS 4b | ★★ |
| 24 | Grip Factor | E1 5b | |
| 25 | Silent Sun | E2 5b | ★ |

Troutdale Pinnacle Direct VS - Richard Tolley 📷 Ron Kenyon

**17  Troutdale Pinnacle    99m    VS 4c    ★★★
Direct**
JD Oliver, M Nixon, K Pepper – 27 Jul 1952

An attractive and varied route, well-protected and a good introduction to the VS grade.
1    25m 4b    Climb the steep slab behind the fallen tree to a ledge. Go up the flake/crack over an overlap to another ledge and traverse right. Climb up 2m to a block belay.
2    25m 4c    Move left a little and climb straight up the immaculate wall on small positive holds; after 10m step left and continue more easily to a small ledge.
3    24m 4a    Move right and climb a steep wall to a small ledge and belay.
4    25m    P5 and 6 of *Troutdale Pinnacle*.
Photo opposite.

**⑤ 18  Troutdale Pinnacle    96m    HVS 5a    ★★★
Superdirect**
P Ross, D Oliver – 26 Aug 1954

An entertaining combination of delicate and strenuous climbing. Start as for *Troutdale Pinnacle Direct*.
1    50m 4c    P1 and 2 of *Troutdale Pinnacle Direct*.
2    33m 5a    Climb the steep exposed wall and wide crack left of the stance to an accommodating ledge. If there is a queue you can belay here. The way forward is the obvious finger traverse rightwards; good footwork pays dividends here. Fix some protection and make an awkward long reach to gain the best holds which lead into an easier groove and the top of the pinnacle. Those with fat fingers may prefer to move right from the stance and up a groove in the front of the pinnacle, to belay on its top, this defeats the object and is no easier.
3    13m    The final pitch of *Troutdale Pinnacle*.

**⑤ 19  Troutdale Pinnacle    105m    S    ★★★**
F Mallinson, R Mayson – 4 May 1914

Originally known as Black Crag Buttress, this magnificent route navigates its way through a complex maze of walls, grooves and overhangs, before reaching a stunning finale. Burnished in places to a fine patina which serves to enhance the experience. Start either at a well-marked short broken crack just left of the arrival point, or at the back of the queue!
1    21m    Climb the crack to a big ledge then walk on to an oak tree at the right end of the ledge. Climb the wall behind for 6m to another ledge then follow a broken groove to a large block belay.
2    28m    Follow a groove on the right onto

slabs. Follow these more easily rightwards to a ledge and block belay below a corner.
3    10m    Climb the steep and awkward corner on good holds then make difficult moves up and left to a small stance on the right extremity of a fine sweep of slabs.
4    21m    Traverse left and down the slabs to below a steep wall. A committing swing leftwards across the wall, on large polished holds, leads to some ledges and a spike belay.
5    12m    Continue easily up to the top of the pinnacle and a spectacular belay.
6    13m    The steep exposed groove above the pinnacle ends below some overhangs where sensational moves up and left lead to easy ground. Photo page 29.

**20  Wasp    86m    E1 5b**
C Read, GL Swainbank - 22 Jul 2000;
Lower part of p2 MG Mortimer, MG Allen - 23 Sep 1978

Another contrived route that gives some worthwhile climbing. The original sting in the tail was too terrible to contemplate being 'serious and worrying' and is not described.
1    25m 4b    P1 of *Troutdale Pinnacle Direct*.
2    38m 5b    Climb diagonally left to reach and climb a thin crack; move up a crack on the right for a couple of metres until moves left lead up the wall above to a small ledge right of the crack of *The Mortician*. Move easily right for 2m, then directly up the wall left of the crack of *Troutdale Pinnacle Superdirect*, until a move up and left leads onto the slab above. Continue to a block belay below the finger-traverse of *Troutdale Pinnacle Superdirect*.
4    10m 5b    Move well round to the right and step into a right-slanting groove and follow this to belay, 4m below the top of the pinnacle, at a good block.
5    13m    The final pitch of *Troutdale Pinnacle*.

**21  Wack    28m    E4 6b**
P Ross, G Woodhouse, F Carroll – 15 Mar 1959;
FFA J Lamb - 12 Jul 1981

The prominent roof, above the slab traverse of *Troutdale Pinnacle*, gives a short strenuous boulder problem in the sky. From the top of p3 of *Troutdale Pinnacle*, climb the slab rightwards to a steep wall. Climb this and the right-hand crack in the large roof to a notch in the lip (peg). Move up left, then back right above the overhang, to finish up the easier wall. The left-hand crack through the roof, **High Explosion** (A1 4c), is yet to be climbed free.

**22  Raindrop**    90m   El 5b    ★★★
P Livesey, J Sheard - Jun 1973

This very direct line up the pinnacle gives great climbing in airy positions and is probably the best E1 on the crag. Start in the centre of the steep slab at a very obvious left-slanting crack.

1    42m 5b   Technical moves up the short crack lead to a large ledge. Trend left up the slab to break through the left end of the heather moustache. Climb straight up to the left end of a small overhang and move left along a diagonal crack to below a shallow scoop; follow this to a stance.
2    33m 5b   Climb the wall, just right of the crack of *Troutdale Pinnacle Superdirect*, to a good foothold on the right. Move left then go straight up friendly cracks to gain a rightward-slanting groove. Climb this and the arête on the right to the top of the pinnacle.
3    15m 4c   Climb a little way up the groove behind then swing round the arête to the left and so to the top or, like most people, finish up *Troutdale Pinnacle*. Photo page 8.

**23  Holly Tree Corner**    87m   VS 4b    ★
P1 A Marr, P Bean – 30 May 1966
P3 & 4 G Ward, CR Wilson – 17 Jul 1937

An interesting and worthwhile climb where a confident approach pays dividends. Start below a mossy slab behind a large birch tree.

1    35m 4b   Climb the slab and shallow corner to a ledge. Move right up the slab to a tree. Follow the slab in the corner above until a steep move left leads into a groove. Climb direct to belay below a steep polished corner (top of p2 of *Troutdale Pinnacle*).
2    10m      P3 of *Troutdale Pinnacle*.
3    30m 4b   Climb the slab rightwards, below the overhang of *Wack*. Make a steep move onto a gangway which is followed rightwards to its top. Easier climbing leads to an oak tree. An atmospheric pitch.
4    12m      Easily up left to finish.

**24  Grip Factor**    82m   E1 5b
K Neal, J Hume, M Trowbridge – 28 Aug 1977

Provides a much harder and bolder start to *Holly Tree Corner*. Take care to protect the second on the slab traverse; a high runner can be placed above the traverse by climbing a short way above the first belay. Start just right of a holly tree.

1    30m 5b   Climb a slab past a tree at 10m to a small ledge. Follow a thin crack up right until a vertical crack splitting a wall is reached. Climb this to the top of the overhung slabs right of *Holly Tree Corner*. Traverse left across the slab to a short wall which is climbed to a stance at the top of p2 of *Troutdale Pinnacle*.
2    10m      P3 of *Troutdale Pinnacle*.
3    42m 4b   Finish up the final 2 pitches of *Holly Tree Corner*.

**25  Silent Sun**    60m   E2 5b    ★
P Botterill, R Parker – 30 Aug 1978

A good route though care is required with some of the rock on p2. Start as for *Grip Factor*.

1    38m 5b   Climb the slab, past a tree, to a ledge. Step up and left onto a slab, climb this and follow the break through the centre of the overhangs to a short groove. Climb the right arête to a small ledge and belay.
2    22m 5b   Enter the thin groove above and left of the belay and climb it until it is possible to swing up left onto *Holly Tree Corner*, which is followed to the top. Serious.

**26  Troutdale Ridge**    65m   MVS 4b    ★
CD Frankland,  B Beetham - 1921

Pleasant climbing with a short bold crux. Start at a short rib below a large oak growing from the crag.

1    23m      Climb the easy rib and right-slanting ramp above to belay at its top, below a short steep wall.
2    30m 4b   The wall is climbed to a ledge. Move up and left then make an exposed step around the arête onto a slab. Go up this, step left and belay at an oak.
3    12m      Easily up left to finish.

| 9 | Prana | E3 5c | ★★★ |
| 12 | Obituary Grooves | HVS 5a | ★★ |
| 13 | Tumbling Dice | E2 5c | |
| 14 | The Mortician | HVS 5a | ★★★ |
| 15 | Black Crag Eliminate | E1 5b | ★ |
| 16 | The Mortuary | E2 5b | |
| 17 | Troutdale Pinnacle Direct | VS 4c | ★★★ |
| 18 | Troutdale Pinnacle Superdirect | HVS 5a | ★★★ |

| 19 | Troutdale Pinnacle | S | ★★★ |
| 21 | Wack | E4 6b | |

| 22 | Raindrop | E1 5b | ★★★ |
| 23 | Holly Tree Corner | VS 4b | ★ |
| 24 | Grip Factor | E1 5b | |
| 25 | Silent Sun | E2 5b | |
| 26 | Troutdale Ridge | MVS 4b | ★ |

**27  Girdle Traverse**         165m  VS 5a        ★★
PJ Greenwood, DW English, P Ross -16 Jul 1955

An enjoyable expedition at a reasonable grade; a good introduction to the peculiarly British habit of girdle traversing. Best done on a very quiet day; leader and second should both be competent at the grade.

1  12m 4b   P1 of *The Shroud*.
2  15m 4c   P2 of *The Shroud*.
3  24m 4b   Traverse the long narrow slab to the right and go up to an oak tree belay in the gully.
4  26m 4c   Ascend slabs to the right and traverse diagonally right to a tree. Continue up to a ledge and belay.
5  10m 5a   From the groove above, a well-protected awkward move right gains the slanting finger crack, the finger traverse of the *Superdirect*. Follow this airily to a groove and the top of the pinnacle. This is by far the hardest pitch; those with fat fingers can avoid it by climbing rightwards from the stance to reach a groove in the front of the pinnacle then following this to belay on top, this is no easier.
6  33m 4a   Reverse p5 and 4 of *Troutdale Pinnacle*.
7  18m 4b   Descend to the slab on the right which is climbed to a junction with *Troutdale Ridge*.
8  15m       Climb the slab above to a stance at an oak.
9  12m       Easily up left to finish.

**FAVOURITE ROUTES** ⑤
*James McHaffie*

**The Niche** (E2) was one of dad's new climbs and became a regular solo for me. A technical traverse on the 1st pitch leads to a cool hanging belay. The 2nd pitch is burly but leads to a good ledge where a lovely VS pitch leads up to the top on perfect rough rock. *Route 1* and *Dry Gasp* on the upper cliff are also amazing.

**Banzai Pipeline** (E1) is in a lovely setting and is always quiet with stunning views back over Derwentwater. The most difficult and bold bits are in the first 30 metres but the rest is varied and has a memorable 5a move to step across the groove near the end.

**Grand Alliance** (E4) looks very improbable from below and offers committing climbing on perfect rock. A contender for the best E4 in the valley.

**Bitter Oasis** (E4) is a Pete Livesey masterpiece. Once having a peg to protect the tricky moves starting the 2nd pitch it now gives a more lonely lead spacewalking over the 'Great Butress'. One of the best in Britain.

**Tumbleweed Connection** (E2) weaves about on the best rock giving two delicate pitches. Goat and Falcon crags were my two favourite cliffs in Borrowdale.

Prana E3 (page 111) - Peter Sterling    Sterling col.

# Christmas Crag

NY 262 167          ⊖ West          ⚠ 340m          🏃 30 mins

This is a small quick-drying crag of rough rock offering good mid-grade routes in an attractive setting. The upper tier offers the best climbing.

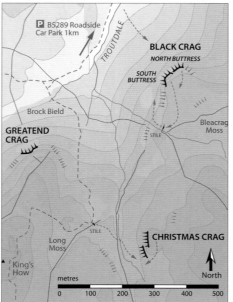

**Approach:** Follow the path into Troutdale and continue up a steep well-made path. Where this levels out, cross the stile over a fence on the left and follow the path over a small col where the crag comes into view. This point may also be reached from the Bowderstone Car Park (NT) by following the path northwards. Just before the second dry-stone wall fork right and up the steep path to the stile and col.

**Descent:** To the right.

## Upper Tier

The Upper Tier is reached by walking to the right of the crag and traversing left to the terrace below the climbs.

**1   Stocking Filler**          14m   S 4a
BJ Clarke – 19 Feb 2006

The arête and curving crack at the far left end of the terrace.

**2   Christmas Tree Groove** 16m   HVS 5a
R McHaffie, T Richardson – 2 Jan 1993

Poor protection. Climb the mossy groove directly, move right and finish as for *1993*.

**3   1993**                      16m   E1 5b   ★★
R McHaffie, T Richardson – 3 Jan 1993
A Dunhill – 13 Aug 2008 (Groove start)

Start at a small tree right of the rib. Climb up (small wires) then make a delicate move up and left to gain the rib; follow this to the top. Alternatively, start up the groove on the left.

**4   Christmas Decoration** 16m   VS 4b
R McHaffie – 25 Dec 1992

**5   One Horse Open**          17m   S 4a
BJ Clarke - 17 Dec 2007

**6   Sleigh Ride**             16m   HS 4a
R McHaffie – 25 Dec 1992

**7   Jingle Bells**            16m   MVS 4a
R McHaffie – 25 Dec 1992

**8   Happy Christmas**         14m   VS 4b   ★
R McHaffie – 25 Dec 1992

Climb leftwards from the foot of the buttress then finish straight up. Photo page 124.

**9   Sherry Trifle**           14m   HVS 5a  ★★
BJ Clarke, L Hibbert – 7 Aug 2005

Climb the front of the buttress trending right-wards, using a good but doubtful jug to overcome the smooth central section.

**10  Alka Salsa**              14m   HVS 5a  ★★
BJ Clarke, P Foster, T Coates - 26 May 2007

A good pitch up the right edge of the buttress. Climb a short rib and pull over a small overhang. Step right and go up a shallow groove to reach a ledge on *Christmas Pudding*. Move up left and finish up a rib.

**11  Christmas Pudding**       14m   VS 4c
R McHaffie, T Richardson – 3 Jan1993

Climb the leftward-slanting chimney/groove on the right side of the buttress.

There is a steep unclimbed wall to the right with some loose rock. Right again is a short wall of good rock with a small pinnacle at its base.

## 12 Christmas Rib 10m HVS 5b
R McHaffie - 25 Dec 1992

The rib has a difficult start

## 13 Christmas Groove 10m S
R McHaffie, T Richardson – 2 Jan 1993

The groove left of the small pinnacle.

## 14 White 9m VS 4b
BJ Clarke - 9 Nov 2007

Start at the small pinnacle and climb the clean left side of the mossy groove to finish up the left arête.

## 15 Soda Stream 9m VS 4c
BJ Clarke – 27 Oct 2007

Climb the wall and arête direct keeping just right of the mossy groove.

## 16 Tinsel Trail 9m S
BJ Clarke - 1 Feb 2006

Step right from the pinnacle and follow the slanting shallow grooves, trending right to finish.

## 17 Light Fairy 9m VS 5a
BJ Clarke - 2 Feb 2006

The obvious undercut slab 2m right of the pinnacle gives an intriguing couple of moves. Gain the slab from the left and smear warily rightwards across it. Finish up and slightly left

## 18 Boxing Day 8m VS 5a
A Dunhill - 1 May 2007

The slim groove 4m right of the pinnacle. Make a strenuous pull up the groove to the top of the slab of *Light Fairy* then finish direct over the dubious block or on the left

### Lower Tier

The lower tier offers a few indistinct climbs and two reasonable ones.

## 19 Easy Ridge 16m VD
R McHaffie - 25 Dec 1992

## 20 Reindeer 16m E1 5b ★
A Dunhill, M Dale, C Thistlethwaite - 17 May 2014

Climb the open right-slanting groove to the base of the steep wall. Move up and traverse left to the edge then climb directly to a ledge at the left end of the overlap, avoiding the dubious block. Continue up the left side of the arête above

## 21 Gargoyle Groove 15m HVS 5a
R McHaffie, T Richardson – 3 Jan 1993

The obvious corner with an exit right

## 22 Yule Be Surprised 15m HVS 5a ★
M Dale, A Dunhill, C Thistlethwaite - 17 May 2014

Move up and right until below the corner. Pull up left into the corner then swing out left, in a fine position, to gain the front of the buttress and up this more easily to the top.

## 23 Royal Oak 15m HS
BJ Clarke - 7 Sep 2006

## 24 Troika 16m MVS
BJ Clarke – 9 Nov 2007

## 25 Plum Duff 8m MS
BJ Clarke – 9 Nov 2007

South of the crag is a prominent black slab that is often wet; when it's dry it provides a pleasant climb especially in the evening sun. Oddly called - 26 **Black Slab** (HS, 2008), the line is obvious.

# Christmas Crag

| 1 | Stocking Filler | S 4a | 20 | Reindeer | E1 5b |
| 2 | Christmas Tree Groove | HVS 5a | 21 | Gargoyle Groove | HVS 5a |
| 3 | 1993 | E1 5b | 22 | Yule Be Surprised | HVS 5a |
| 4 | Christmas Decoration | VS 4b | 23 | Royal Oak | HS |
| 5 | One Horse Open | S 4a | 24 | Troika | MVS |
| 6 | Sleigh Ride | HS 4a | 25 | Plum Duff | MS |
| 7 | Jingle Bells | MVS 4a | 26 | Black Slab | HS |
| 8 | Happy Christmas | VS 4b | | | |
| 9 | Sherry Trifle | HVS 5a | | | |
| 10 | Alka Salsa | HVS 5a | | | |
| 11 | Christmas Pudding | VS 4c | | | |
| 12 | Christmas Rib | HVS 5b | | | |
| 13 | Christmas Groove | S | | | |
| 14 | White | VS 4b | | | |
| 15 | Soda Stream | VS 4c | | | |
| 16 | Tinsel Trail | S | | | |
| 17 | Light Fairy | VS 5a | | | |
| 18 | Boxing Day | VS 5a | | | |
| 19 | Easy Ridge | VD | | | |

Black Slab
100m south

Happy Christmas VS (page 120) - Sarah Bailey    Ian Grimshaw

## Greatend Crag

NY 260 170     ⊘ North West     ▲ 225m     🏃 25 mins

This imposing crag towers above Grange. With its northerly aspect and vegetated drapery it is forbidding in appearance. After a fire raged here for more than a week in 1940 a number of routes were climbed. The vegetation returned through the remains of dead trees and ashen soil, and the popularity of the crag diminished. A local group of 'sodbusters' reclaimed the crag in the 1970s and a number of excellent routes were added. Today much of the crag has returned to nature.

**Approach:** Parking at Bowderstone Quarry. Take the path north towards Troutdale to the dry-stone wall. Go through the gate and follow the wall rightwards until it begins to peter out. Cross the wall then follow the wire fence south for a short distance before heading up to the foot of the cliff.

**Descent:** Go up and rightwards to indistinct paths leading down the right side of the crag. Alternatively, head left to join the path from King's How then head back up to the foot of the crag.

---

⑤ **1   Nagasaki Grooves**    90m   E4 6b   ☆☆☆
C Reid, J Adams - 24 Jul 1972; FFA P Livesey - 22 Jun 1974

This superb climb follows a line of interlinking grooves and corners up the steep wall left of *Banzai Pipeline*.
1   30m 5b   Pitch 1 of *Banzai Pipeline*.
2   45m 6b   Climb on the left until it is possible to move up rightwards to the foot of a long smooth groove. Gain and climb it with some difficulty. Move left and up to a bulge. Surmount this on the right and continue up the thin poorly protected groove above to a ledge.
3   15m   Continue more easily to the top.

---

★ **2   Banzai Pipeline**    90m   E1 5b   ☆☆☆
⑤ D Nicol, C Downer, H Cobb, C Bacon - 26 Jun 1977

A brilliant route giving varied and interesting climbing with a bold first pitch. Start on the right-hand side of a pinnacle, 16m down and left of *Greatend Corner*.
1   30m 5b   Ascend the pinnacle and follow a white diedre. Move left over an overlap then up to climb the corner above. Move left and ascend a further corner over a bulge to a slab. Belay below a crack.
2   30m 5b   Climb the crack to a ledge then the chimney/crack above to a ledge and belay.
3   30m 5a   Move up left to stand on a spike. Either swing left round a rib into a slanting groove and follow it; or climb direct from the spike then continue up the walls above to the top.

---

**3   Greatend Corner**    72m   E1 5b   ☆☆☆
D Nichol, C Downer, I Conway, D Hellier – 28 April 1975

A striking climb which goes up the obvious long corner in the centre of the crag. Once very popular, this route now sees less traffic than it used to, yet still provides a memorable outing.
1   15m   Go up an easy chimney and step left onto a ledge.
2   45m 5b   Climb up past rattly flakes to easier ground and an overhang. Continue up a vertical groove and either make an exit right to the rib, or continue up the groove, with difficulty, and move right to a pedestal and belay.
3   12 m 5a   Climb the wall to a corner/crack on the left and climb it to the top.

---

**4   No Holds Barred**    45m   E2 5b   ☆☆☆ ♂
C Downer, S Kysow – 13 May 1982

An excellent and direct line up the slab.
Climb *Greatend Corner* for 3m. Step right and climb directly up an obvious line of slim grooves and a difficult crack to belay at a tree.

# Quayfoot Buttress

NY 254 167          ⊙ West North West          ⛰ 135m          🏃 5 mins

This popular crag offers very accessible high quality climbing on superb compact rock: a HVS – E2 climbers' paradise! It is especially enjoyable to climb here in the afternoon or evening sun.

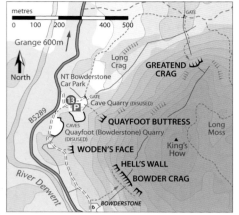

The first climb starts well up and left of the fence at the foot of the crag.

### 1    The Mound          30m    VS 4b          ★
R McHaffie, P Phillips - 13 Apr 1969

A surprisingly good route that winds its way between patches of vegetation. Start at a clean slab below and right of a long overhang. Climb the steep slab and the V-groove above before stepping left onto a narrowing gangway. Pull onto the slabby wall and climb the cleanest rock to the top; the upper section has spaced protection.

### 2    Quayfoot Buttress          56m    VD          ★★
B Beetham - 4 Apr 1946

Enjoyable varied climbing which becomes more interesting as height is gained. Start 3m right of the fence at the foot of the crag.
1    31m    Climb a groove rightwards to a block overhang which is avoided on the left; continue to a ledge. Move left to a small tree then climb the arête and groove to a good ledge.
2    25m    Climb the scoop on the left then make an awkward move onto a ledge. Follow the slab above to the top.

The next seven routes start from ledges below the conspicuous right-facing corner taken by *Aberration*.

### 3    The Crypt          40m    HVS 5a          ★★
R McHaffie, JG Alderson -1 May 1969

Cracking climbing up the shallow scoop. Start from the left end of the ledges. Climb up a few metres then pull over an awkward bulge and continue to a tree. Move up to gain and climb the fine scoop; at the overlap move left to the rib and follow this to the top. Photo page 130.

### 4    The Crypt Direct          40m    E1 5b          ★★
K Rudd - 17 Apr 1971

This short and sharp alternative finish climbs the overlap and wall avoided by the original route.

### 5    The Go Between          40m    E2 5c          ★★
J Lamb, P Botterill - 20 Jun 1981

A steep start leads to satisfying technical climbing up the wall between *The Crypt Direct* and *Aberration*. The steep crack leads to easier ground and a ledge. Follow a vague crack-line in the middle of the wall above to a horizontal break; continue directly up the wall above to the top. If the initial crack is wet, start up *Mandrake*.

### 6    Brain Stain          42m    E4 6a          ★
N Dixon, S Walker, P Whitfield - 10 Aug 1982

Thought-provoking climbing up the wall above the traverse on *Mandrake*. May benefit from a brush up before leading. Start as for *The Go Between*. Follow *The Go Between* to the ledge. Step right and climb the delicate slab to the traverse of *Mandrake*. Move up left then pull up right, over the overlap, onto an oval hanging slab. Climb up right past a sickle-shaped flake to a second overlap; continue over this and up the short groove.

### 7    Aberration          44m    VS 4c          ★★
O Woolcock, P Nunn - 2 May 1965

Technical and delicate climbing in good positions. Start below the right-facing corner in the centre of the buttress. Gain the corner, which gives interesting moves, leading to a short narrow chimney then an overhung ledge. Establish yourself on the rib to the left then go diagonally left crossing *Mandrake* to a chimney/groove which is climbed, past a tree, to the top. Photo page 132.

**5** **8   Mandrake**           44m   HVS 5a   ★★★
A Liddell, M Burbage - Jul 1964

Simply superb; one of the valley's finest single pitch HVSs. From the base of *Aberration's* corner, hand-traverse left for 3m then climb up to a ledge. Continue up the thin crack leading to the bottom of the chimney/groove on *Aberration*. Traverse right for 6m to another crack and climb this to an overhang; thrilling moves over this lead to a grand finish. Photo page 105.

Two obvious direct hybrid pitches are possible; perhaps not when the crag is busy!

**Aberration Direct** (36m VS 5a ★★) follows *Mandrake* until it joins *Aberration*.

**Mandrake Superdirect** (36m HVS 5a ★★) climbs *Aberration* to the rib then continues to join *Mandrake*.

| 2 | Quayfoot Buttress | VD |
| 3 | The Crypt | HVS 5a |
| 4 | The Crypt Direct | E1 5b |
| 5 | The Go Between | E2 5c |
| 6 | Brain Stain | E4 6a |
| 7 | Aberration | VS 4c |

| 8 | Mandrake | HVS 5a | ★★★ |
| 9 | Mandrake Direct | E1 5b | ★ |
| 10 | Morceau | HVS 5a | ★★ |
| 11 | Dark Angel | E5 6b | ★ |
| 12 | Irony | HVS 5a | ★★★ |
| 13 | The Creep | E1 5c | ★ |
| 14 | Sidewinder | E2 5b | ★★ |

The Crypt HVS (page 128) - Justin Shiels    Richard Tolley

### 9 Mandrake Direct   40m   E1 5b   ★
R Graham, P Graham - 3 Sep 2001

Not as satisfying as the original. Follow *Mandrake* to the start of the hand-traverse; ignore this and climb straight up to the left end of a grass and heather ledge. Traverse right on or below this to move up onto the blunt arête left of *Aberration*. Climb this to join and finish up *Mandrake*.

The short left-facing overhanging corner at the base of the right side of the crag is the start of *Irony*. The next two routes also use this start.

### 10 Morceau   45m   HVS 5a   ★★
D Bodecott, T Knowles - 18 Jul 1995

Very enjoyable climbing on an indirect line that crosses many routes; for a quiet day only. Climb the corner of *Irony*, step left and follow the groove until moves can be made up and left to *Aberration's* narrow chimney, which leads to an overhung ledge. Pull right over the bulge to join the crack of *Irony* leading to the end of the large horizontal break. Make a sensational hand-traverse crossing *Dark Angel*, *Mandrake* and *Brain Stain* to the tree on *Aberration* and easy ground.

### 11 Dark Angel   40m   E5 6b   ★
M Pryzgrodzki, R McHaffie - 19 Oct 1997

An eliminate squeezed onto the narrow wall between the upper sections of *Mandrake* and *Irony*. Climb the corner of *Irony* then pull over the nose of a blunt pillar with difficulty; continue up to join *Irony* which is followed until it is possible to step left above an overhang. The steep wall immediately right of a thin crack leads to the overlap right of *Mandrake*. Pull over the overlap with great difficulty to a right-slanting ramp, reach a pocket

and re-join *Irony*. Go up to a break and finish just right of *Mandrake*.

### ⑤ 12 Irony   40m   HVS 5a   ★★★
R Belden - 1961; FFA A Liddell, R McHaffie - 1961

Sustained absorbing climbing leading to a memorable and spectacular overhang. The short stiff overhanging corner to the right of *Aberration* leads to a ledge. Follow a groove and slab on the left before moving slightly right to a crack which is climbed to a ledge. Cross the broken overhang and climb the thin crack; swing right at the top to another ledge. Move left under the large overhang and pull over with great difficulty; continue more easily to the top.

### 13 The Creep   35m   E1 5c   ★
CJS Bonington, R Lawson, I Lawson - Jun 1965

Start in the gully below a steep corner/crack which proves to be particularly uncooperative. Fight your way up the crack then move out right to a slab and climb to a ledge on the left. The mossy wall above leads to the ledge below the overhang of *Irony*. Climb the steep groove on the right to a roof which is passed on the left; finish up the wall.

### 14 Sidewinder   33m   E2 5b   ★★
J McHaffie, R McHaffie - 22 Mar 1998

Start a few metres further up the gully from *The Creep* near a wide crack.  Climb the wall left of the crack to reach the top of a flake. Pull onto the slab using twin cracks on the right. Continue over a small overlap in the corner onto the top slab. Climb up to the large overhang in the corner, pull over and move up to a good hold. Either traverse left through the ever-widening crack to the top or finish directly up the steep wall.

Abberation VS (page 128) - Andy Cairns   Keith Sanders

# Woden's Face                                    🎋

NY 253 166          ⊖ West              🔺 110m              🚶 5 mins

This delightfully sunny wall of immaculate ice-planed rock offers a nice selection of routes in the S – VS grades. There is a good picnic site on the rocky knoll facing the crag. Popularity has resulted in some wear and tear but this does not detract from the quality of the climbing.

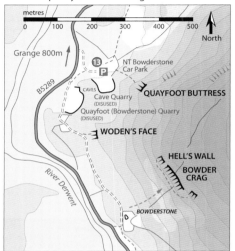

**Approach:** Bowderstone Quarry car park. From the car park take the Bowderstone track.

| 1 | **Left Hand Route** | 13m | VD | |
R McHaffie - 1989

The obvious groove and crack.

| 2 | **Family Outing** | 15m | S | |
R McHaffie, JM McHaffie, JR McHaffie - 7 Jun 1989

James McHaffie's first new route! From the lowest point of the wall, climb to the obvious slabby ramp leading to the top.

| 3 | **Blue Riband** | 15m | HS 4b | ★ |
R McHaffie - 4 Jun 1989

The enjoyable steep cracked face.

| 4 | **Jaffa Cake** | 15m | S | |
R McHaffie - 4 Jun 1989

The ramp behind the tree.

The remaining routes lead to a terrace just below the top; a scramble down left from here is possible with care; alternatively climb a short easy wall to the top.

| 5 | **Wimpey Way** | 24m | S | ★★ |
W Robinson, K Perry - 1970

Start 3m right of the large oak at an obvious stepped groove. Some layaway moves lead to the groove which is followed to the terrace.

To the right, a large block overhang at 6m is a prominent feature.

| 6 | **Woden's Face** | 25m | MVS 4b | ★★ |
B Beetham, CD Frankland - 1921

A popular route characterised by exposed and exciting climbing in its upper half. Teeter up the wall to the overhang then make delicate moves left to join *Wimpey Way*. From a short distance up the groove, step right and follow the precarious scoop in the edge of the buttress to the terrace. The scoop can be avoided to the right; this reduces the grade to S 4a with no loss of quality.

| 7 | **Woden's Face Direct** | 24m | S 4a | ★★ |
B Beetham, CD Frankland - 1921

Good climbing up the centre of the wall. Follow *Woden's Face* to the block overhang and reach the top of the block by skirting either side; left is easier. Step off the block, move right a metre or so, then gain and climb a shallow scoop. At its top move left then climb directly to the terrace.

| 8 | **Woden's Wotsit** | 24m | E2 5b | ★ |
R Kenyon, C Eckersall - 4 Jul 1984

This direct route up the right side of the front face offers good climbing with no real line. Start from a ledge below the wall left of *Woden's Cheek*. A few stiff pulls up the wall lead to easier ground and a ledge. Continue up the wall and slab between *Woden's Face Direct* and *Woden's Cheek*.

| 9 | **Woden's Cheek** | 22m | VS 4c | ★★ |
B Beetham - 12 Sep 1935

An awkward start leads to an airy finish. On the right side of the crag there is a short groove above a small overhanging wall. Enter the groove by a decisive and difficult pull and follow it to a good ledge. Continue up the groove above, moving right to finish.

Derwentwater | Watendlath | Grange | Stonethwaite | Combe Gill | Seathwaite

Derwentwater

Watendlath

Grange

### 10  Wodentops          20m   E2 6a
P Carling - 29 Jul 1989

The thin crack in the overhanging wall right of
*Woden's Cheek* is uncooperative but eases when
a ledge and good holds are reached.  Climb the
groove between *Woden's Cheek* and *Tantalus* past
a poor spike, then move over a bulge and finish up
twin cracks.

### 11  Tantalus          20m   VS 4c          ★
K Jones, W Baddet - 10 May 1969

An enjoyable test piece at the grade starting at a
greenish wall up and right of *Woden's Cheek*. After
a few easy moves move right to gain the top of the
obvious flake; climb the technical groove and crack
above to the terrace. Photo opposite.

| | | | |
|---|---|---|---|
| 1 | Left Hand Route | VD | |
| 2 | Family Outing | S | |
| 3 | Blue Riband | HS 4b | ★ |
| 4 | Jaffa Cake | S | |
| 5 | Wimpey Way | S | ★★ |
| 6 | Woden's Face | MVS 4b | ★★ |
| 7 | Woden's Face Direct | S 4a | ★★ |
| 8 | Woden's Wotsit | E2 5b | ★ |
| 9 | Woden's Cheek | VS 4c | ★★ |
| 10 | Wodentops | E2 6a | |
| 11 | Tantalus | VS 4c | ★ |

Tantalus VS - Chris Campbell   Ron Kenyon

⊘ South West   ▲ 220m   ⚹ 20 mins

...erstone are a number of but-
...ge variety of popular routes across
...r the grades.

**Approach:** From the Bowderstone Quarry car park a track leads to the Bowderstone, passing below Woden's Face. Just before the Bowderstone take a track on the left to below Bowderstone Pinnacle with Hell's Wall up to the left.

| 1 | Just and So | E2 5c | ✦✦ |
| 2 | Fleur de Lys | MS | |
| 3 | Woden's Needle | S | ✦✦✦ |
| 4 | Creeping Bentley | VS 4c | ✦ |
| 5 | Needle Wall | HVS 4c | ✦✦ |
| 7 | Woden's Crack | VS 4c | ✦✦ |
| 9 | Hell's Wall | E6 6c F7c+ | ✦✦✦ |
| 15 | Valhalla | E1 5c | ✦✦✦ |
| 16 | The Bulger | E5 6b | ✦✦✦ |
| 17 | Heaven's Gate | E3 6a | ✦✦✦ |

## Left Hand Section

To the left of Bowderstone Pinnacle is the imposing Hell's Wall and about 50m down and left is a small open buttress fronted by a prominent pinnacle: Woden's Needle. A further 60m up and left is another buttress.

**Approach:** Scramble up the lower rocks to behind an oak tree below a groove with a crack sprouting a birch tree.

**Descent:** The best descent is by the gully just right of *Just and So* – and well left of Hell's Wall.

| 1 | Just and So | 26m | E2 5c | ★★ |
|---|---|---|---|---|

P Norman, R Henderson - 31 May 1988

A hidden gem starting 4m left of *Fleur de Lys*.

1   12m 5a   Follow the obvious thin crack (can be dirty) to a large grass ledge and holly tree belay.

2   14m 5c   Step right into the scoop and follow the thin crack for 2m to a hand-traverse. Move 3m right and ascend the small overhang to the top.

| 2 | Fleur de Lys | 36m | MS | ★ |
|---|---|---|---|---|

GB Fisher, GB Withington - 9 Mar 1950

A good climb with a short mossy section. Ascend the groove, past the tree, then traverse diagonally right to an oak. Continue up the fine steep crack above. Finish up a short pleasant wall and slab above.

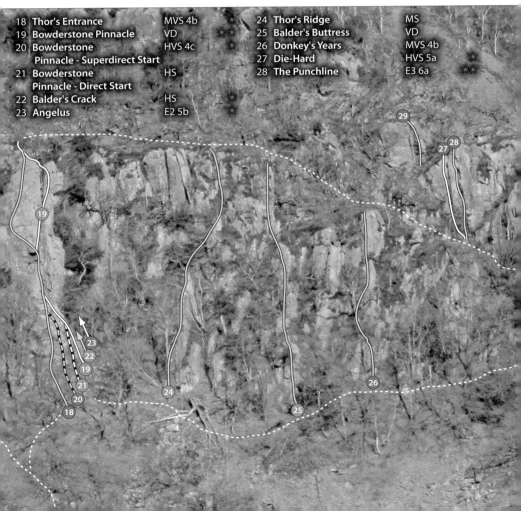

| 18 | Thor's Entrance | MVS 4b |
|---|---|---|
| 19 | Bowderstone Pinnacle | VD |
| 20 | Bowderstone Pinnacle - Superdirect Start | HVS 4c |
| 21 | Bowderstone Pinnacle - Direct Start | HS |
| 22 | Balder's Crack | HS |
| 23 | Angelus | E2 5b |

| 24 | Thor's Ridge | MS |
|---|---|---|
| 25 | Balder's Buttress | VD |
| 26 | Donkey's Years | MVS 4b |
| 27 | Die-Hard | HVS 5a |
| 28 | The Punchline | E3 6a |

Derwentwater

Watendlath

## Woden's Needle

A small buttress fronted by a prominent pinnacle; well worth the detour.

**Descent:** To the left, by the gully as for the Left-Hand Section.

---

**3   Woden's Needle**       30m   S       ★★
B Beetham - 26 Aug 1936

A delightful climb taking flakey cracks to the top of the Needle. Move left and finish up the stepped wall above.

---

**4   Creeping Bentley**     30m   VS 4c       ★
R Smithson, D Heard - 20 Aug 2004

Move up right, on the front of the Needle and climb a crack past a wobbling flake and gain the top using an obvious pocket. Move up then left and ascend the left edge of the wall.

---

**5   Needle Wall**          24m   HVS 4c
D Armstrong - Jul 1978

Good climbing but a bit dirty and with poor protection. Climb the groove right of *Woden's Needle*, with a holly at the base, to a corner above. Pull up to a small vegetated ledge on the right and finish directly up the wall above.

---

Borrowdale is the valley for getting your trad head on in the early season, for slow mornings and for hard projects when it's dry and crisp. And all days in Borrowdale should start with milky coffees, tea, scones and a fudge slice from Shepherd's Café. Or you might as well stay in Langdale.

**White Noise** (E3) Any of the routes at Reecastle could be in a top 5 but *White Noise* is the line of the crag. I backed off it on my first attempt when trying to make the step up to Lake District E3s. And even after multiple repeats the start is still serious and pumpy enough to make it inadvisable for a warm up.

**Bleed in Hell** (E8) A cold sunny day makes Hell's Wall the best place to be and I should know because I've spent many days there. *Bleed in Hell* takes the direct line up the arête. The climbing is fingery and very technical with just enough tiny footholds making it a real boot test. When your edges are worn they start rolling off and you follow. The view from the top of the crag is the finest in the valley.

**Dry Gasp** (E4) I must admit I've only ever climbed the top pitch, we backed off the bottom pitches as they seemed to be collapsing under us, so slogging up the scree and abseiling in is recommended. This was one of my first E4s, climbed after work on a sunny summer evening. The crux is poky but from there it's pleasure all the way to the top.

**FAVOURITE ROUTES** ⑤
*Mary Jenner*

**Gillercombe Buttress** (S) Gillercomb is a mountain crag with the shortest walk in and the classic *Gillercombe Buttress* is a climb that should be done again and again, it's almost as good as Shepherd's Café. It felt hard on my latest ascent as I was very pregnant but hopefully next time it will feel easy again.

**Slab Happy** (E2) I climbed this route to get going early in the season and got more than I bargained for. It was particularly memorable for the amount of time I spent dithering about, trying to commit to the crux, feeling fairly sure I'd hit the ground if I got it wrong. The rock is bubbly and rough like Sergeant's Crag Slabs but the climbing will stay with you a lot longer.

Hell's Wall E6 (page 140) - Karin Magog / 📷 Steve Crowe

## Hell's Wall

An impressive area, for most just to be looked at, for some it provides several modern test pieces.

**Descent:** Follow a broken ramp to the left.

### 6  Lucifer                30 m   E5 6a      ★★
P Whillance, D Armstrong - 19 May 1981

An entertaining route which takes the steep groove in the wall. Start left of *Hell's Wall* and climb up into an open groove or more easily just right. Go up to a ledge then easily up left to the next ledge. Pull up right into the slim hanging groove (peg) and climb it, exiting left at the top.

### 7  Woden's Crack          30m    VS 4c      ★★
D Armstrong - 1975

Climb the wide crack, at the left arête of the *Hell's Wall*, and continue up the gangway, past a large flake, to a steep little corner. Climb this and the crack above on the right to a heathery finish.

### 8  De Quincy              30m    E7 6b F7a  ★★
J Moffatt, P Kirton - Jun 1982

A mind-blowing, poorly protected route, which climbs the impending wall to the right of *Lucifer* and just left of the arête.  Climb thin cracks up the left side of the wall until moves round left lead to the ledge of *Hell's Wall*. Climb straight up above the ledge, just left of the arête (hidden peg), passing the final crack on the left.

### ⑤ 9  Hell's Wall          30m    E6 6c F7c+ ★★★
S Clark, B Henderson - Feb 1964; FFA  R Fawcett, C Gibb - 1979

The original testpiece of the wall is furnished with in-situ pegs. Climb the wide crack to a ledge then go up to a ledge on the arête. Move up and right to gain a crack. Go up this then move out right and up rightwards to below a curving groove, which is followed boldly to the top. Photo page 139.

### ⑤ 10  Bleed in Hell       30m    E8 6c F8a  ★★★
D Birkett - 5 May 1992

The stunning arête.

### 11  Inferno               30m    E7 6c F8a  ★★
P Ingham, I Cummins - 4 Jun 1988

A sensational line - follow *Hell's Wall* through its crux crack to the first jug. Traverse left along some good handholds (stacked pegs) and dyno to reach a good small ledge (crux). Stand on the ledge (peg) then pull round left to join and follow *De Quincy* to its finish.

### 12  Mesrine               40m    E6 6b F7c+ ★★★
D Booth - 1990

Follow *Hell's Wall* to the point where it follows the leftwards-rising groove. At this point move out right to a large flake beneath a diagonal roof. Excellent climbing leads through the roof to good jugs over the lip. Continue up the thin and sustained wall above, crossing *Wheels of Fire* and climb directly to the top.

### 13  Hellish               35m    E8 6c F7c
D Birkett - 14 Jul 1992

"Quite gnarly" Dave Birkett. Climb the corner to a ledge. Move left and up (peg) until hard moves lead to a loose undercut (poor small wires). Move right, then back left to join and finish up *Hell's Wall* and the first good protection!

### 14  Wheels of Fire        35m    E4 6a      ★★★
P Whillance, D Armstrong - 22 Apr 1979

The awkward first corner leads to a very good top pitch above the impressive wall. Start in the slabby corner behind a large block.
1   15m 6a   Ascend the corner to a ledge. Climb directly up the steep corner and crack above to a tree belay.
2   20m 6a   Traverse diagonally left along the lip of the overhang. Pull up (long reach) then finish up the short wall and groove on the left.

### 15  Valhalla              32m    E1 5c      ★★
W Barnes, DA Elliott (aid) - 22 Sep 1962

The obvious corner to the right of *Hell's Wall*.
1   18m 4c   Climb up the corner to a ledge. Move right across a slab and up steep cracked rock to a rowan tree below the corner.
2   14m 5c   Follow the corner to a square-cut overhang; pull up left and continue up the corner above to the top.

### 16  The Bulger            36m    E5 6b      ★★★
S Clark, R McHaffie - 4 Sep 1971 ; FFA P Botterill, J Lamb - 30 May 1981

An exciting and strenuous pitch and a must for fans of finger-jamming through roofs.
1   18m 4c   P1 of *Valhalla*.
1   18m 6b   Step down right and climb the vague crack in the wall above until a pull out right can be made below the roof. Pull up to the thin crack above and follow it rightwards to the top.

### 17  Heaven's Gate         35m    E3 6a      ★★★
J Lamb, P Botterill - 1 Jun 1981

Climbs the arched groove right of *The Bulger*.
1   15m       Scramble up past a holly and an oak to a large oak tree below the groove.
2   20m 6a   Enter the groove above and follow it until forced out right at the top onto the rib. Climb the wall on the right of the rib direct to a ledge on the left.

## Hell's Wall

## Bowderstone Pinnacle Area

The prominent buttress, at the centre of the crag, above where the approach path arrives.

**Descent:** Traverse horizontally well to the right and down a ramp to reach a good steep path or go to the left and down the ramp left of Hell's Wall. Care is needed if it is wet.

### 18  Thor's Entrance        55m   MVS 4b   ★
R Miller, AC Cain - 6 Dec 1953

An interesting route with excellent climbing and situations on the second pitch. Start 2m left of the arête of the Pinnacle at a groove.
1    20m 4a   Climb up and leftwards to a crack behind a tree and follow this to a ledge. The crack above leads to the arête stance on *Bowderstone Pinnacle*.
2    25m 4b   Continue up the short V-groove onto the rib. Immediately traverse delicately left, with hands on the obvious ledge, to reach good holds in a shallow recess. Boldly climb steeply to a good spike on the arête and continue up the arête to the top of the buttress.
3    10m       Continue along the buttress to a step down and finish up the wall above.

### 19  Bowderstone Pinnacle 50m   VD      ★★
F Mallinson R Mayson - May 1914

The classic route of the crag, ascending the prominent buttress. Start in a rocky bay by the large tree up and right from the foot of the buttress.
1    12m       Climb diagonally left on polished holds to a stance on the arête.
2    28m       Continue up the buttress to a short V-groove. Climb this onto the rib on the right and continue to a dead tree in the cleft between the buttress on the left and the pinnacle on the right. Now either bridge up the cleft, step right and up to the top of the pinnacle then move along the pinnacle and make a long step across the cleft to the buttress or climb the left arête of the buttress and belay.
3    10m       Continue along the buttress to a step down and finish up the wall above.

### 20  Bowderstone Pinnacle 16m   HVS 4c   ★
Superdirect Start
M Przygrodzki - 18 Oct 1997

Climb the arête direct.

### 21  Bowderstone Pinnacle 16m   HS
Direct Start
CJA Cooper, E Wood-Johnson - 20 Sep 1933

Climb the arête for 5m then move right and ascend a strenuous crack to join the ordinary route.

### 22  Balder's Crack          38m   HS      ★
B Beetham - 30 Aug 1944

An interesting route starting at the back of the bay.
1    20m       Climb past yew and oak trees and up a V-groove to a large ledge.
2    18m       Ascend the awkward crack in the line of the groove to the top.

### 23  Angelus                 35m   E2 5b   ★
B Thompson, WA Barnes - 1965

An eliminate and serious line taking the steep upper wall to the right of *Balder's Crack*.
1    20m       Climb through the yew and oak trees to the large ledge and belay on the right.
2    15m 5b   Climb the obvious crack to a tree. Move up using the tree then traverse delicately 4m left and move up to a ledge near the top of the Pinnacle.

### 24  Thor's Ridge            50m   MS
B Beetham - 16 Apr 1944

Start at the foot of the rib.
1    30m       Climb broken rocks then move left to ascend the clean ridge to a tree. Traverse right to belay at an oak.
2    20m       Climb up behind the oak, more or less direct up vegetated rock, to a grass terrace and tree belays.

### 25  Balder's Buttress       49m   VD
B Beetham - 12 Apr 1945

An interesting climb starting at a pedestal block, just above the remnants of a stone wall.
1    31m       Climb a steep flake/crack on the right then up the ridge, passing two gendarmes.
2    18m       Climb a mossy open V-chimney then the right-hand of three cracks

**26  Donkey's Years**        30m    MVS 4b
BJ Clarke - 6 Mar 2006

After a poor start, an ascent of the two clean arêtes high up gives a worthwhile outing. Start 12m right and 4m up from *Balder's Buttress* at some scrappy cracks.
1    13m 4b    Climb the deceptive cracks and move up left to belay on the second larger multi-stemmed tree.
2    8m 4a     Move right, step off the spike and climb the first arête via its left-trending ramp to a cosy ledge behind a juniper.
3    9m 4a     Climb the upper arête direct at first, then use a series of holds on its left side to reach the top.

## Far Right Buttress

Approach:  Follow the path, on the right of the crag, until underneath the buttress with its pronounced arête and a well-defined groove on its left.

**27  Die-Hard**        20m    HVS 5a    ★
R McHaffie, T Richardson - Jun 1992

Climb the strenuous well-protected groove.

**28  The Punchline**        15m    E3 6a    ★★
K Wilkinson, R McHaffie - 23 Feb 1992

Traverse into the hanging groove from the left with difficulty then make a hard move to better holds. More hard moves lead to the top. Easier for the tall.

**29  Bros' Climb**        12m    E2 5c    ★
A Horsfield, G Horsfield - 19 Mar 2016

On the buttress just left of the top of *Die-Hard*. Climb the rounded arête moving left at the top.

# Dalt Quarry

NY 249 165 ⓨ North and South ▲ 120m 🚶 20 mins

The slate quarry hidden away in the trees below Castle Crag has short and pleasant sports routes in a sheltered setting. A clip stick may be useful for the first bolt! The rock, in the main, is sound. For conservation reasons, do not disturb the pool – The Dalt Loch – beware there may be monsters in there!

**Approach:** A track from Grange leads past Hollows Farm Campsite then alongside the river; branch right for 125m into the quarry.

## North (Sunny) Side

| 1 | **Little Sydney** | F5 |
A Nichol, D Nichol - 1990s

Pleasant wall.

| 2 | **Baywatch** | F6b |
A Nichol, D Nichol - 1990s

Desperate corner!

| 3 | **Legless in Gaza** | F6c | ★ |
A Nichol, D Nichol - 1990s

Long way to the first bolt – then rattle up the arête.

| 4 | **Bury my Heart** | F3+ |
A Nichol, D Nichol - 1990s

Pleasant corner.

| 5 | **Ian's Day Off** | HVS 5a |
M Johnson, A Hocking - 13 Aug 1995

V-Groove.

| 6 | **Wounded Knee** | F5 |
A Nichol, D Nichol - 1990s

V-groove and wall.

| 7 | **Dalt Loch Chimney** | F5 |
A Nichol, D Nichol - 1990s

Broken corner and wall above.

| 8 | **Dalt Loch Monster** | F6a |
A Nichol, D Nichol - 1990s

Start up the broken corner and crack on left!

| 9 | **The Seam** | F5 |
A Nichol, D Nichol - 1990s

Slanting corner.

| 10 | **Chickenhawk** | F5+ | ★ |
A Nichol, D Nichol - 1990s

Interesting corner.

## 11 Zipcode     F5+
A Nichol, D Nichol - 1990s

Athletic start – easier above.

## 12 Blue Oyster Cult     F6a   ★
A Nichol, D Nichol - 1990s

Fine cracked arête - F6b when taken direct.
Photo page 146.

## 13 Laguna Verde     F5+   ★
A Nichol, D Nichol - 1990s

Fine ledgey groove.

## 14 Better Red than Dead     F5+
A Nichol, D Nichol - 1990s

The reachy wall.

## 15 Heart of Glass     F6b
A Nichol, D Nichol - 1990s

Awkward crackline.

## 16 Panzerfaust     F6c+   ★
A Nichol, D Nichol - 1990s

Rib and slab gives a fine challenge.

## 17 Al's Slab     F5+
A Nichol, D Nichol -1990s

Sustained groove line.

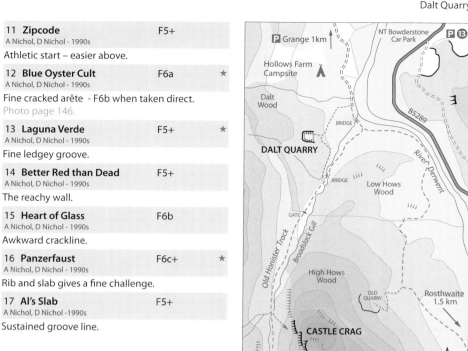

146

Blue Oyster Cult F6a (page 145) - Shaw Brown   Ron Kenyon

## South (Dark) Side

**18  Valdez is Coming**                     F6b+
A Nichol, D Nichol - 1990s

Arête with layaways to left.

**19  Zima Junction**                        F6a+
A Nichol, D Nichol - 1990s

Shot-hole may help start up corner.

**20  Nameless**                             F5
A Nichol, D Nichol - 1990s

Wall past poised block

**21  Backfire**                             F6b
A Nichol, D Nichol  - 1990s

Right side of arête – not quite like Archangel.

**22  Hothouse**                             F6b+
A Nichol, D Nichol - 1990s

Left side of arête – even less like Saul's Arête.

**23  Skegness is so Bracing**               F6a+
A Nichol, D Nichol - 1990s

Amazing layaway on flakes.

**24  Bat out of Hell (a.k.a Mac's Crack)**  HVS 5a
R McHaffie, J Bosher - 21 Nov 1993

There will be no queues for this!

## The Pink Wall
The distinct colour does not help with climbing!

**25  Shadow Warrior**                    F7c
M Johnson - 5 Jul 1994

Technical wall to crackline.

**26  Dark Angel**                        F7b+
M Johnson, A Hocking - 13 Aug 1995

Gymnastic pocketed wall.

# Castle Crag

NY 248 160          ⊖ West          ▲ 200m          🏃 20 mins

The prominent triangular peak of Castle Crag over-looks the picturesque narrowing, the 'Jaws', of the Borrowdale Valley, about 1½ km south of Grange. The rock dries reasonably quickly and there are some good interesting climbs. It can be windy in strong westerlies.

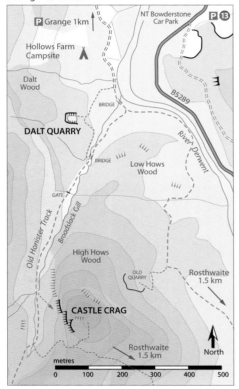

**Approach:** From Grange take the bridleway south. From Rosthwaite take the lane west, cross the river, then head up the path by Tongue Gill to join the bridleway. Cross over the col and head down towards the crag.

## Lower Buttress

The left-hand and lowest buttress is short, steep and unbroken.

**Descent:** To the right down a ramp.

**1    Gardeners' World          36m    VS 4c**
R McHaffie, D Brownlee - 1974

Ascend the right-hand side of the arête to a ledge at 20m, then follow blocks and a groove on the left, to a ledge leading up right to a tree belay.

**2    Swine Trek Direct          38m    E1 5b          ★**
T Stephenson, C Sice, R Parker – 1977
Direct Finish A Dunhill, P Clarke - 23 Aug 2014

Ascend the pinnacle, the overhang and the wall above to the base of a rib. Climb this for 3m then traverse right and step down to gain a shallow black groove and climb it to a ledge. Step out left and climb the wall in a fine position.

**3    Epithet          36m    HVS 5a          ★★**
AN Boydell, T Taylor - 2 Dec 1963

An interesting climb. Climb the V-groove for 8m to the overhang. Pull out left on excellent holds to join *Swine Trek*. Continue up the left side of the arête; awkward moves right at half-height.

**4    Vortigern          36m    E1 5b          ★★**
J Roper, P Shackleton - 19 Nov 1963
FFA T Stephenson, C Sice, R Parker - 22 Oct 1977

Climb the slabby right wall of the groove to the second flake on the arête. Move up left into the groove where it steepens and make an awkward move right to gain a shallow black groove which is followed to a ledge. Continue up the open groove above.

**5    Zoar          36m    E1 5b          ★★**
WL Robinson, C Read – 2 May1970

Follow the grass ramp behind the tree left into the corner above using the right wall to gain a ledge. From the right end of the ledge, make a bold pull up the bulging wall and continue up the crack above.

**6    A Face in the Crowd          36m    E3 6a          ★**
S Miller, T Stephenson, G Rowley – 9 Sep 1989

A steep route taking the upper wall right of *Zoar*. Scramble up to a pinnacle then climb the short groove to a square ledge. Step right and follow indefinite cracks directly, until fingery moves lead to good holds on the right. Move up left to finish.

### 7  Disillusion          40m   HS 4a
P Ross, W Aughton – 21 Mar 1959

Start at the foot of the grass ramp. Follow a diagonal line up rightwards to a ledge at 12m, below the wide hand crack. Move right and step down awkwardly. Make a high step right and follow broken ledges, until moves left across the smooth face lead to a broken crack. Climb this to the top.

### 8  The Five Planets      36m   E1 5b    ★
M Bagness, S Wood – 2 May 2002

This climbs the right arête of the *Zoar* headwall. Start just right of the grass ramp. Climb the smooth brown wall to a ledge then the right-slanting handcrack to another ledge. Pull left onto the headwall using a small flat-topped spike to good holds and climb up just left of the edge to ledges. Finish up the crack in the prominent arête.

### 9  Lyre                  32m   VS 5a
DA Elliott, W Young – 25 Sep 1962

Climb the pock-marked wall to a heather ledge and the corner on the left, with a sting in its tail.

## Central Buttress

The central buttress is much larger and more complex.

**Descent:** Up and rightwards to join a path.

### 10  Irrawaddy            65m   HVS 5a   ★★
PJ Greenwood, I Smeaton – 29 July 1955

A fine route.
1    40m 5a   Climb the steep wall behind the tree until moves right lead to the arête and a ledge. Move right and climb the steep wall on good holds to a tree-covered ledge. Walk to the right and belay below a leaning pinnacle.
2    25m 4c   Reach the top of the pinnacle; climb a steep stepped crack to easier ground.

### 11  Vortex               40m   E1 5b
C Read, J Adams 15 Apr 1968; FFA T Marr - 1968

Pull into the hanging groove with difficulty and climb boldly to pass the small overhang on the right. Climb the wall above to the second overhang. Overcome this on the left and gain the ledge above to join *Irrawaddy*.

## Upper Buttress

### 12  R.I.P.               53m   E1 5b    ★★
P1 R McHaffie and party - 6 Mar 1963
P2 NJ Soper, P Nunn, A Wright - 2 Apr 1963

An intriguing route, with an exciting first pitch and an airy top pitch. Start below a groove at the lowest point of the buttress.
1    30m 5b   Ascend the groove (peg). Bridge up awkwardly until it is possible to pull out left and enter a narrow groove precariously. Move up past a small tree, into a corner and follow this to a belay ledge on the right.
2    23m 5a   Step back down the corner and traverse left a little. Ascend past a detached block and go diagonally right to the arête, which is followed to the top.

## Castle Crag

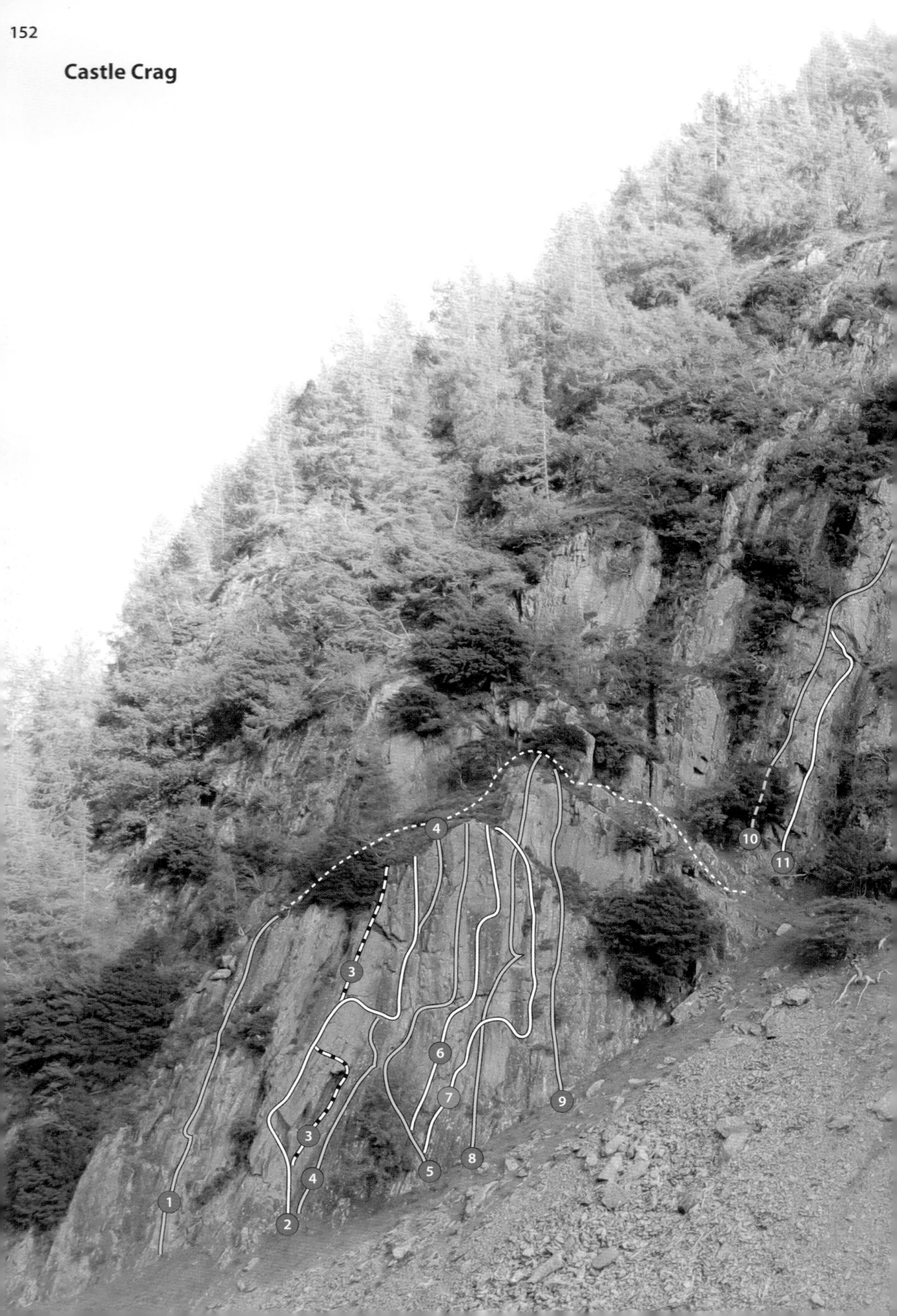

| 1 | Gardeners' World | VS 4c | | 8 | The Five Planets | E1 5b | ★ |
|---|---|---|---|---|---|---|---|
| 2 | Swine Trek | E1 5b | | 9 | Lyre | VS 5a | |
| 3 | Epithet | HVS 5a | ★★ | 10 | Irrawaddy | HVS 5a | ★★ |
| 4 | Vortigern | E1 5b | ★★ | 11 | Vortex | E1 5b | |
| 5 | Zoar | E1 5b | ★★ | 12 | R.I.P. | E1 5b | ★★ |
| 6 | A Face in the Crowd | E3 6a | ★ | | | | |
| 7 | Disillusion | HS 4a | | | | | |

## Lobstone Buttress
NY 246 159     ⊝ East     ⚠ 280m     🏃 40 mins

This long route makes a good way to the top of Maiden Moor and a walk along the ridge.

**Approach:** Strike diagonally right up the fell.

**Descent:** If making for the base of the crag, first continue up the hillside to cross the gill, then easily down the grassy slopes to the south.

**1   Lobstone Buttress     86m   HS   ★**
B Beetham - 23 Apr 1942

Start by a small needle of rock, below a holly, at the foot of the buttress

1   26m     Mount the needle then climb past the holly and up the wide crack to the top of a pinnacle.

2   25m     Move left, up a corner and broken rocks above. Move back right and up past unstable blocks to the top of the outcrop.

Scramble leftwards across the hillside for 80m to the upper buttress. To the left of the centre is a steep flake chimney.

3   20m     Climb the flake chimney, passing several chockstones, to the great pinnacle flake summit.

4   15m     Step across the chasm and follow slabs to a large ledge. Easy rocks lead to the top.

**Variation Start     18m   VS 5a**

The steep strenuous crack on the left of the needle.

# Perched Block Buttress

NY 245 160    ⊕ East    ▲ 300m    🏃 50 mins

**Approach:** Strike diagonally right up the fellside to the foot of Lobstone Buttress. From here a path leads up rightwards to the short grassy gully leading to the perched block, a large detached slab standing on a terrace above the steep lower wall.

**Descent:** Continue up for 50m to where the hillside levels out then traverse left to gain and follow the gully down and under the pillar of *Azania*.

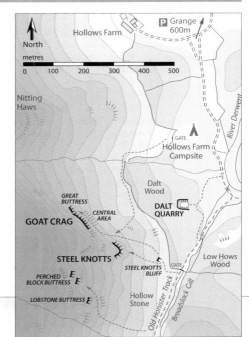

Lobstone Buttress

Perched Block Buttress

Fank Wall
Page 164

Steel Knotts
Page 159

## Upper Buttress

**1    Azania**    30m    E1 5b
S Prior, A Davis – Jul 1994

Start at the foot of the pillar, below and left of the deep chimney. Follow the obvious crack to a sloping ledge. Step left to follow a flake/crack continuation and a groove leading to a twin spike. Climb the serious but fine wall above on good holds.

**2    Grumpy Old Men**    28m    E4 5c
J Williams, P Rigby – 18 Oct 2003

A serious route which traverses below the overhang left of *Brass Monkey*. Climb *Brass Monkey* to below the overhang. Delicately traverse left under the overhang to an obvious downward pointing spike (skyhook at foot level). Pull up steeply to gain a sloping ledge on the left. Step back right and climb the wall to the top. Tree belay.

**3    Brass Monkey**    20m    E1 5b    ★★
K Wilkinson, S Holmes – 23 Nov 1988

Just to the left of the perched block is a clean steep wall with an obvious groove/crack, situated immediately above the hole beneath the block. Layback the flake crack to make a difficult move over the overlap. Finish up an easy groove.

**4    Peregrine Wall**    23m    HVS 5a
R Jackson, AR Barlett – 11 Apr 1955

Start just right of the perched block below a dirty green wall. Climb the wall for 3m using a crack and continue into a steep crack, just right of the top of the perched block. Continue upwards via a jammed flake to the top.

5    **African Skies**         43m    E2 5c         ★★
S Miller, W Young – 14 May 1988

An airy and enjoyable traverse above the large roof
on the right of the perched block. Start at the left
end of the roof by a detached pinnacle. Step off
the pinnacle and gain the groove above. Follow
the diagonal crack right and gain the groove of
*Well Heeled*. Climb the groove for 2m to swing right
on pockets to an easier-angled gangway. Step
down and right, then climb the steep wall and step
right across an overhanging groove. Step down
and traverse right to a good pocket in the middle
of the wall. Climb straight up finishing in a shallow
corner right of the grass ledge and tree. Well-protected but beware of rope drag.

The following climb starts at a small tree 6m right
and below the start of *African Skies*. This is accessed
by traversing below the perched block and continuing down, before scrambling back up to the
foot of the route. Alternatively descend from the
start of *African Skies*.

6    **Well Heeled**          30m    E3 5c          ★
S Miller, D Johnson – 21 May 1988

The roof and groove directly above the yellow
shield of rock below the left side of the large
roof. Climb a groove left of the yellow shield of
rock until excellent jams lead out right under the
roof (large cam and nuts). At its narrowest point,
surmount the roof on good holds and climb the
groove above leading left. Gain a good ledge and
continue to the top.

## Steel Knotts Bluff

NY 248 162          South East          160m          20 mins

This beautiful little slab of well-textured rock offers some very enjoyable short routes with bolt belays at the top! It is a great place for a family to enjoy a picnic and the children can have a climb. The first few moves of each route are normally the hardest.

**Approach:** From Grange follow the bridleway south to the gate. Follow the wall on your right to the crag.

| 1 | **Picnic** | 11m | D | |
|---|---|---|---|---|

This route has nice flake holds.

| 2 | **Sandwich** | 13m | VD | ★ |
|---|---|---|---|---|

The easiest start is on the left.

| 3 | **Pop** | 15m | S 4a | ★ |
|---|---|---|---|---|

After a delicate start climb direct through the white scar.

| 4 | **Biscuit** | 15m | HS 4c | |
|---|---|---|---|---|

Barely independent, a thin start but the upper section is easier than it looks.

| 5 | **Cake** | 15m | HS 4a | ★ |
|---|---|---|---|---|

Very pleasant.

# Steel Knotts

NY 246 162          ⓨ South and East          ▲ 240m          🏃 20 mins

Steel Knotts is composed of excellent clean rock which dries quickly and provides some very good quality climbing. Photo-plan on page 155.

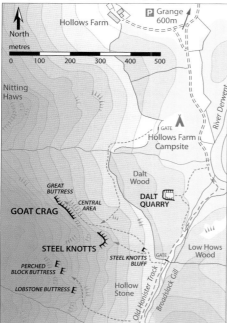

**Approach:** From Grange take the bridleway south and immediately after the gate take a path up the fellside on the right. From Rosthwaite take the lane west, cross the river, then head up the path by Tongue Gill to join the bridleway. Cross over the col and head down. Just before the gate take a path on your left passing below Steel Knotts Bluff.

**Descent:** Down scree to the left.

## South Face

**1    Stinger**          21m    E2 5c          ★
J Williams, P Rigby - 17 Aug 2003

Climb the groove right of the large holly, with difficulty, then make a hard move into the short groove on the left. Move up easily to a corner. Step onto the front of the narrow pillar on the right and climb this to the top.

**2    The Sting**          23m    E2 5c          ★★★
R Mardon, TE Dunsby - 1973

A fine route giving good jamming. Climb the crack, past a small ledge at half-height, to finish up the short rib on the left.

**3    Smoker's Delight**          21m    E2 6a          ★
M de Vaal, C Reid, T Suddaby - 28 Jul 2004

High in the grade. A fine line up the thin crack 3m right of *The Sting*. Climb the crack with difficulty to good undercuts, step left and climb directly up to the left of the overhang. Step back right on to the overhang and climb directly to the top.

**4    Meandering Maggot**    30m    E1 5b          ★★
R Kenyon, T Price - 1984

Start just left of *Lurching Leech*. Ascend a crack to gain the niche on the left, below an overhang. Climb up the corner, avoiding the overhang on its left, to follow pleasant cracks then the short arête to the top.

**5    Lurching Leech**          30m    HVS 5a          ★★
     **(Route 1)**
K Leech, T Taylor - 23 Aug 1965

A deceptively awkward climb. Start at a large block at the centre of the crag. Ascend the crack above to a corner. Finish up the final wide crack with interest.

**6    Samurai Jack**          30m    E4 6a          ★
T Suddaby, C Reid - 28 Jul 2004

Takes the centre of the steep clean wall right of the large block. Step up and left onto the wall from a block and continue straight up to a ledge (serious). Climb the short corner and wall through an overlap, and then up to the top. High in the grade.

**7    Rashomon**          30m    E3 5c
J Timney, M Dunne - 6 Oct 2012

The fractured-looking arête. Start from the obvious block on the right side of the steep wall. Climb the arête on its left side using opposing edges to where difficulties ease and the first real protection. Ascend a pair of cracks with ease, passing to the left of a hollow-sounding flake and up to finish.

### 8    Ambling Ant    30m    MVS 4b    ★★
R Kenyon, T Price, L Jordan - 20 Oct 1985

A pleasant open climb starting on a block 6m down and right of *Lurching Leech*. Step off the block then go up a corner/crack to a ledge, just left of a holly. Pass the corner above by moves on the left to gain a ledge. Continue up the wall above, passing a large detached block, to easier rock and the top.

### 9    Route 2    30m    VS 4c    ★
The obvious crack forming the left side of the pinnacle. Climb the crack exiting awkwardly, (junction with *The Lost Boys*), move up then climb the steep short wall just right of the corner. Move 2m left and follow a slabby wall to the top

### 10    Tottering Tortoise    30m    HVS 5a    ★★
T Taylor, K Leech - 23 Aug 1965

An entertaining climb which takes the obvious snaking corner/crack forming the right side of the pinnacle. Ascend the off-width crack with interest to join *Route 2* and finish up this. A large cam or two would be useful.

## East Face

### 11    Loss Adjustor    30m    E2 5c    ★★
R Graham, P Graham - 31 May 2013

Start at the foot of the arête just left of *The Lost Boys*. Pull directly up and climb the wall on the right of the arête to finish as for *The Lost Boys*.

### 12    Lost in Space    40m    HVS 5a    ★★
R Kenyon, M Kenyon - 8 Jun 2014

A good trip across the crag. Start as for *The Lost Boys* following this to the step out left onto the pinnacle and up to the corner on *Route 2*. Climb the large flake above on the right then step left and follow the crackline rising leftwards to reach *Lurching Leech*. Climb the awkward off-width crack and continue up the crack above to the top.

### 13    The Lost Boys    30m    HVS 5a    ★★★
P Whillance, D Armstrong - 8 Apr 1984

This follows the prominent arête right of the pinnacle. Start at a short corner, just right of the arête. Surmount the corner with difficulty, cross *Loss Adjustor*, and climb diagonally left to step onto the pinnacle; junction with *Route 2*. Make a couple of

7    Rashomon    E3 5c
8    Ambling Ant    MVS 4b
9    Route 2    VS 4c

1    Stinger    E2 5c
2    The Sting    E2 5c
3    Smoker's Delight    E2 6a
4    Meandering Maggot    E1 5b
5    Lurching Leech (Route 1)    HVS 5a
6    Samurai Jack    E4 6a

moves up the wall and pull right to the arête. Climb this and the short wall above. Photo page 163.

### 14  Paint it Black          30m    E3 5c    ★★
B Davison, D Smart - 24 Jul 1982

Start as for *The Lost Boys*. Climb the corner onto a large ledge on the right. Climb the obvious black crack until it becomes thin. Move left onto the wall and make a hard move right, up to a large hold. Stand on this and then continue to a large ledge. Climb the wall and crack, right of a holly tree.

### 15  Free Falling          28m    E4 6a    ★★
D Messenger, J Sharpe - 17 Sep 1995

Low in the grade. Start in the centre of the steep wall 3m left of *B.M.C. 1*. Climb the broken ribs to a small niche at around 4m. Make some awkward moves up and continue through the left-hand side of the shallow scoop to the large ledge. Finish as for *Paint it Black*.

### 16  Terminal Velocity          28m    E3 5c    ★★
P Graham, R Graham - 31 May 2013

High in the grade. Start between *Free Falling* and *B.M.C. 1*. Climb the wall direct moving slightly left of a small black overlap at mid-height to reach the large ledge and the same finish right of the holly as for *Paint it Black*.

### 17  B.M.C. 1          30m    VS 4c    ★
M Armitage, J Unsworth - 6 Sep 1986

This takes the groove bounding the right-hand side of the steep face and then the wall above the large ledge. Climb the groove to a ledge on the right and then up to the large ledge. Move left along this ledge towards a holly tree. Climb the wall and crack, right of the holly tree, to finish up the slabs above.

| 10 | **Tottering Tortoise** | HVS 5a | ★★ |
| 11 | **Loss Adjustor** | E2 5c | |
| 12 | **Lost in Space** | HVS 5a | ★★ |
| 13 | **The Lost Boys** | HVS 5a | ★★★ |
| 14 | **Paint it Black** | E3 5c | ★★ |

| 15 | **Free Falling** | E4 6a | ★★ |
| 16 | **Terminal Velocity** | E3 5c | ★★ |
| 17 | **B.M.C. 1** | VS 4c | ★ |

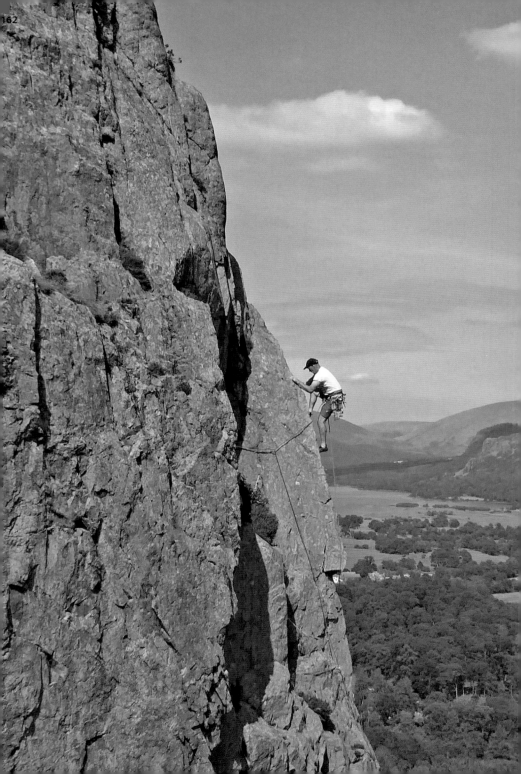

The Lost Boys HVS (page 160) - Paul Clarke 📷 Richard Tolley

## Fank Wall

50m above Steel Knotts, and just above a sheep fank, is a clean area of rock identified by a blank-looking wall with a rounded overhang on its right and bounded on the left by a tree-filled gully.

**Descent:** Rightwards through the small juniper trees then carefully down broken rocks.

### 18  Unfank          12m    VS 4c
BJ Clarke - 29 Mar 2006

Start at the foot of the tree-filled gully, 4m above a thriving juniper. Step right and climb a shallow groove, pulling over its capping roof to reach flakes. Move right to a large spike and follow the arête to the top.

### 19  Shuttle's Finale          12m    E1 5c
A Dunhill, S Wrigley - 24 Jul 2011

Start at the arête on the left side of the wall. Step onto ledges and move left to the arête. Climb this with difficulty (small wires) to a wide crack then up to a ledge and large spike. Step left and climb the slab.

### 20  Fank Wall Right          12m    HVS 5b
BJ Clarke, S Broatch, J Simpson, J Holden - 6 May 2006

The shallow groove system on the right side of the smooth wall and left of the rounded overhang. Start just right of the thriving juniper. Climb up to the niche below the smooth wall, then move up and right to follow the shallow groove system to a ledge. Finish up the corner, stepping left at the top.

# Goat Crag
### NY 245 165    Ⓝ North    ⛰ 350m    🏃 50 mins

Goat is a special and iconic crag; steep, uncompromising, yet thrilling and rewarding for those willing to make the effort to climb here. Towering above the valley, its oppressive walls dominate the fell above Grange.

Arriving at the airy vantage of the grassy gearing up point you can contemplate what lies ahead. Great Buttress, the meat of the crag, offers probably the finest collection of extreme challenges in the valley. Most of the pegs were replaced in 2011.

Even after a long dry spell there is some seepage at the base of the routes; steepness defies the damp and most routes can be climbed after a couple of dry days. Early starts will catch the sun.

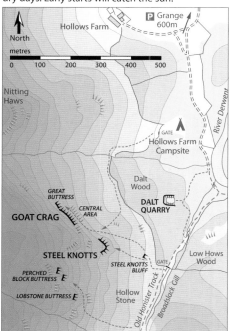

**Approach:** Take the track towards Castle Crag then, at a gate, go right. A wet rake finally leads up to a sunny belvedere near a large boulder, or approach through Hollows Farm campsite.

**Descent:** ♂ - two 50m ropes are just long enough; 60m ropes are preferable.

A word about trees – pulling your ropes after abseiling directly from trees damages the bark and eventually the tree will die. In Borrowdale several trees have been lost already. Use the designated abseil points which have fixed gear to protect the tree. These are clearly indicated on the photo-diagrams.

## Central Area

An impressive area of rock in the middle of the crag leads to mossy slabs. It's probably best to climb the lower pitches then abseil off.

| 1 | **Manpower** | 75m | E3 5c | ☆☆☆ ♂ |
|---|---|---|---|---|

C Downer, A Hall 20 May 1983

Bold thin climbing provides a demanding challenge. Start 5m right of a flake below a crack.
1   36m 5c   Climb the crack, over a bulge and up a narrow ramp and corner to below the overhangs. Pull left across the overhangs to a short groove and a corner leading to a grassy ledge; thread belay. (Traverse right to abseil.)
2   26m 5b   Follow the slab above to a steep headwall. Move right and climb the wall to a ledge.
3   13m 5a   Cross a little way up the wall on the right then back left into a corner. Follow this to a ledge and trees.

| 2 | **The Rat Race** | 101m | E2 5c | ☆ ♂ |
|---|---|---|---|---|

P1 B Henderson, J Cook, R McHaffie - 11 Apr 1966
P2, 3 & 4 MA Toole, B Henderson, B Robertson – 1966
FFA P Botterill, S Clegg - 15 Jun 1975

Steep climbing on sloping holds through the overhangs. Start as for *Manpower*.
1   42m 5c   Climb the crack, over a bulge, and move right to some ledges. Ascend the luminous green slab to below the steep right wall. Step left into the corner and go up this to a good hold on the right at the top. Immediately step left round a bulge to a groove. Climb this and the corner above, pulling right at the top to a small ledge. (Traverse right to abseil.)
2   26m 5a   Cross the mossy slab leftwards to a crack which leads to a short steep wall, just right of an undercut rib. Go up and left to a small ledge on the arête to another ledge.
3   13m   The corner above is followed to a ledge.
4   20m 4c   Descend slightly to the right and traverse diagonally right across a steep wall to the arête. Good holds lead to the top.

| 1 | Manpower | E3 5c |
| 2 | The Rat Race | E2 5c |
| 3 | The Cursing Caterpillar | HVS 5a |
| 4 | Alone in Space | E1 5b |

**3    The Cursing Caterpillar** 53m    HVS 5a    ★★ ♂
B Henderson, P Ross (aid) - 14 Aug 1965

This route weaves up the crag. Start at a small flake.
1    23m 4b    Climb the flake and slab above. Move
right and up a groove, past a holly, to a large
ledge and tree belay.
2    30m 5a    Move left round a bulge into a scoop
below an overhanging wall. Traverse left to
a small overhang at its left end. Pull over
this and climb up steeply to a resting place.
Traverse left then follow the ramp on the right
to an excellent thread belay.

**4    Alone in Space** 100m    E1 5b    ★★ ♂
T Stephenson, C Sice, R Parker - 24 Sep 1977

A great route with a thought-provoking well-protected crux. Not to be underestimated.
1    26m 5a    Climb the flake and slab to a move
left to gain and climb a short crack in a bulge.
Move right to a ledge (peg).
2    28m 5b    Step up right to a thin crack below
a break in the bulge. Pull up, step left and
ascend the slab and corner to a thread belay
below an overhang.
3    15m 5a    Climb the overhang and continuation groove. Step right to a grass ledge below
a green wall.
4    31m 5a    Quite run out - from the right side of
the ledge, make an ascending traverse left to
a tree. Climb the crack above and swing left
onto an arête. Easier climbing leads to trees.

### The Great Buttress

An impressive area of excellent steep rock topped
by 'beetling yellow overhangs' sports an awesome
collection of hard extremes.

**5    Fear of Flying** 36m    E3 6a    ☆☆ ♂
C Downer, A Hunter, C Bacon, D Nicol - 8 May 1978
FFA D Mullen, J Lamb - May 1978

Thin serious climbing. Climb the crack and step left
at its top to a tiny ledge. The wall leads to a small
overhang which relents after some difficulty. Cross
a small ledge and continue up the grooves above
to a ledge and tree on the left.

**6    Wild Times** 34m    E5 6b    ☆☆ ♂
P Botterill, P Rigby - 30 Jul 1983

Very strenuous and sustained with protection difficult to arrange. Climb a wall and short V-groove
to overhangs. Above on the left is a block; stand on
this and climb the steep wall, using three vertical
slots. Climb the right rib of a short groove on the
left and continue up the wall above to a ledge and
tree.

**7    Day of the Jackals** 30m    E4 6b    ☆ ♂
M Wilford, K Lindhorne, C Downer 14 Jul 1981

Steep and strenuous with easier climbing above.
Climb a short wall to a horizontal break, pull over a
bulge into a small niche and follow the crack above
to a ledge (junction with *Point Blank*). Step up leftwards and climb the arête to a ledge and tree.

**8    Point Blank** 65m    HVS 5a    ♂
C Downer, H Cobb, D Nicol - Jun 1977

Climb the groove to an overhang and traverse
left to a ledge. Climb the crack and continuation
groove to a ledge and tree. A short wall leads to
another ledge.

**9    D.D.T.** 65m    E1 5a    ★★★ ♂
J Lee, A Jackman, P Ross - 17 Oct 1965; FFA A Liddell

The impressive corner shouts to be climbed and
doesn't disappoint. Best done as a magnificent
single pitch climb using 60m ropes.
1    35m 5a    Climb the corner; a short excursion
onto the steep right wall sidesteps the bulge.
The wide crack above leads to a ledge and tree
on the left.
2    30m 4c    A short wall on the right leads
to a V-groove. Climb this past an awkward
steepening onto an upper slab. Climb up and
rightwards to an unprotected dirty finish into
trees. The abseil point is to the right.

⑤ **10    The Voyage** 83m    E3 5c    ★★★
S Clegg, P Botterill - 26 Jun 1976

A magnificent involved trip, space-walking across
very impressive ground. With sustained, absorbing,
technical climbing this passage ranks as one of the
great E3s of the Lakes.
1    30m 5c    Climb *D.D.T.* for 10m then traverse
right to a junction with *Tumbleweed Connection* below a bulge. Go straight up (peg),
traverse right to a groove in the arête and follow this onto the base of a ramp below a holly.
2    30m 5c    Step down and traverse right below
an overlap. Continue rightwards to reach
and follow a higher ramp (aged bolt, pegs).
Traverse down rightwards onto an easy slab to
reach a ledge.
3    23m 5c    Go up left then move steeply right
and follow a flake/crack over a bulge to a
foothold below a corner. Climb the corner and
wall above to the top.

Tumbleweed Connection E2 (page 170) - Justin Shiels    📷 Richard Tolley

## 11  Lithuania          64m    E4 6b
P1 A Phizacklea, A Kells, S Wood, J Holden - 29 Apr 1990
P2 FA P Ross, J Lee, I Wilson 13 Oct 1965 (aid)
FFA A Liddell, J Cook - 30 April 1966

A direct that struggles for independence on the steep ground right of *D.D.T.*

1    42m 6b    Climb *D.D.T.* to the first small bulge at 6m. Traverse steeply right on pockets to gain a shallow scoop; climb this to join a traverse line. Step left and follow a small groove to a sloping hold; continue up a short crack to reach a good slot out on the right. Trend left on tiny holds to gain a conspicuous round pocket, then climb directly up to the base of a large left-facing groove. Step right and climb the right-hand side of the arête to a belay.
2    22m 5c    Climb a shallow groove in the overhangs (thread), pulling right onto the final slabs.

## 12  Altered Images/          60m    E3 6a    ★★
## The Ruptured Duck
M Berzins, P Botterill – 1977; B Wayman, C Downer - 10 Jun 1979
C Downer, A Hall, R Graham - 29 May 1983
P Rigby, A Greig - 15 Jun 1991

Uses much existing work to construct an engrossing route tackling the soaring blunt arête and upper wall avoided by *Tumbleweed Connection*. There are always some holds to stitch together and this is a superb way up the crag. Gain the arête using either two parallel cracks 3m right of *D.D.T.* which lead to the bottom of a groove then follow a hand traverse right to the arête, or starting directly below, climb the arête. After 20m traverse left onto the wall to the bottom of an open groove. Make an awkward move right past an obvious undercut to the arête. Climb up to the bottom of a groove (*Tumbleweed Connection*), step left and climb the shallow scoop to reach and follow a diagonal break rightwards. Climb the slabby wall to the V-groove and a finish; or from the groove finish up *Tumbleweed Connection*.

## 13  Tumbleweed          56m    E2 5c    ★★★
## Connection
P Botterill, D Rawcliffe - 24/25 Jun 1976

Awesome climbing. Once engaged, the isolation requires total commitment.

1    26m 5c    Follow the prominent traverse line left to the arête. Step up and traverse left for 6m passing twin thin cracks. Move up and cross a bulge (peg) to reach a traverse. Move delicately right for 3m to a groove in the arête; follow this to belay at the base of a ramp.
2    30m 5b    Follow the ramp leftwards. Take the prominent groove and wall until a sensational

pull leftwards can be made across the undercut arête onto the finishing slab.
Photo page 168.

## 14  Tumbleweed By-Pass    50m    E2 5c    ★★★
B Wayman, C Downer - 10 Jun 1979

Follow *Tumbleweed Connection* to the peg. Continue up the wall above and link with the groove on p2.

## ⑤ 15  Praying Mantis        85m    El 5b    ★★★
L Brown, S Bradshaw - 30 May 1965

A UK mega-classic insolently finding a devious way up the frowning buttress. The apparent insecurity, exposure and circuitous route finding increase the emotional commitment.

1    25m 5b    Climb the square-cut groove and slippery crack to a niche. Step left and move up to belay at the foot of a ramp. Or continue in the same line and step down left to the stance.
2    16m 4c    Follow the ramp then work left across a steep smooth wall to reach a hidden left-facing V-groove. Climb the groove until a bold swing right leads to a small airy stance below overhangs.
3    44m 4c    Traverse horizontally right (peg), selecting the line carefully, to a small ledge. Ascend the wall on the right to a vague depression. Climb this steeply until a step left gains a final slab leading to heather and trees.

## 16  Mantis Direct          63m    E2 5b
L Brown, K Jackson – 1965 (now free)

Cuts off the big loop. Climb to the ramp of p2, above and left of a holly then follow a rightward-leading scoop. Continue up to join p3 at the traverse rightwards towards the vague depression.

## 17  Mantis –          55m    E1 5b    ★★★
## Tumbleweed Connection

A brilliant technical and exposed adventure combining p1 of *Praying Mantis* and p2 of *Tumbleweed Connection*.

| | | |
|---|---|---|
| Fear of Flying | E3 6a | |
| Wild Times | E5 6b | |
| Day of the Jackals | E4 6b | |
| Point Blank | HVS 5a | |
| D.D.T. | E1 5a | ★★★ |
| 3 Tumbleweed Connection | E2 5c | |
| 4 Tumbleweed By-Pass | E2 5c | ★★★ |
| 5 Praying Mantis | E1 5b | ★★★ |
| 6 Mantis Direct | E2 5b | |

| | | | |
|---|---|---|---|
| 19 Athanor | E3 6a | ★★★ | |
| 21 Footless Crow | E6 6c | ★★★ | |
| 23 Trojan Horse | E6 6b | ★★ | |
| 24 Mirage | E5 6b | ★★★ |
| 25 Bitter Oasis | E4 5c | ★★★ |

### 18 The Thieving Magpie    65m    E3 6a
R Berzins, M Berzins, J Lamb - 8 Jun 1979

With a fine first pitch and a strenuous and exposed upper section, this makes an interesting eliminate.
1   25m 5c   Climb the groove until forced into the curving right-hand groove and follow this up to a roof. Climb flakes leftwards to belay at the foot of a ramp.
2   40m 6a   Go up and right to the foot of a V-groove and climb this to an overhang (as for p2 of *Athanor*). Traverse right on undercuts for about 6m. Climb through bulges to finish on a slab.

### ⑤ 19 Athanor    73m    E3 6a    ★★★
J Adams, C Read - 14 Sep 1968; FFA J Lamb, K Rudd - 19 Aug 1974

This fusion of technical and steep maintains the heat and sustains the pressure.
1   28m 6a   The rib on the left of a dirty groove leads to a large flake. The blank-looking groove above gives access to a short steep crack; move up leftwards to traverse under a small overlap and up to the sanctuary of the belay at the foot of the ramp. ♂
   Or continue; it is well worth the effort to clean this pitch.
2   45m 5c   Go right and up a prominent V-groove to overhangs (peg). Continue up to a small ledge. Climb directly up the groove above towards the top overhang until a pull right gains mossy slabs. Belay on a tree to the left.

### 20 Legless Lizard    56m    E5 6b    ☆☆
D Dinwoodie, D Hawthorn - 9 Aug 1985

A link pitch from *Athanor* to *The Thieving Magpie* which climbs the wall and twisting crack through the orange bulges 5m left of *Footless Crow*. Climb *Footless Crow* to the niche. From a good foothold up and left, go straight up the wall to a small ledge. Climb the wall and bulge right of a crack to gain a good flake. Haul leftwards over the bulge to a chockstone. Move right and go up a flake/crack to a small ledge. Finish directly over the bulge and up the slab.

### ⑤ 21 Footless Crow    56m    E6 6c F7c+★★★
P Livesey - 19 Apr 1974

Historical, futuristic and epic: altered by the loss of crucial holds (and protection) it remains an incredible and audacious undertaking. Climb the rib and the blank-looking groove to below a steep crack. Pull up into the niche above, then go up right to gain and follow a rightward-trending ramp above (ancient bolt and pegs). Step up and left below the overhangs (peg). Improvise to eventually gain the tantalising crack. Step left round the rib to a little green wall and climb up to the overhangs. Pull through and step left above the overhang to continue straight up the slabby wall and final short corner.

### 22 Footless Horse    60m    E6 6b    ★★★
                                                       F7b+
C Hope - 3 Jul 2003

The powerful combination of *Footless Crow* and *Trojan Horse* gives arguably the best E6 in the valley. Climb Footless into the niche and up right to gain the rightward-trending ramp. Pass below the roof (ancient bolt and pegs). Climb directly up the undercuts (peg) and continue (peg) to the undercut fang. Continue directly moving right to the top.

### 23 Trojan Horse    60m    E6 6b    ★★
                                                       F7b+
N Foster, M Berzins - 26 May 1990

An impressive eliminate. Follow *Athanor* for about 6m to where it steps left to a big flake. Continue up the scoop above and then climb the wall trending slightly rightwards to arrive at a smooth groove. Gain the undercuts in the bulge above then make a tricky sequence up and right round the rib to a good slot. Climb straight up the slab (ancient bolt). Then directly up the undercuts (peg) and continue (peg) to the undercut fang. Power over this using a detached spike. Continue up directly until a move right leads to a steep little wall. Finish up this.

### ⑤ 24 Mirage    60m    E5 6b    ★★★
Lower section R Graham, D Lyle - 15 Apr 1981
Upper section P Botterill, M Berzins - 22 Jun 1981

At first delicate and bold, then very steep and strenuous. Climb the groove 3m right of *Athanor*, and gain the beckoning undercuts. Work up leftwards then climb a thin crack to an awkward pull up right. Above is a large flat hold; stand on it, then step right, round a rib and up rightwards to a pocket. Traverse left from the pocket to a slight rib and then go straight up (aged bolt and pegs). Climb up rightwards (old bolt) and move straight up to beneath a bulge (old bolt). Step left and

Praying Mantis E1 (page 170) - Stephen Reid 📷 Tom Ripley

climb the weakness through the bulges (thread) to pull into the scoop beneath a down-pointing spike. Climb the left side of the spike and continue directly on finger pockets to a ledge. Now more easily up leftwards to finish.

### 25  Bitter Oasis          54m    E4 5c    ★★★
P Livesey, J Sheard - 12 May 1974

The tension builds spectacularly on this magnificent and heart-stopping route.
1    28m 5c   From a birch, reached by scrambling from the right, head leftwards then step right into the groove. The bulge gives onto the 'bitter oasis', a slab which is followed diagonally rightwards to a welcome commodious stance.
2    26m 5c   From a pedestal on the left, gain the wall above and traverse leftwards to a small foothold below a hanging spike. Moving out of sight of your second, confidently climb the left side of the spike and continue directly on finger pockets to a ledge. Now more easily up leftwards to finish.

### 26  Sweet Waters         54m    E5 6a    ★★
A Jones, D Kirby - 16 Jun 1990

A challenging direct on *Bitter Oasis*.
1    28m 6a   From the birch, climb the short wall on the right to the overhang. Pull over then climb the wall above rightwards to a niche then up left slightly to a slab. Follow this diagonally rightwards to a good ledge.
2    26m 6a   From a pedestal on the left, gain the wall above and start traversing leftwards before going up to the sharp overhang. With some urgency pull over; step right then pull over the bulge leftwards to a good ledge and belay.

### 27  Midsummer at the     23m    E4 6a    ★★
###     Oasis
S Crowe, K Magog - 26 Jun 1995

Gain the arête above the stance of *Bitter Oasis*. Difficult moves (peg) now lead to the final sequence of *The Voyage*. Finish up the corner and wall above to the top.

**FAVOURITE ROUTES** ⑤  *Rick Graham*

Shepherd's Crag is the classic Lakes poor weather option, quick drying clean rock, done all I can too many times to count. Never tire of visiting, but what to climb? Walking past other favourites, inevitably start up the compelling crackline of **Finale**, can't resist, sustained steep well protected and varied climbing, always easier at the start of a session. Perhaps I should do it as a finishing route as well.

Got to include **Footless Crow**, the route that inspired a generation (mine). This route (along with Right Wall) were real game changers in 1974. Slightly tamed by modern gear, this was probably also its demise. A cam (and numerous weightings) were probably too much for the crucial third undercut. Wish I could find the missing piece to glue it back on.

**Phillistine.** The best single pitch E1. It's really special. Only 3 km over the pass. I climbed for years in the honeypots of Borrowdale and Langdale, it took the FRCC and a Buttermere guidebook authorship for me to to look past the Valley.

**Raindrop.** Good all the way. Our nickname for P2 is " the pure pleasure pitch". Enjoy.

**Corvus** is touted as enjoyable in all conditions and it is. Traditionally recommended for a wet day, the clean incut holds seem purposely designed for climbing in mountain  boots. I prefer a quiet dry summers evening.

# Stonethwaite

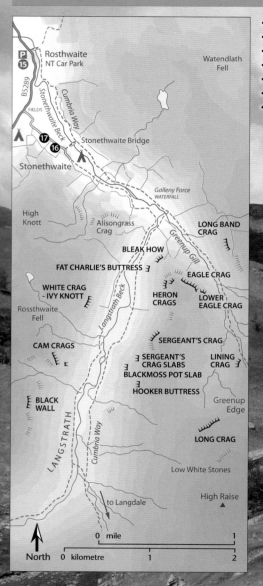

# Long Band Crag

NY 282 125          West          430m          60 mins

This is an impressive crag of superb rock giving good quality sustained routes. It is split by a large roof at half-height which is cut vertically by the fine bottomless groove of *The Technician*.

**Descent:** To the right.

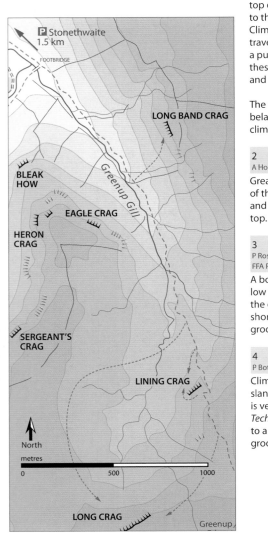

P Stonethwaite
1.5 km

FOOTBRIDGE

LONG BAND CRAG

BLEAK HOW

Greenup Gill

EAGLE CRAG

HERON CRAG

SERGEANT'S CRAG

LINING CRAG

North

metres

0          500          1000

LONG CRAG

Greenup

| 1    **The Apprentice**         30m   E4 6a        ★ |
| A Jones, S Mackay – May 1987 |

Airy and exciting climbing. Start at the foot of a groove by a large spike in the wall left of *The Technician*. Climb the groove making a hard move at its top onto a leftwards-rising traverse line. Climb this to the left end of the large roof - poor protection. Climb the corner for 1m then make a hard bold traverse right, across the lip of the overhang, where a pull up onto a ledge leads to some slabs. Climb these pleasantly, keeping to the left of a large crack and loose block.

The following three climbs may be best done by belaying at the flake before the start of the hard climbing especially if the initial groove is wet.

| 2    **The Gymnast**         33m   E7 6c F7c      ★★ |
| A Hocking, M Norbury – 1 May 2011 |

Great climbing. Follow *The Technician* to the base of the smooth groove then make wild moves left and up to better holds and follow the arête to the top.

| 3    **The Technician**         33m   E5 6b      ★★★ |
| P Ross, D Byrne-Peare - 2 Jun 1965 |
| FFA P Botterill, P Whillance, D Armstrong – 18 Jun 1978. |

A bold route through the impressive roof. Start below the centre of the overhang at a groove. Climb the groove to the overhang. Pull up left into a short corner and climb over the roof to the smooth groove above. Finish up this.

| 4    **Masochist**         34m   E5 6a        ★ |
| P Botterill – 26 Aug 1976 |

Climbs the impressive overhanging rightward-slanting groove to the right of *The Technician*. It is very serious and poorly protected. Follow *The Technician* to the overhang. Move up rightwards to a niche under the main groove (nuts). Gain the groove and follow it to the top.

### 5   The Mastercraftsman   30m   E5 6b   ★★★
A Jones, W Hannah – Jun 1987

A great route, following the shallow groove right of *Masochist*. Start at the foot of the groove at some quartz overhangs. Pull over the overhangs and climb the groove to the corner on the left. Go up this to the top of some large blocks. Move up rightwards then make very hard moves up to good jugs. More hard climbing leads past a bulge to a rest in a groove on the right. Ignore the easy finish right and step left to climb a difficult crack in the wall leading to a hard finishing move.

### 6   The Sado-Masochist   25m   E6 6b F7b+   ★
D Booth, J Robertson – 26 Jun 2004

Start at the detached flake of *The Machinist*. Pull up and left into a steep groove capped by an overhang. Climb diagonally up left (poor peg), then rightwards through the overhang, making difficult technical moves (poor peg) to reach good holds. Continue directly up the steep groove above, pulling out left at its apex onto a slab and easier climbing.

### 7   The Machinist   25m   E6 6b F7b+   ★★★
C Hope, A Wilson – 5 Jul 2003

Start at a large detached flake below an obvious right-facing groove 2m left of *The Professional*. Step off the flake and enter the groove. Climb the groove to the obvious large undercut on the right. Make tricky moves directly above to join *The Pro-*

*fessional* at the top of the groove.

### 8   The Professional   28m
D Armstrong, P Whillance – 29 May 1983

The grey wall at the right-hand side of the crag gives interesting climbing. Start on a ledge 12m right of *Masochist*, just right of a large pointed block. Climb the steep wall, moving slightly rightwards to a groove. Follow this up leftwards to its top. Cross the wall on the left to a slim groove/crack and climb this to below the obvious slanting overhang. Pull leftwards over the overhang to a thin crack and climb up to the top.

### 9   Professional Direct   25m   E5 6b   ★★★
D Booth, J Robertson – 20 Jun 2004

Start 3m right of *The Professional*. Climb the short blank wall to pull onto the gangway. Move up, place good gear and continue up the wall above, veering slightly right at the top.

### 10   The Sadist   30m   E2 5c   ★
R Wightman, K Long, A Phizacklea – 26 Oct 1985

Climbs the lichenous slabby wall right of *The Professional*, starting 6m to its right at a pointed block. Climb a shallow groove to gain a slab and traverse delicately left up a ramp to gain the groove of *The Professional*. Go up this to where *The Professional* traverses left and follow the rightward-slanting crack to the top.

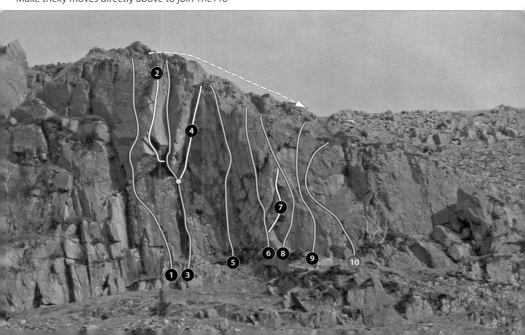

...etting above Greenup ..., it should offer a quiet ... generally excellent ...thwhile. It is situated ...up Edge, below the path ...asmere.

**Approach:** ... ...nwaite take the path over Stonethwaite Beck, turn right and follow the valley path.

**Descent:** To either side.

The crag forms a large open corner with easy climbing up each of the end ridges and a green groove in the centre. There are fine slabs on each side of the centre. With little traffic, the crag becomes mossy relatively quickly, especially the right-hand side.

| 1 | **Crucifix** | 50m | S |
|---|---|---|---|

JDJ Wildridge, H Hall – Jul 1952

Climb the slab to grass ledges then the slab above to the arête which is followed more easily to the top.

| 2 | **Ullscarf Edge** | 50m | VD | ★★ |
|---|---|---|---|---|

DJ Cameron, W Heaton Cooper - 1936

1   20m    Climb the blunt arête to belay at the dubious blocks below the left end of the line of overlaps.

2   16m    Follow the corner in the arête directly and continue up to the ledge; move right to belay

3   14m    Climb the wall above to the top

| 3 | **Evening Wall** | 76m | HS | ★★ |
|---|---|---|---|---|

DJ Cameron, W Heaton Cooper - 1936

An exciting route starting 3m right of *Ullscarf Edge*.

1   22m    Ascend the steep slab to a ledge and belay as for *Ullscarf Edge*.

2   14m    Traverse right, taking care with the loose blocks, then descend to a grass ledge. Now climb rightwards to pass right of the band of overlaps then up to gain a ledge and belay.

3   10m    After a delicate step up left, traverse left above the overlaps and climb up to a ledge. Move right to belay as for *Ullscarf Edge*. Spaced protection.

4   30m    Traverse right and climb a short chimney. Step right and continue up the arête above at first on its left side to a ledge. Move right and finish up the slab above.

| 4 | **The Borrowdale Pyramids** | 54m | HVS 5a | ★ |
|---|---|---|---|---|

J Arnold, K Arnold, A Hewison – 1 Jul 2003

1   40m 5a    Climb directly up to an obvious nose of rock. Pull right onto this and go straight up the slab to a belay.

2   14m    P3 of *Ullscarf Edge*.

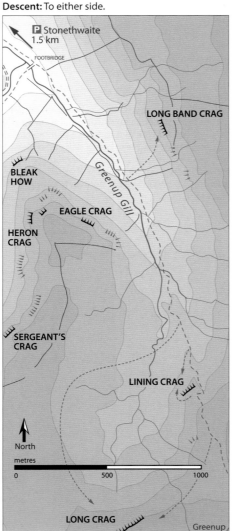

P Stonethwaite
1.5 km
FOOTBRIDGE

LONG BAND CRAG

BLEAK HOW

EAGLE CRAG

HERON CRAG

Greenup Gill

SERGEANT'S CRAG

LINING CRAG

North

metres

0      500      1000

LONG CRAG

Greenup

Long Band Crag
...e and finish up this.
179

Derwentwater
...dlath

Grange

Stonethwaite

Combe Gill

Seathwaite

### 5    City of Love and Ashes  54m    E1 5a    ★★
A Hewison, J Meeks, G Baum – 1 May 2000

A fine route on immaculate rock throughout.
1    40m 5a    Climb up to the hanging boulder then ascend the clean slab above heading up and slightly left to the open corner just right of a jagged nose. Climb up the corner until it is possible to move right to below the large overlap; pull through this and the next overlap to gain a fine slab. Go up this and move left to the belay of *Ullscarf Edge*.
2    14m    P3 of *Ullscarf Edge*.

### 6    Uncle Warren    54m    MVS 4b    ★
A Davis, A Hewison – 6 May 2000

A good route starting 10m right of *Ullscarf Edge* at a short right-facing corner.
1    40m 4b    Climb the corner for 4m to a ledge, step left and follow the open groove system all the way, passing the overlaps on the right. Traverse left above these as for *Evening Wall*.
2    14m    P3 of *Ullscarf Edge*.

### 7    Solitaire    72m    VS 4b    ★★
MA Toole – 30 May 1970

A pleasant route with an exciting second pitch.
1    30m 4a    Climb up to and over the overlap then the slab above, passing left of a grass ledge to belay on the large grassy ledge below the left end of the overhangs.
2    42m 4b    Climb the groove on the left to join *Evening Wall* at the short chimney on p3. Climb the chimney for 3m until it is possible to make an exposed traverse right, round the arête. Climb up trending slightly right over grassy ledges and the slab above to the top.

### 8    Gorgoroth    64m    HVS 4c    ★
MA Toole, B Henderson, N Wilson – 12 Feb 1967

In its upper half this route takes the central corner which gives an impressive finale. It is well worthwhile, cleaner than it looks and well-protected where it matters.
1    30m 4a    Ascend a faint groove in the slab to a ledge, move right and continue up the slab to the ledge below the overhang. Block belay on the right
2    34m 4c    Traverse up right under the overhangs then enter and climb the groove to the top. Belay well back.

### 9    Shemezim Grooves    67m    HVS 5a    ★
S Miller, R Allen – 30 May 1980

This climb follows a line of grooves parallel to the right-hand skyline of the crag.
1    42m 5a    Climb the slab to gain a tree-covered ledge. Follow the leftward-slanting gangway initially on the left then the right to a smaller grass ledge. Move left and climb the wall left of a thin crack until level with the central ledge. Move right to the arête and belay a few metres to the right.
2    25m    Finish up the arête of *Greenup Edge*.

### 10    Greenup Edge    70m    D    ★★
W Heaton Cooper - 1934

A good climb starting at the lowest point on the right of the crag.
1    35m    Climb the slab for 12m and continue up, skirting the grass ledges on the right. Spike belay in a grassy trough on the right of the arête.
2    35m    Climb up two shallow corners, move left and climb more or less directly to the top on excellent rough rock. Spike belay several metres higher.

### 11    Black Gills Slab    70m    VD
A Dunhill, C Thistlethwaite - 12 Sept 2014

The obvious clean slab 8m right of *Greenup Edge*. P1 makes a worthwhile D.
1    37m    Climb the slab and continue up to the grassy ramp to belay a little higher than *Greenup Edge*.
2    33m    Climb the slab 10m right of the obvious downward-pointing block. Surmount the bulge above taking care with the doubtful block and continue up to a large block. Step rightwards off the block and continue up to belay.

## Lining Crag

| | | | |
|---|---|---|---|
| 1 | Crucifix | S | |
| 2 | Ullscarf Edge | VD | ★★ |
| 3 | Evening Wall | HS | ★★ |
| 4 | The Borrowdale Pyramids | HVS 5a | ★ |
| 5 | City of Love and Ashes | E1 5a | ★★ |
| 6 | Uncle Warren | MVS 4b | ★ |
| 7 | Solitaire | VS 4b | ★★ |
| 8 | Gorgoroth | HVS 4c | ★ |

Derwentwater

# Long Crag

NY 279 105          ⊙ North West          ▲ 600m          🚶 90 mins

Situated in a wonderfully quiet and remote part of the valley, offering excellent views over the northern fells, the crag is only 20m high but is, nevertheless, impressive. The rock is very good and compact although the left-hand end of the main wall does take some time to dry.

**Approach:** From Stonethwaite to the top of Greenup Gill where the crag comes into view in the distance.

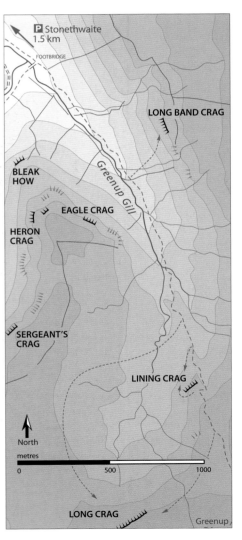

**1    Roadside Picnic**          20m    HVS 5a          ★
J Sparks, M Walsh - 6 May 1990

Gain and climb the series of right-facing grooves in the slab. Go up to the bilberry ledges and continue more dynamically using a steep little flake/crack. At its top step right and up to belays.

**2    The Foad Factor**          20m    MVS 4c
J Sparks, M Walsh - 6 May 1990

Climb the vegetated groove to gain the obvious mossy chimney which proves to be not so obvious after all! Better than it looks although needs time to dry.

To the right is a prominent pointed boulder.

**3    Double Lip Trip**          20m    E3 5c
J Clay, J Davidson – 28 Aug 1993

Ascend the left-hand of the twin cracks, about 3m left of the large pointed boulder, by steep and technical climbing to reach the overhanging chimney. Finish up this.

**4    Borrowdale Volcanic**    20m    E6 6b F6c    ★★
M Greenbank, P Cornforth - Jul 1996

The fierce thin crack line (peg) to gain the slanting gangway-cum-groove.

**5    Hock Clock**          20m    E7 6b F7b    ★★
J McHaffie, A Hocking – 15 Apr 2002

Climb the thin groove to a good hold (gear), then go up the wall (gear) with a hard move up to a big break. Move up right and more easily to the top.

**6    Rock Lobster**          20 m    E7 6b F7a    ★★
M Greenbank, P Cornforth - Jul 1996

The stunning slim groove line in the centre of the crag is both strenuous and serious. Unprotected tricky moves lead to a good flat hold (RP1 up and right). From here launch up the steep wall above for about 5m to good holds in a horizontal break (Friend 2). Continue up the wall above.

Derwentwater

### 7  Not with a Bang  20m  E3 5c  ★★
J Clay, J Sparks, M Walsh – 27 May 1990

Gain and climb a right-facing open pinkish groove (peg) then step left onto a mossy slab and move up to a bilberry ledge. Finish through the bulges above the left end of the ledge.

### 8  Paddy's Arête  10m  E3 6a  ★
J Clay – May 27 1990

Climb the arête starting on the right. Sustained.

# Eagle Crag

NY 277 121        ⊙ East North East        ◢ 440m        🏃 45 mins

Eagle dominates the view south-east from Stone-thwaite. Its clean-cut rectangular vertical wall screams "climb me"! Closer acquaintance reveals a complex mix of good steep, sometimes green and lichenous, rock – difficult to approach and slow to dry. Those who do venture onto this imposing face will discover climbs of real character, sadly no longer fashionable, with solitude, adventure and striking memories guaranteed.

**Approach:** From Stonethwaite via the east side of Stonethwaite Beck and Greenup Gill. Cross the beck near a large boulder and up the fellside to a grass bank, between the Lower and Main Crags. Gain the base of the left hand wall by abseil. For the Main Crag follow a short rake up rightwards to a large flake at the left end of vegetated ledges below the climbs.

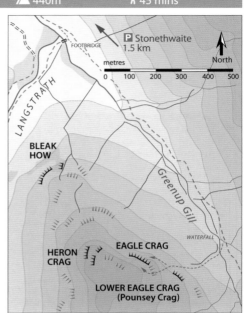

## Lower Eagle Crag
### NY 278 121    Ⓐ    🔺420m    🧍45 mins

The smaller more amenable neighbour of the Main Crag gives a number of short sustained routes on excellent rough rock that may need cleaning.

**Approach:** Traverse left across either one of two grass ledges from the gully.

**Descent:** Use the gully to the right.

### 1    Birdie            36m    E1 5b        ☆
R Kenyon, C Kenyon - 7 Aug 1988

A companion route to *Double Bogey* starting as for that route.
1    24m 5b    Climb the corner/crack to a grassy ledge at 10m. Continue up a short crack and wall above to gain an obvious layback flake. Finish up the corner/crack above.
2    12m 5a    Climb the smooth buttress trending right to finish up twin cracks.

### 2    Double Bogey        36m    El 5b        ☆☆
P Whillance, D Armstong - 2 Aug 1981

1    24m 5b    Climb the obvious corner for 8m, then move right and up a flake crack onto a large block. Move up the steep wall, slightly leftwards, to reach a thin crack and follow this, passing a small square overhang, to the terrace.
2    12m        Finish up the thin crack in the slab left of the easy corner.

### 3    Pitch and Putt        36m    E2 5c        ☆☆
P Whillance, D Armstrong - 23 Aug 1981

A good route up the steep wall. Start 4m up to the right of the corner of *Double Bogey*.
1    24m 5c    Start easily up a short wall and slab above to where the angle steepens. Move up and climb a thin crack and the twin cracks above.
2    12m 5b    Move 2m right and climb a wall to reach a thin crack in a rib. Finish up this, moving right into a scoop at the top.

### 4    Fear and Loathing    36m    E4 6a        ☆
T Stephenson, H Sterling - 10 Jul 1983

Start 6m up the terrace above *Pitch and Putt* at a thin crack.
1    18m 6a    Climb the crack to a large handhold. Swing right on flakes and pull up to a small spike runner. Go up left to a thin crack and pull up round the overhang on the right. Pull up leftwards onto the terrace.
2    18m 5b    The thin corner/crack, 5m right, is followed past a small triangular overhang. Pull out at the top onto easier rock which is followed to the top.

| | | |
|---|---|---|
| 1 | Birdie | E1 5b |
| 2 | Double Bogey | El 5b |
| 3 | Pitch and Putt | E2 5c |
| 4 | Fear and Loathing | E4 6a |
| 5 | Hole in Yan | E4 6a |

# Bleak How
NY 273 125          ⊙ North West          ▲ 270m          ⫪ 40 mins

A justifiably popular crag with good rock and a lovely outlook. Late May - Sep: midges can be seriously annoying.

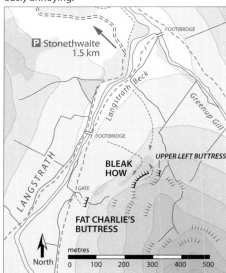

**Approach:** From Stonethwaite either side of the beck.

**Descent:** To the left along a ledge system for climbs on the *Brush Off* slab; by abseil from the tree at the top of *The Reiver* for climbs on Bleak How Buttress; or by heading uphill then descending the grassy gully behind the Upper Left Buttress.

**1   BX Breakdown          40m   E1 5b**
PC Bennett, P Chapman, C Chapman – 9 Jul 1994

Climb the slab left of the overlap then up to the right-hand end of the grass ledge. Move 2m left then climb up the slab first leftwards on obvious holds then right to move up and right of the moss. Climb straight up the slab to a ledge then move right to finish.

**2   Rub Off          40m   HVS 5a   ★★**
M Armitage, D Falcon – 19 Jul 1984

Climb the steep wall and slab to gain the right-hand end of the vegetated ledge. Climb the thin crack above and swing left to a small niche. Continue direct to join and finish up *Brush Off* at a big ledge.

**3   Brush Off          35m   HVS 4c   ★★★**
C Downer, C Bacon, S Kysow – 24 May 1984

An extremely good route requiring a bold approach. Start just right of the small roof. Climb the featureless slab until forced left at 8m to a shallow triangular pocket. Move back right, away from the line of *Rub Off*, then go directly up to a ledge. Finish up the short wall above.

**4   Pop Goes the Asteroid  35m   E2 5c   ★**
C Dale - Apr 1985

Start just right of *Brush Off*. Climb directly up the slab, over two tiny overlaps, to better holds. Move right and up to a vegetated ledge. Minimal protection without side runners. Move left to finish.

**5   Seconds Out          35m   E1 5b   ★**
C Downer – 29 May 1985

Start 2m right of *Brush Off* at a thin crack. Climb the crack to an overlap. Step left and pull over on good holds. Climb more easily towards the vegetated ledge above. Move left to finish as for *Brush Off*.

**6   Footloose          35m   E2 5c**
C Downer, C Bacon, S Kysow - 25 May 1984

Start in the corner on the right of the slabs. Poor protection. Often wet. Bridge up the black corner to reach holds on the left. Pull up and continue up the corner until easier climbing leads left to the finish of *Brush Off*.

**7   Fancy Free          30m   E1 5a   ☆☆ ♂**
C Downer, C Bacon, S Kysow – 24 May 1984

A striking route up the curving bold arête right of the slabs; sadly now becoming very mossy. Climb the arête from the right, with a short deviation to the left at half-height, to a small overhang. Pull over on good holds and follow the edge of a narrow white slab up rightwards to a tree belay.

**8   Steel Pulse          30m   E3 5c   ☆ ♂**
C Downer, J Waters – 15 Jun 1984

A pulsating climb starting just right of *Fancy Free*. Climb the slab directly to a small groove below an overhang. Traverse right to a steep corner. Bridge up to a good hold in the crack at its top. Pull up onto the left wall to some undercuts and then go up right (thread). Climb steeply up left on good holds to finish up the slab of *Fancy Free*.

### 9 Breathless 30m E3 6a ☆
C Downer, S Kysow – 25 May 1984

Challenging steep technical climbing up the hanging groove in the back right-hand side of the central bay with protection where it counts. Start at a large block. Climb a wall and groove to an overhang. Move over and, where the groove steepens, swing right and pull up onto a small ledge. Easier climbing leads to a tree belay.

### 10 Boston Strangler 28m E5 6b ☆
A Murray, R Parker – 2 Jun 1984

A problematic climb up the overhanging groove, just right of *Breathless*. Follow *Breathless* for 3m then step right onto a grassy ledge. Climb the groove above to an overhang. A difficult move gains the groove above. Swing right onto the arête and continue up the wall above to a tree belay.

### 11 The Boj Eliminate 36m HVS 5a ★★
SJH Reid, L Steer – 20 Jun 1985

Start at a short corner behind trees just right of the gearing up boulder. Climb the corner and go up to a good spike. Climb the groove above (as for *Bleak How Buttress*) and move up rightwards to pull up

onto a large slab in the middle of the face. Climb the slab up leftwards, under the steep headwall, to some cracks (junction with *Bleak How Buttress*). Climb 2m up the cracks and make an exposed traverse horizontally rightwards on superb quartz holds to gain good holds on *The Reiver*. Step back left and climb flakes leftwards to the final break and up to a tree belay.

### ⑤ 12 Bleak How Buttress 36m E2 5c ★★★
D Hellier – 15 Nov 1983

A first class route, with a distinct short crux. From the lowest point of the buttress, a short groove leads onto the oval slab. A couple of thin moves lead up and leftwards to a spike runner. Start up a short groove to a swing left on a huge jug. Mantel onto this then follow easier grooves to a tree belay.

### 13 Bleak Beauty 36m E4 6a ☆
M Dale, T Robinson - 18 Aug 2015

A bold eliminate. Follow *Bleak How Buttress* to good holds at the top of the oval slab and continue up the wall above heading for the obvious hanging corner (small cam). Climb the wall just right of the corner and move left to good holds. Go up leftwards across the slab and climb the wall direct

| 1 | BX Breakdown | E1 5b | 7 | Fancy Free | E1 5a |
| 2 | Rub Off | HVS 5a | 8 | Steel Pulse | E3 5c |
| 3 | Brush Off | HVS 4c | 9 | Breathless | E3 6a |
| 4 | Pop Goes the Asteroid | E2 5c | 10 | Boston Strangler | E5 6b |
| 5 | Seconds Out | E1 5b | 11 | The Boj Eliminate | HVS 5a |
| 6 | Footloose | E2 5c | 12 | Bleak How Buttress | E2 5c |

| 13 | Bleak Beauty | E4 6a | 16 | Front Runner | E1 5a |
| 14 | The Reiver | HVS 5a | 17 | Psyched Out | E3 5c |
| 15 | Fun Run | MVS 4c | 18 | Bleak How Eliminate | E5 6a |

at the brown Mare's Tail streak to reach good slots at the quartz band. Climb direct on spaced finger edges and step right below the final steepening to belay as for *The Reiver*.

⑤ **14   The Reiver**          36m    HVS 5a ★★★ ♂
C Downer - 5 Jun 1984

A compelling climb taking the right-hand side of the main buttress. Interesting throughout. Follow *Bleak How Buttress* for 6m. Step right and climb a rib and reddish wall to a ledge. Where the wall steepens climb slightly leftwards on good holds, then go directly to the top.

The slabs right of the main buttress tend to be mossy but offer two good climbs.

**15   Fun Run**          30m    MVS 4c
A Hall, H Bingham – 28 May 1984

Follow the left-slanting crack and slab right of two trees. Move right past an overlap and climb up to a groove. Climb steeply up the rib on the left to finish on the grass ledges. Belay block up to the left.

**16   Front Runner**          30m    E1 5a
C Downer, C Bacon – 28 May 1984

Go straight up the centre of the slab, over an overlap and up to a steep wall. Move left and pull onto a ledge on the rib on the right. Gain a jug on the wall above and move right onto the arête (bold); follow this to the top. Belay well back.

About 40m up and right of *Front Runner* is a very obvious smooth left-leaning slab with a groove on its right-hand side.

**17   Psyched Out**          20m    E3 5c
M Morton, J Church - 1997

Start at the bottom right-hand side of the slab. Step onto the slab and traverse left to its centre. Climb straight up to the top of the groove and then trend left to a small tree belay.

**18   Bleak How Eliminate**   20m    E5 6a    ★★
D Birkett, P Ross – 3 May 1995

Climb the groove with difficulty, then move out right and climb the headwall above. As the difficulty eases so the protection becomes sparser.

## Upper Left Buttress

This is the small buttress up and left of the main buttress which offers some good short climbs. Descend to the left down the grassy gully.

**19   First Footing**          20m    MVS 4c
M Naftalin, R Henderson – 29 Apr 1988

Start at the top of the leftward-slanting ramp. Move up and right into a groove. Follow this moving right at a tree then climb a rib to the top, finishing as for *Manuel*.

**20   Amistad Con El Diablo** 20m   E2 5c          ★
S Sena, R Kenyon, D Smith – 5 Jul 1986

Start on the ramp at a weakness in the steep lower wall. Overcome the overhung base and ascend rightwards to an overlap. Surmount this with difficulty and climb up precariously to an obvious thin crack. Follow this to the top.

### 21 Catching Up    20m    E1 5b    ★
F Dooley, C Scammel – 2 May 1995

Start at the lowest point of the buttress at an obvious block. Use a finger flake to surmount the steep lower wall and follow a faint crack crossing the overlap to a junction with *Manuel*. Continue up *Amistad*, *Dago* or *Manuel*.

### 22 Dago    20m    VS 5a    ★
S Sena, R Kenyon, D Smith , C Kenyon – 5 Jul 1986

Start below small ledges, 2m to the right of the left-slanting ramp. Gain the ledges and climb the wall above to a shallow groove. Climb this and the short bulge to finish.

### 23 Manuel    25m    HVS 4c    ★
M Park, A Irving, P Osliff – 26 Apr 1987

Start at two distinct vertical gouges low on the wall. Climb up to a junction with *Dago*, then move diagonally left above an overlap (poorly protected) to the finish up the left-hand skyline rib.

### 24 Basil    20m    E1 5b    ★
C King, A Hewison – 14 Apr 1997

Start as for *Manuel*. Climb straight up to the left-hand end of the higher overlap. Make a delicate move up and right into a vague scoop and finish direct.

**Langstrath East**

High
Page 205

Upper
Page 202

Heron Crag
Page 201

Upper Bleak How
Page 195

Bleak How
Page 193

Fat Charlie's Buttress
Page 199

## 25  Que?                    20m   E1 5b         ★
M Dale, A Dunhill – 16 Jun 2013

Start 3m right of *Manuel* at a small very shallow
corner below the right end of the overlap. Climb
up right to gain the right end of a couple of
gangways. Step right and climb the slab above to
a bulge. Gain and climb the bulge with difficulty.
Continue up the wall above exiting leftwards at its
top. Belay well back.

Derwentwater

Watendlath

ergeant's Crag
Page 207

Sergeant's Crag Slabs
Page 209

Hooker Buttress
Page 216

Blackmoss Pot Slab
Page 214

Cellulite E2 (page 200) - Tony Whitehouse 📷 Andy Birtwistle

# Fat Charlie's Buttress

NY 272 124          ⊖West          ▲ 160m          🏃 20 mins

A small crag with several short but worthwhile routes on excellent rock.

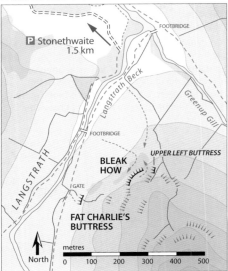

**Approach:** From Stonethwaite either side of the beck. The buttress is 50m above the large solitary fir tree.

**1    Myth of Fingerprints    15m    VS 4b    ★**
M Boniface, N Wallis, C Phillips – 26 Feb 1988

Climb the curving slabby arête on the left-hand side of the buttress in a fine delicate situation. Photo page 177.

**2    Supermodel    15m    E1 5b    ★★**
A Hewison, G Baum – 19 Jun 1996

Start 2m right of the fence at a scoop. Climb up the left side of the scoop then straight up moving slightly left, avoiding the option of the easy finish, to end up on top of the arête.

**3    Blubber    13m    VS 4c**
G Baum, A Hewison – 19 Jun 1996

Start 4m right of the fence and climb straight up following a vague crack to finish below the fence.

**4    Islay Wait    13m    MS**
G Baum, A Hewison – 19 Jun 1996

Go up to below a small overlap then move up and diagonally left using parallel cracks.

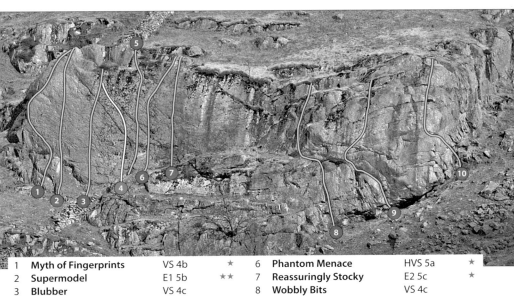

| 1 | Myth of Fingerprints | VS 4b | ★ | 6 | Phantom Menace | HVS 5a | ★ |
|---|---|---|---|---|---|---|---|
| 2 | Supermodel | E1 5b | ★★ | 7 | Reassuringly Stocky | E2 5c | ★ |
| 3 | Blubber | VS 4c | | 8 | Wobbly Bits | VS 4c | |
| 4 | Islay Wait | MS | | 9 | Cholesterol Corner | E1 5b | ★ |
| 5 | Joss's Route | VS 4c | | 10 | Cellulite | E2 5c | ★★ |

**5    Joss's Route**          14m    VS 4c
T Langhorne – 5 Jun 2004

Climb directly to and up the thin crack left of *Phantom Menace* stepping left from the small niche just below the top.

**6    Phantom Menace**          13m    HVS 5a    ★
M Lynch, D Kay – 25 Apr 1999

Start on the grass ledge. Climb up to gain the rightward-leaning diagonal crack at two-thirds height. Follow this to a monster jug finish.

**7    Reassuringly Stocky**    11m    E2 5c    ★
A Hewison, G Baum, J Meeks – 11 Jul 1996

Climb the enjoyable slab to hard finishing moves. High runners possible on the left.

**8    Wobbly Bits**          15m    VS 4c
SJH Reid, A Hewison – 16 Apr 1997

Start at an undercut groove. Climb up and step right into the groove which leads to a break. Follow this left, under a boss, to the right end of a long grass ledge. Step up onto a light-coloured slab then direct to the top.

**9    Cholesterol Corner**    12m    E1 5b    ★
A Hewison, G Baum – 19 Jun 1996

Climb the undercut corner 4m left of the arête and pull out onto a rounded ledge. Move up to gain good holds and (hidden) protection at the base of a depression. A hard move leads to better holds and the top.

**10    Cellulite**          10m    E2 5c    ★★
A Hewison, G Baum - 5 Apr 2000

Start just right of the arête and make strenuous moves up the undercut wall leading to better holds. Move left to the arête and continue more easily to the top or climb the upper groove direct at 6a. Photo page 198.

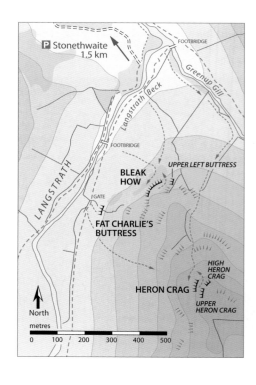

# Heron Crag

NY 274 121     ⊖ West     ▲ 360m     ✦ 60 mins

This group of crags is situated in a prominent position on the ridge at the junction of the Greenup and Langstrath valleys.

Good rock broken by large heathery ledges becoming more abundantly verdant as height is gained; you are likely to meet more sheep than climbers here. Technical problems can be discovered in abundance and the crag provides that unique Lakeland mountaineering experience. There is one route of merit that is probably best done in cold conditions.

**Approach:** From Stonethwaite take the path to the bridge across Greenup Gill. Take the west side of the gill to the second dry-stone wall. Turn right uphill by the wall, cross a stile and continue up for 100m to a shoulder.

To reach Upper Heron Crag, traverse across and slightly down to pleasant grassy terraces along the bottom of the climbs. For High Heron, continue up the path for a short distance. For Heron Main Buttress, leave sacks at the start of the terraces then descend to the foot of the buttress.

| 1 | **Heron Crag Buttress** | 103m HS 4c | ★ |
B Beetham - 18 Sep 1940

Takes the ribs to the left of Heron Crag Gully starting at the foot of the buttress. The lower pitches are dirty but the upper section follows a ridge in a delightful exposed position.

1   35m     Climb the nose to gain a ledge. Continue up past a tree to belay near the gully.

2   20m 4a    Climb leftwards to a big heather terrace and belay on the right at the foot of the buttress.

3   30m 4c    Climb past a block to a large flake. Continue to a small slab and climb a short groove to a ledge on the right. Surmount the awkward wall above (crux) to reach a ledge.

4   18m 4a    Continue up the ridge, moving right off the crest to follow a crack to the final terraces.

# Upper Heron Crag

NY 275 122        North West        ▲ 440m        🏃 60 mins

A short steep wall of very good rock with a concentration of excellent single pitch climbs. The superb situation, catching the afternoon sun, and the quality of the climbs make the walk well worthwhile. The bilberry topping of vegetation, heather cornices and a small spring make finishing the routes adventurous. Fixing a rope is advised.

**Descent:** To the left.

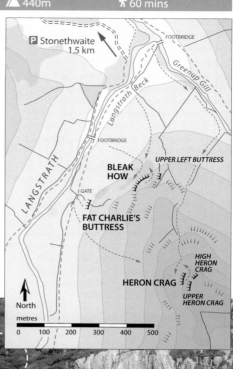

**2    Traverse of the Frogs**   30m   E2 5b   ★★
J Hughes, SJH Reid – 26 Jun 1996

An extremely strenuous pitch with hard-won but excellent protection. Climb a short crack to gain the rightward-slanting break.

**3    Heaven Knows I'm**   22m   E1 5b   ★★
       **Miserable Now!**
C Dale, R Curley – 17 Jun 1984

After a commiting start, the interest is maintained on jagged brittle spikes. A good warm up.

**4    Flamingo Fandango    22m    E1 5b    ★★**
R Kenyon, C King – 17 Jun 1984

A crack and wall leads to the flutings. Move over a slight bulge to finish up an overhanging crack in the nose above or, more sensibly, skirt to the left of the nose.

**5    Big Foot    24m    E2 5c    ★★★**
C Dale, R Curley – 17 Jun 1984

A reachy route. A crack leads to a ledge and a little higher is a jug, beyond which a sinuous crack is followed. Finish up the nose on the left.

**6    The One that    28m    E2 5c    ★**
      **Got Away**
J Arnold, K Arnold - 28 Jun 2001

A direct finish to *Little Nose* climbing the superb flake/crack.

**7    Little Nose    30m    E2 5b    ★★**
C Dale, R Curley – 17 Jun 1984

A sustained route. Climb the shallow corner and the wall above to a hollow flake overlap. Stand on this then move right to a good jug. From here a long reach gains the groove above.

**8    Shooting Fish in a    28m    E4 6a    ★**
      **Barrel**
J Arnold, K Arnold, S Prior - 23 Jun 2001

Good climbing up the obvious clean wall. Pull left on to the ramp, step right and climb the wall past two horizontal breaks. Difficult moves left above the top break gain a crack (junction with *Little Nose*). Step back right and climb the wall and slab with difficulty. Continuing up *Little Nose* makes an E3 5c.

⑤ **9    The Question    28m    E2 5c    ★★★**
R Kenyon, C King – 17 Jun 1984

The technically demanding conspicuous grooved arête in the centre of the crag.

**10  Little Corner    28m    E1 5b**
D Armstrong – 11 Aug 1984

The gangway slanting left leads into a short awkward corner. Finish leftwards.

**11  Joie Pur    28m    E2 5c**
C Dale, C King, R Kenyon, R Curley – 17 Jun 1984

A deceptively steep climb up a loose green crack above the start of *Little Corner*. Gain the crack from the left and follow it until moves on the right enable a ledge on the left to be gained. Continue up the wall behind to a ledge. Climb a short wall above to the top.

**12  Barefoot    28m    E2 5c**
C Dale, C King, R Kenyon, R Curley – 17 Jun 1984

A varied route starting below a slightly slanting crack. Go up a short wall to gain the crack which is followed, with interest, to a ledge on the right. Follow a crack rightwards to a ledge. Climb the pinnacle, crack and groove above to a bilberry-covered ledge. Finish up the short wall.

Derwentwater
Watendlath
Grange
Stonethwaite
Combe Gill
Seathwaite

## 13  Bilberry Topping        28m   E2 5c      ★★
R Kenyon, M Armitage – Jul 1999.

Climb the short wall and tricky slanting crackline.
Move up rightwards to an open groove below a
crack in the upper wall. On the right is a ledge with
a vital block. Use a good handhold to get established on the wall, overcome a small overlap and
use the 'bilberry topping' to gain the large ledge
above. Move slightly left and climb the obvious
corner in the short wall.

High Heron Crag

# High Heron Crag

NY 275 122　　⊕ North　　　　🔺 480m　　　　🏃 60 mins

Offering medium grade climbs in a wonderful panoramic position, this is the conspicuous crag on the skyline above and left of Upper Heron Crag.

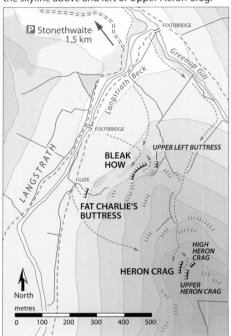

P Stonethwaite
1.5 km

FOOTBRIDGE

Greenup Gill

Langstrath Beck

FOOTBRIDGE

LANGSTRATH

UPPER LEFT BUTTRESS

BLEAK
HOW

GATE

FAT CHARLIE'S
BUTTRESS

HIGH
HERON
CRAG

HERON CRAG

UPPER
HERON CRAG

North

metres

0　100　200　300　400　500

**Descent:** To the right.

| 14 | **Pot Pourri** | 42m | HS 4b |
|----|----------------|-----|-------|

BJ Clarke – 7 Aug 2006

Three entertaining pitches up the rather discontinuous rib at the left end of the crag. Start just up and left of the lowest point of the rib, on a shelf.
1　11m 4b　Climb the crimpy wall to a ledge. Step right and move up a short wall, before trending left to reach a large triangular ledge.
2　23m 4a　Climb the slab on the left to the arête. Scramble up for 15m to reach a quartz wall riven by two cracks.
3　8m 4a　Climb the left-hand crack on amazing holds.

| 15 | **High Heron Cracks** | 30m | HVS 5a |
|----|----------------------|-----|--------|

A Dunhill, C Thistlethwaite - 11 Sep 2014

Climb the crack to the heather ramp and continue up parallel cracks to pull out right onto a grass shelf. Climb the crack in the open groove above to a belay ledge. Scramble off diagonally left.

The next two climbs start from the higher level terrace above and right.

| 16 | **Up the Khyber** | 25m | HVS 5a |
|----|-------------------|-----|--------|

J Fotheringham, C Bonington - 1986

Climb the steep groove.

| 17 | **Solar Toupee** | 30m | HVS 5a |
|----|------------------|-----|--------|

J Fotheringham, C Bonington - 1986

Start up the open groove just right of *Up The Khyber* and then pull up left onto the nose on good jugs. Finish up steep ground.

30m right at the same level is a slabby wall defined on its right by a fine arête above a series of sinuous cracks.

|  | **Sheherazade** | 11m | VS 4c |
|--|-----------------|-----|-------|

BJ Clarke – 7 Aug 2006

Climb the cracks then move right to a ledge on the arête. Follow the arête to finish.

Derwentwater　Watendlath　Grange　Stonethwaite　Combe Gill　Seathwaite

## Sergeant's Crag

| | | | |
|---|---|---|---|
| 1 | Sergeant's Crag Gully | S | |
| 2 | The Redoubt | HVS | |
| 3 | Echoes of Zechariah | E1 5b | ★ |
| 4 | Broadway | HS | ★ |
| 5 | The Great Wall | HS | ★ |
| 6 | The Diagonal Crack | HVS 5b | ★★ |
| 7 | West Face Route | VD | |
| 8 | Now for Something Completely Different | | |
| 9 | Doberman | E1 5a | |

# Sergeant's Crag

NY 274 115          ⊘ North to West          ▲ 400m          🏃 50 mins

This large complex crag features prominently overlooking Langstrath. The prominent deep cleft on its left side is *Sergeant's Crag Gully*, a classic Victorian tour de force. Climbing with a sac makes sense on these long mountaineering routes to avoid a return to the base of the crag.

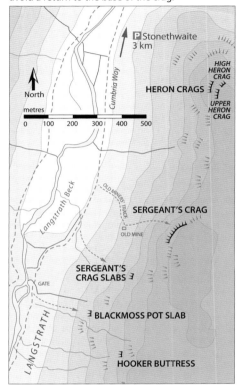

**Approach:** From the west side of Langstrath Beck.

**Descent:** From the top of the crag, a long grassy ramp drops down to the right. To return to the base of the crag, drop down carefully just above Sergeant's Crag Slabs.

To return to the valley floor, continue following a line to the fell wall and descend to its right (looking down). It is also possible to descend well to the left of the crag.

---

**1   Sergeant's Crag Gully**   110m  S          ★★★
WA Wilson, JW Robinson - 1 Sep 1893

A traditional gully climb of considerable merit.
1   36m       Climb the left wall, past a chockstone, and continue up the wall. Pass another chockstone on its right. Scramble up to the next chockstone.
2   8m        Climb the left wall with interest (also possible on the right).
3   30m       Continue past another chockstone to below a further steepening.
4   36m       Climb the right wall of the gully to avoid the chockstone and finish up easier ground above.

---

**2   The Redoubt**          56m   HVS
P Nunn, B Henderson - 23 Jul 1967

This climb attacks the rounded buttress starting at a pinnacle 20m to the right of *Sergeant's Crag Gully*.
1   16m 4c   Climb the obvious ramp rightwards past poised blocks to a niche then traverse back left under the overhang to a detached block.
2   40m 5a   Traverse back right and ascend the short slabby groove to the right of the overhangs until a slab leads left between the roofs (peg) to a good crack above the stance. Climb this to a ledge and the diagonal crack then move left to a ledge. Slabs lead rightwards to a heather traverse.

---

**3   Echoes of Zechariah**   40m   E1 5b      ★
S Prior, RJ Kenyon - 2 Jul 1993

This route weaves up the small overhanging ribs on the corner of the buttress. Start 2m right of *The Redoubt* below an obvious crack above a detached flake. Follow a ramp up rightwards to a point where an awkward move gains a slab between overlaps. Move left across the back of a groove and surmount an overhang to gain the upper part of the groove. Continue with interest moving slightly left to gain and climb a crack. Continue up easier rock to a grass ledge.

The following two routes can be easily reached. At the top continue up almost anywhere, climb *The Diagonal Crack* or descend grassy ramps on right.

### 4    Broadway                33m   HS            ★
B Beetham - 6 Sep 1945

Climb up the wall on excellent holds, passing a small ledge. Move up slightly leftwards and follow the nose and rock above to the heather terrace.

### 5    The Great Wall           30m   HS          ★★
B Beetham - 6 Sep 1945

A fine climb starting just left of the foot of a chimney; Two-Way Traffic Chimney. Climb up past a small holly tree. Continue up the corner and the wall on the right, on superb holds, to a heather terrace.

### 6    The Diagonal Crack   22m   HVS 5b         ★
R Kenyon, C Kenyon  - 12 May 1985

An interesting and exposed pitch above *The Great Wall* starting on the heather ledge above that route. Gain the obvious diagonal crack in the wall on the right and follow it rightwards to its top. Either continue up the crag above or descend grassy ramps on the right.

### 7    West Face Route          270m  VD          ★
B Beetham, TH Somervell, TB Meldrum,
TR Burnett, LW Somervell - 28 Aug 1945

An expedition for aspirant pioneers and overall one of the longest routes in the Lakes. Start at a small cairn at the toe of the crag.
1    30m        Up slabs to a grass terrace.
2    20m        Walk left towards the prow of the buttress.
3    36m        Surmount short walls and terraces to below a gully – Two-Way Traffic Chimney.
4    25m        Fight up the left chimney, over a fence (with care) and grass slope.
5    14m        Climb an irregular crack and wall to a heather terrace and belay to the right of the line of metal spikes.
6    20m        Climb up to and follow a shallow corner to a stemple belay.
    125m       Either continue rightwards up a series of walls and terraces or finish less traditionally up the via ferrata.

### 8    Now for Something        100m
### Completely Different

Starting in a corner left of *Doberman* then continuing leftwards and on up the crag, linking with *West Face Route*, is a line of metal spikes (rope in place in 2015). Its ascent makes an interesting outing.

### 9    Doberman                 30m   E1 5a
R Kenyon, B Barnard, SJH Reid, D Scott, S Prahbu - 29 Jun 1993

Start at the foot of the vegetated chimney/ramp in the centre of the buttress. Climb up the ramp for about 7m until it is possible to move awkwardly left onto a slab. Continue up rightwards, aiming for the highest point of the buttress finishing on the left. Descend down the grass/heather ramp to the left.

# Sergeant's Crag Slabs

NY 271 113          ⊖ West          ⛰ 360m          🚶 45 mins

Superb routes on immaculate rock in magnificent surroundings make this, justifiably, one of Borrowdale's most popular crags for the HVS – E2 climber.

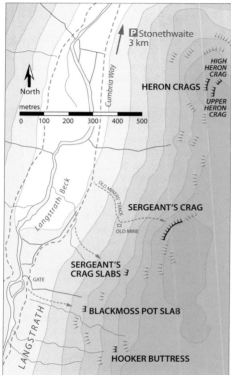

**Descent:** Abseil. There are fixed abseil stations at the top to help protect the fragile habitats found in the gullies on either side of the crag.

### 1   Revelation          45m   VS 4c   ★★ ♂●●
R McHaffie, J Bosher - 7 Jul 1991

From the left-hand side of the main slab, climb leftwards towards a block step in the overhang; pull through this and follow the crack above until it peters out then move right and up a groove.

### 2   Cedric in Space          45m   HVS 5a   ★ ♂●●
R Kenyon, S Prior - 13 Jul 1995

Interesting, but barely independent, climbing up the seriously-squeezed slab between *Revelation* and *Endurance* finishing up a blunt rib; blinkers essential. If you avoid using either crack getting over the overlap it is 5c.

### 3   Endurance          45m   HVS 5a   ★★★ ♂●
R McHaffie, J Bosher - 7 Jul 1991

The thin crack left of the prominent central crack of *Lakeland Cragsman* with an interesting sequence of moves through the overlap. The hardest of the three star HVSs but protection is excellent.

### 4   Between the Lines          45m   E1 5b   ★★ ♂
J Campbell, SJH Reid - 15 May 1995

Climbs the slab and overlaps between the cracks of *Endurance* and *Lakeland Cragsman*.
Start up *Lakeland Cragsman*; after a few metres step left and climb between the two cracklines without recourse to either. The pebbly pillar above gives a teasing finish.

### ⑤ 5   Lakeland Cragsman          45m   HVS 5a ★★★ ♂
R McHaffie, J Bosher - 7 Jul 1991

The wider central crackline has great moves and superb protection; sustained yet low in the grade. A good first HVS lead. Climb the slab passing a blocky overhang on the left. Continue up the crack over three small overlaps to finish up an easier corner. Photo page 212.

### 6   Terminator 2          45m   HVS 5a ★★★ ♂
R McHaffie, J Bosher - 8 Sep 1991

A superb companion to *Lakeland Cragsman*. Climb the thin crack right of *Lakeland Cragsman* through the left-hand of three breaks in the overhang. Delicate moves lead up and left to a right-slanting ramp/groove leading to a narrow ledge. Pull into a corner on the right and follow the horizontal crack leftwards to finish.

### 7   Boris in Wonderland          45m   E2 5b   ★★ ♂
R Kenyon, C King - 21 May 1995

A direct pitch starting just right of *Terminator 2* and giving similar but harder climbing. Climb to the central of the three breaks through the overlap and gain the slab above. Continue directly until moves left lead onto the rightward-slanting rampline of *Terminator 2*. Move up, then pull through the overlap and climb the slab leftwards to a ledge. Continue direct past another ledge.

**8  An Turas**     45m   E4 5c   ☆ ♂
M Przygrodzki, V Crookes - 21 Aug 2010

This eliminate squeezed between *Terminator 2* and *Aphasia* is a route where blinkers are essential.
Go up the slab just left of *Aphasia* to the central overlap; climb this direct (skyhook) and move up the slab to a good pocket. Overcome the bulge, keeping in a parallel line to *Aphasia* and cross another bulge (thread) to gain the large ledge. Finish direct or as for *Aphasia*.

⑤ **9  Aphasia**     45m   E2 5b   ★★★ ♂
C Downer, C Bacon, R HcHaffie - 8 Jun 1992

The centre of the slab left of *Holly Tree Crack* gives one of Lakeland's finest slab pitches. Very sustained and intricate climbing with reasonable protection keeps your attention right to the top.
Climb the short steep slab to below the right-hand break in the overlap. Pull up right and go straight up to a bulge where a hard move leads to a good hold. Continue up until moves right lead to a thin crack which ends at a narrow ledge. Pull up into the slight corner via a horizontal crack and climb the wall above directly to the top.

**10  Hookworm**     50m   E3 5c   ★★ ♂
D Nichol, A Nichol - Jul 1993

Climbs directly up the slab just left of *Holly Tree Crack*; spaced protection adds spice.
Climb to the overlap and pull directly over this to gain a slab. Go straight up, with a hard move over the steepening, to reach *Aphasia* and cracks. Step right and then move up the slab to a ledge. Pull over the overhang and climb a thin crack to the right of the final crack of *Aphasia*.

**11  Holly Tree Crack**     50m   E1 5b   ★★ ♂
R Mc Haffie, J Bosher - 17 Jul 1991

Start below a holly! Low in the grade and well-protected.
1   35m 5b   Climb the groove past the holly to a niche. Follow the crack out of the top of the niche to a ledge.
2   15m 5a   Climb the awkward corner to a ledge then follow a right-slanting crack to the top.

**12  Holly Tree Ramp**     35m   E1 5a   ★★ ♂
SJH Reid, J Campbell - 15 May 1995

Pleasant and increasingly bold climbing up the ramp right of *Holly Tree Crack*. Climb *Holly Tree Crack* to the niche and move up right onto the obvious right-slanting ramp/groove line. Follow it, avoiding a bulge on the right, to a small overlap containing a prominent crack. Climb this to a ledge.

**13  Quicksilver**     35m   E1 5b   ★★ ♂💧
C Downer, R McHaffie - 11 Jun 1992

Start 3m right of *Holly Tree Crack*. Bold in its upper half. Climb the crack, moving left and up into the right-slanting groove of *Holly Tree Ramp*. Pull over the bulge into a higher groove; climb this awkwardly and then pull left onto the arête which is followed to a ledge.

**14  The Death Stroke**     35m   E1 5b   ★★ ♂💧
R McHaffie, J Bosher - 17 Jul 1991

Start 3m right of *Quicksilver* and climb thin cracks to join *Holly Tree Ramp* which is followed to the belay.

**FAVOURITE ROUTES** ⑤
Ron Kenyon

My first climbing trips were by bus to Keswick and then on to Shepherd's, 50 years ago! Borrowdale is a lovely valley with varied crags from the popular Shepherd's to the more remote crags of Langstrath.

**True Cross** (VS) - Girdles are not everyone's cup of tea but try this one, best not on a busy day, then go back and do it again.

**The Question** (E2) – Checking crags out for the 1986 guide I saw Colin Downer, Chris Bacon and Sue Kysow gardening a crag at the start of Langstrath, this turned out to be Bleak How. Colin was rather defensive when I pointed at a line to be done that became *The Reiver*. We went up and climbed Heron Crag Buttress and saw a clean looking crag on the way down. A few weeks later saw seven new routes on Upper Heron Crag. The first was *The Question* which answered the question of how good the crag was and was just after I had "popped the Question" to Chris.

**Praying Mantis** (E1) - A Les Brown route always seems to be special. It opened up this fine though now often neglected crag weaving a way up the crag. An awkward crack on pitch one and a memorable traverse back right leading to the middle of the crag and get the heart beating.

**Gillercombe Buttress** (S) - I like to be in the fells with views across the Lakes and reach a summit. Best start at Honister Youth Hostel and take the track round to Gillercomb and climb the route then continue to the summit of Grey Knotts. A good route to do on Boxing Day.

**Aphasia** (E2) - I love slabs, a silence seems to descend as you work your way up. This is another Downer route – this time with Chris Bacon and Ray McHaffie. What a tally of routes these guys have – and this is one of the best.

**Sergeant's Crag Slabs**

| | | | |
|---|---|---|---|
| 1 | Revelation | VS 4c | ★★ |
| 3 | Endurance | HVS 5a | ★★★ |
| 5 | Lakeland Cragsman | HVS 5a | ★★★ |
| 6 | Terminator 2 | HVS 5a | ★★ |
| 7 | Boris in Wonderland | E2 5b | ★★ |
| 9 | Aphasia | E2 5b | ★★★ |
| 11 | Holly Tree Crack | E1 5b | ★★★ |
| 12 | Holly Tree Ramp | E1 5a | ★★ |
| 13 | Quicksilver | E1 5b | ★★ |
| 14 | The Death Stroke | E1 5b | ★★ |

Lakeland Cragsman HVS (page 209) – Martin Bennett 📷 Richard Tolley

# Blackmoss Pot Slab

NY 269 112  ⊖West  ▲ 310m  ⚡ 45 mins

The crag offers excellent climbing on solid clean rock.

**Approach:** Direct from the valley floor to ledges below the slab gained from the right.

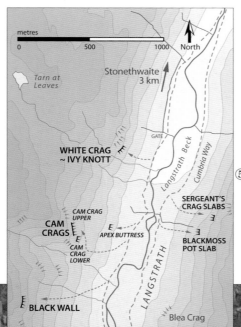

1 **Pebble Lane** 27m HVS 5b ★
P Ross, P Armstrong – 15 May 1996

Start below and left of the main slab behind a large spike. Climb the rib on pebbles starting on the right, moving left to follow the thin crack/groove to a ledge. Traverse right to climb a short prominent crack, or continue straight up to reach a grass ledge. Twin cracks are followed to the top.

2 **Posidriver** 20m E4 5c ★
S Jones, D Simmonite – 21 Jul 1996

From the left end of the ledge, climb the seam/crack to the overlap, step right and follow the slanting groove until it fades. Gain a short horizontal break to finish directly up the top wall.

⑤ 3 **Slab Happy** 20m E2 5c ★★★
K Wilkinson, R McHaffie – 18 Aug 1991

An excellent pitch. Start from the ledge (peg). Climb the corner then go directly to the apex of the slab on improving holds.

**4   Pot Luck**                20m     HVS 5a          ★
P Ross, P Armstrong - 15 May 1996

Start to the right of *Slab Happy* where a thin indefinite crack starts one metre above a smooth slab. Gain the crack and follow more cracks directly.

**5   Cannon Slab**            30m     S
BJ Clarke – 18 Jun 2005
Lower section A Dunhill, C Thistlethwaite - 20 Aug 2014

A pleasant climb. Start at the base of the lower buttress directly below a large tree. Follow grey ledges up and left then make an awkward move right into a short groove; up this then head up and left to the ledge leading to the main slab. Gain a heather ledge 3m higher then climb a thin left-slanting crack to join *Pot Luck*. Follow the ramp up right and climb a short wall to the finishing cracks.

FAVOURITE ROUTES
Pete Botterill

Top of my list is **The Niche** on Lower Falcon Crag as it was my first days climbing ever, with Jeff Lamb, in The Lakes. I had only ever done a few HVSs up to then and he sent me to lead the first pitch poorly protected (in 1974) into the niche itself as he wanted to climb the second pitch free. The same day we did *Dedication*, *Interloper* and *MGC* and *Finale* on Shepherd's, my first encounter with Lakes extremes! After, Jeff said he was planning a trip to Yosemite that September and asked if I wanted to go. Of course I did and that's another story.

Next Livesey's masterpiece **Dry Gasp**, mistakenly called Dry Grasp even by guidebook writers! Jeff had heard Pete had climbed the blank wall left of *Original Route*, we had no description but easily found the initial pitches due to the gardening. To start the crux pitch we mistakenly traversed out of the corner of *Original Route* missing the correct line but I still remember it being hard. It was a couple of years later, after a wet morning in Keswick it cleared and I got to lead the main pitch with Johnny Adams. Superb pitch.

**Grand Alliance** has to be on my list. It took me three attempts before success. A fantastic route by our South Lakes rivals (it was friendly really) Cleasby and Matheson.

Next **White Noise** only one pitch but good and varied. The route name refers to Jeff's second - Mac, those who knew Mac will know why!

Being only allowed one more route it has to be **The Voyage**. Steve and I, having climbed all the lines on Goat's North Buttress (with one notable exception), set off from *DDT* crossing the crux of *Tumbleweed Connection* (incidentally the one route of mine that gets the most praise from people I meet) and worked our way across the whole of that fine buttress to a neat finish.

Derwentwater
Watendlath
Grange
Stonethwaite
Combe Gill
Seathwaite

# Hooker Buttress

NY 271 112          West          410m          60 mins

A small buttress composed of good rock.

**Approach:** Strike southwards diagonally up across the hillside from Blackmoss Pot Slab or Sergeant's Crag Slabs.

**1   Boogy Chillen**          14m   VS 4c
A Dunhill, C Barbier – 9 Sep 2001

Make bold moves up to good holds then straight up to a dubious block. Continue up the rib above. Side runners in *The Healer*.

**2   The Healer**          14m   S 4a
A Dunhill, C Barbier – 9 Sep 2001

Climb the corner and follow the easy line slightly leftwards to the top.

**3   Boom, Boom**          14m   S 4b          ★
A Dunhill, C Barbier – 9 Sep 2001

The obvious crack.

**4   Dimples**          14m   VS 4c
A Dunhill, C Barbier – 9 Sep 2001

Climb the crack past a V-shaped groove, then follow the crack above and continue direct.

**5   Tupeledo**          14m   HVS 5a          ★
A Dunhill, C Barbier – 9 Sep 2001

Climb the slab via a crack to a small recess. Continue directly up the slab, passing a T-shaped crack.

# Black Wall

NY 258 107          ⊙ East          ⛰ 500m          🚶 60 mins

A place for those wishing to escape the crowds.

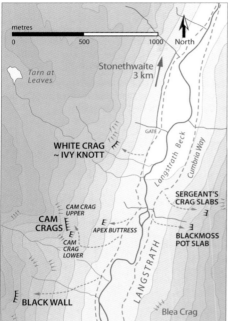

Tarn at Leaves

Stonethwaite
3 km

metres
0        500        1000   North

GATE

WHITE CRAG
~ IVY KNOTT

Langstrath Beck

Cumbria Way

SERGEANT'S
CRAG SLABS

CAM CRAG
UPPER

CAM
CRAGS       APEX BUTTRESS

CAM
CRAG
LOWER

BLACKMOSS
POT SLAB

LANGSTRATH

BLACK WALL

Blea Crag

**Approach:** Up the steep grass slope.

## 1   Garner Grooves          42m    HVS 5a
N Kekus, S Hubball - 1 Aug 1989

Start just above a small pinnacle block.
1   20m 5a   Climb the short rightwards-slanting
    crack to a groove. Follow this until it is possible
    to break out left and up to a good ledge.
2   22m 4c   Follow the steep corners on the right
    to a tree at the foot of a groove. Move awk-
    wardly right round a rib into another groove
    and climb this to the top.

## 2   Upshot          10m   E2 5c
K Wilkinson, R McHaffie - Summer 1990

Good holds and steep. Climb a rib for 3m then
traverse left to reach the ragged crack at a good
hold and nut placement.

## 3   The Codebreaker          20m   E7 6c F7c   ★★
A Hocking, J McHaffie -1 Apr 2001

Start on good holds, move up left (gear), up right
(peg) then right and up to the top (if you crack it).

## 4   Satan's Little Helper          20m   E7 6b F7b ★★★
D Booth, I Turnbull – May 1998

There is a long run-out on the crux of the obvious
line in the centre of the wall.

## 5   Raising Steam          20m   E4 6b
I Turnbull

Climb the right end of the wall (peg) to join *Peregrine Grooves*.

## 6   Peregrine Grooves          33m   HVS 5a
R McHaffie, J Glen - 1982

Start just right of the steep white wall below a
short crack.
Climb the crack and follow a gangway leftwards to
a ledge (peg). Move back right and climb the obvious deep groove.

## 7   Sheer Entertainment          25m   E4 6a
K Wilkinson, A Scott - 1993

Climb steeply passing a couple of broken holds
(RP3) to stand in a break at 8m. Climb the steep
groove above; it is difficult to leave (RP3) a large
sloping hold to reach the first ledge. Above the
second ledge, the innocuous low-angled groove is
stubborn and poorly protected.

## Langstrath's Secret Hermit Cave

A secret, well-hidden cave is rumoured to exist in Langstrath, but only a few folk know for certain that it exists and even fewer know its position. For those who are willing to spend the time looking – it is there, high on the fellside above the valley and the 300m line. It is fantastically well-constructed and equipped, even offering a fireplace and chimney, but you'll need to take some fuel!

What's really exciting about the cave is that it remains a secret: so you will need to devote some time looking or the chances are you won't find it. You don't need to climb to find the door and it isn't anywhere dangerous.

It does make a great base, but just in case you can't find it or you find it occupied you'll need a tent or bivvy. The door is ruggedly constructed with strong fastenings that resonate of a construction yard – shipbuilding or steel erection. It was built to last. And once inside this solid and permanent theme continues with sleeping and cooking platforms, signs of gas pipes and even a wooden lining, you'll be snug and comfortable.

But finding it will be the hardest part: you'll need to be organised and plan your search. Even the top of the flue is disguised in the boulders.

### Langstrath West

Upper
Page 223

Lower
Page 222

Cam
Crags

Black Wall
Page 217

Apex Buttress
Page 221

See more at: www.livefortheoutdoors.com/
Answers/Search-results/Walking/Is-it-true-
theres-a-secret-cave-in-Cumbrias-Langstrath-
Valley/#sthash.JeJQmqVK.dpuf

White Crag - Ivy Knott
Page 224

# Cam Crags

NY 262 111     ⊕ East     ⛰ 340m     🚶 45 mins

These crags offer one of the best scrambles in the Lakes and, in complete contrast, a concentrated selection of very hard climbs on excellent rock. There are some useful boulders to warm up on at the foot of the ridge.

| 1 | **Cam Crag Ridge** | M | ★★★ |
|---|---|---|---|
|   | **NY 262 110** | | |

B Beetham, JB Meldrum and members of the Goldsborough Club - 1943

Solid rock and interesting scrambling combine to make a fine expedition taking the rocky buttress above Black Moss Pot. The ridge is gained over a chaos of boulders and the interest is best maintained by following the crest.

Upper
Page 223

Lower
Page 222

Cam Crags

1

Cam Crag Boulders

Apex Buttress
Page 221

## Cam Crag – Apex Buttress
**NY 264 112** ⊕ ⏶ 280m 🚶 35 mins

This distinctive triangular-shaped buttress is only a short distance above the valley floor. It offers short and steep climbs on good rock with sparse protection.

**2   She is Suffering**       15m    HVS 5a
G Gwynne, M Balmer, P Gordon – 31 Jul 2005

Start one metre left of the obvious boulder. Layback the crack then climb direct to join the left-slanting gangway. Finish direct up the fingery wall and slab above.

**3   Love Triangle**       15m    VS 5a
BJ Clarke - 19 Sep 2005

Start at the left edge of the boulder. Pull up the bulging wall to a hollow thread and up to the gangway. Step left and climb the edge of the slab to the top.

**4   This is Yesterday**       15m    E3 5c    ★
G Gwynne, M Balmer, P Gordon – 31 Jul 2005

From the top of the boulder, pull out right then up left to the start of the main gangway. Move up right and climb the overhanging wall moving left near the top. Serious

**5   Frozen in Exile**       15m    E5 6a    ★★
C Fisher, J Surman – 5 Jun 2008

A superb sustained route on good rock with widely-spaced protection. Start 2m right of the boulder. Pull up the steep wall to a spike; step left (low nut) before stepping back right to attack the wall via a series of layaways and flat holds to gain good holds in the centre of the wall (Friend 0) and continue with difficulty.

Derwentwater

Watendlath

Grange

Stonethwaite

Combe Gill

Seathwaite

## Cam Crag Lower

This and the Upper Crag are round to the right of the base proper of the ridge. The Lower Crag is a steep wall with a prominent band of overhangs containing some hard test pieces.

| 6    Cameleon | 20m | E3 6a | ★ |

P Clarke, A Dunhill – 12 Aug 2015

Climb easy rocks left of the main wall to the obvious overlap. Move right onto the wall then make a committing pull through the overlap moving up and right to reach cracks which are followed to the top

| 7    'Arry 'Ardnose | 20m | E3 6a | ★★ |

K Wilkinson – 23 May 1988

The twin cracks left of the overhang are gained by a layback sequence. There is a step right at 6m.

| 8    Cam Crag Crack | 15m | E4 6b | ★★★ |

K Wilkinson – 23 May 1988

The route tackles the striking crack which cuts through the left end of the roof system starting at the foot of the groove. The crux is overcoming the roof. The crack above is best laybacked and remains difficult.

| 9    Campaign | 15m | E7 6c | ★★ |
|   |   | F7c+/8a |   |

A Hocking, M Norbury, A Wilson, W Hunter – 1 Jul 2011

Start up the steep groove of *Cam Crag Crack*. Moves up the groove lead to small wires and small cams in the roof. Move out to a spike undercut and up via hard moves to better holds. Keep your nerve and follow the crack to the top. RP1 pre-placed.

| 10   Campagnolo | 22m | E6 6b F7b+ | ★★ |

K Phizacklea, C Matheson – 22 Aug 2009

The obvious line under the roof from bottom left to top right. Gain the horizontal break via the left side of the triangular recess. Follow this to where it ends and cross the wall to gain the right end of the capping roof where a short groove leads to a tree

| 11   Cambodia | 15m | E7 6b F7b | ★ |

A Hocking - 22 Mar 2012

Tackles the roof at the right-hand end of the crag. Climb through the roof dynamically (Friend 00), then move left. Now balance your way up the wall to a final bold and tricky move before a step right onto easy ground.

**12 Genocide In Cambodia (Extension)**    15m   E7 7a F7c   ★★
A Hocking - 20 Jun 2012

Follow *Cambodia* to the move right onto easy ground. Step back down and move out through the overhang via some powerful moves. As you move upwards the holds get smaller until a final and very fingery move leads left to better crimps at the top.

## Cam Crag Upper

The Upper Crag is a smooth wall containing several sustained climbs on excellent quality rock.

**13 Camouflage**    25m   E7 6b   ★★★
                                      F7b+
M Dale – 19 Aug 1998

Breaches the wall left of *Camikaze*. Very bold in its upper section. Climb a short overhanging groove; often wet. From a small ledge move left then back right and climb a thin crack in the slab to a ledge. (Small cams in a small horizontal slot above the detached flake). Climb the wall above to the top.
Photo opposite.

**14 Camikaze**    25m   E6 6b F7a   ★★★
P Cornforth, G Cornforth – 25 May 1994

Start in the centre of the crag. Climb straight up to a sloping ledge (peg). Move up to hollow flakes and a horizontal break (stacked knife blades), then continue boldly straight up the wall to the left end of an overlap (Friend 0.5). Pull through the bulge to the top. Serious.

**15 Teenage Kicks**    25m   E4 6a   ★
D Cronshaw, J Ryden, I Vickers – May 1988

Start 3m left of a shallow groove on the right side of the crag. Climb the bulging wall to a large ledge and corner at 10m. Follow the thin crack on the left to a horizontal crack then up to a small ledge on the right. Continue up under the overhang to a jug. Make a long stride left onto the wall then move up to the overhang and surmount this using a hidden side-pull on the right to gain the top. **Flexible Friend** [E4 6a 1989] climbs directly over the over-hang from the jug.

**16 Camalot**    30m   HVS 5a
R Graham, E Rogers – 19 Sep 1996

Climb the obvious grooves and rib right of *Teenage Kicks*. The flake at 8m is a bit of a lottery - be careful.

Camouflage E7 - Paul Clarke   Ron Kenyon

# White Crag - Ivy Knott

NY 265 118    &#x1F73D; South East    &#x25B2; 300m    &#x1F6B6; 45 mins

White Crag offers some good climbing on generally sound, clean and quick-drying rock. It is the
most left-hand and lowest of a small number of
crags on the west side of Langstrath, north of Cam
Crag Ridge and opposite Sergeant's Crag.

**Approach:** Walk up Langstrath, pass through a
gate in the dry-stone wall and continue south
for another 300m before striking directly up the
hillside to the crag.

**Descent:** To the right.

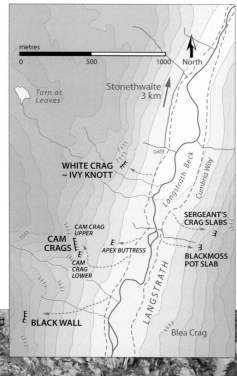

**1   Indiagate**   18m   VS 4c
BJ Clarke – 19 Sep 2005

Has an exciting finish. Climb the slab, then the groove on the left of the overhang, to a ledge and tree. Mount the block on the left then up the slab for a couple of moves to a tree. Traverse right across the steep wall and up to block belays.

**2   Langstrath Buttress**   20m   HVS 4c   ★
SJH Reid, A Hewison - 19 Apr 2000

Start in a bay below a steep groove, 8m left of the large holly tree at the lowest point of the crag. Climb up rightwards following the top of a slim right-slanting ramp, then move out left to the arête and climb this to a hand-traverse line. Traverse rightwards along this and make a bold bridging move into the wide groove on the right and climb its right arête.

**3   Whiter Shade of Pale**   18m   HVS 5a   ★
A Dunhill, C Thistlethwaite – 16 Jun 2014

Straightens out *Langstrath Buttress*. From the top of the ramp, climb direct crossing the hand-traverse and finish directly up the groove above.

My dad's would be:

**Troutdale Pinnacle**: he did this well over 1000 times in all weather conditions. He loved the views and the climb and his ashes are scattered in a small valley just above it.

**FAVOURITE ROUTES**
Ray McHaffie

**Illusion**: Put up in the golden era. Stunning views and the climb takes in wild terrain beneath a huge roof. Close to Keswick so easy to get to without a car.

**The Shroud**: A quiet part of Black Crag with a lovely corner and nice varied climbing above. One of his regulars.

**Lakeland Cragsmen**: Ray discovered this crag in the 1990s whilst working in Langstrath. Under the moss the rock was fantastic and gave some of the best single pitch routes in Borrowdale.

**Praying Mantis**: He did it every decade since the first ascent. Often telling a story about his friend, Les Kendall getting his fingers stuck in the first pitch and being cragfast for ages. An underrated route and cliff.

James McHaffie

Derwentwater

Watendlath

Grange

Esk Pike from Langstrath   Richard Tolley

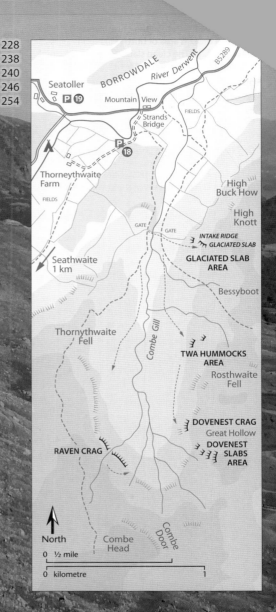

BORROWDALE    River Derwent    B5289

Seatoller

P 19

Mountain View

Strands Bridge

FIELDS

P 18

High Buck How

Thorneythwaite Farm

FIELDS

High Knott

GATE    GATE

INTAKE RIDGE
GLACIATED SLAB

GLACIATED SLAB AREA

Seathwaite 1 km

Bessyboot

Thornythwaite Fell

Combe Gill

TWA HUMMOCKS AREA

Rosthwaite Fell

DOVENEST CRAG

Great Hollow

DOVENEST SLABS AREA

RAVEN CRAG

North

Combe Door

Combe Head

0    ½ mile
0    kilometre    1

For the Record VS (page 256) - Paul Clarke    📷 Richard Tolley

… rance to the
…esses running up
…by outcrop on the
… Slab.

… and up steep grass. To
…ectly below, traverse in
fro… …l with the crag.

---

### 1 Intake Ridge 150m D ★
B Beetham - 5 Sep 1937

A pleasant route linking a series of rock steps up the hummocky ridge left of Glaciated Slab. Start at the lowest rocks 20m right of the south-east corner of the dry-stone wall.

1 15m Climb the short buttress then walk 8m across grass to the right.
2 26m Climb a shallow groove followed by a gently inclined slab.
3 18m Broken rocks lead rightwards to below a steep wall. Move right to belay just above the left-hand edge of Glaciated Slab.
4 18m Climb the steep rightwards-slanting crack above or, more easily, climb a slightly lower slab which slants right, with an awkward move to gain the slab above. Now move left to gain the crest of the ridge and up to the top of Glaciated Slab.
Walk left across scree to an easy-angled broken rib.
5 30m Easily up the broken rib to a grassy saddle.
Walk left to a steeper buttress with a prominent arête at the left-hand end and an easy-angled rib, right of a heather recess.
6 23m Climb the easy-angled rib for 10m then escape up left on big holds. Climb easy rock to a grass platform.
7 20m Move left onto a rough rib, follow a slab and then straight up the obvious line to a nick at the top.

Combe Gill

227

**Glaciated Slab Area**

Grolley Buttress

Upper Buttress

Glaciated Slab

Start of Intake Ridge 1

## Glaciated Slab

Excellent relaxed climbing on an ice-planed slab of immaculate rock, with two serious hard routes on the steep West Face.

**2  Déjà Vu**        25m   E3 5c     ★
P Ross, D Byrne-Peare, R McHaffie - Oct 1988

Steep, clean and quick drying. Climb up to a flake at 6m on the left edge of the buttress. Pull awkwardly over a bulge into a shallow groove. Reach cracks to the right and follow these until they fade. Finish directly.

**3  Prodigal Son**     25m   E5 6a    ★★
P Ross, D Byrne-Peare - Oct 1988

A serious and poorly protected lead on excellent clean rock. Reach a finger crack in the corner and make difficult moves to a small ledge (peg). Pull out left onto a slab and up into a small groove, cross a horizontal crack and continue straight up to finish.

**4  Trod Pip**        14m   VS 4c    ★
D Byrne-Peare, P Ross - Oct 1988

Bridge the corner behind the small holly then pull directly over the bulge to easier ground.

**5  Trod Dovera**      14m   S
B Beetham - 6 Sep 1944

Climb the right-hand side of the recess, step right and climb to the ledge.

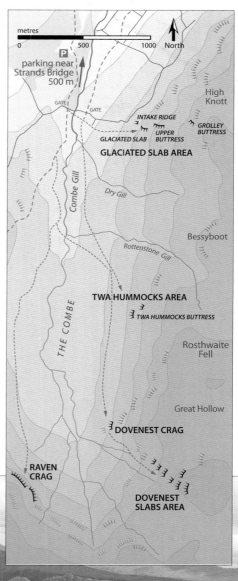

## Glaciated Slab - West Face

| 2 | Déjà Vu | E3 5c |
|---|---|---|
| 3 | Prodigal Son | E5 6a |
| 4 | Trod Pip | VS 4c |
| 5 | Trod Dovera | S |
| 15 | Trod On Their Toes | VS 4c |

**6   Trod Lethera**        30m   D        ★★
B Beetham - 4 Sep 1944

Climb the chimney then move left (exposed) to the ledge on *Intake Ridge*. Finish on the right.

**7   Trod Sethera**        28m   D        ★
B Beetham - 6 Sep 1944

Climb the fissure at the left of the slab.

**8   Trod Too Far**        28m   HS       ★
P Latimer, R Tolley - 18 Sep 2008

An eliminate with independent climbing. The slab is delicate in places if you avoid holds on *Trod Pimp*.

**9   Trod Pimp**           28m   S        ★★
B Beetham - 4 Sep 1944

Excellent climbing. Climb the first crack right of the fissure to gain a small ledge. Move right and finish up the obvious crack. Photo page 234.

**10  Trod Methera**        24m   S        ★★
B Beetham - 6 Sep 1944

Delicately climb the slab on great rock.

**11  Trod Tethera**        22m   VD       ★★
B Beetham - 4 Sep 1944

Climb the enjoyable polished central crack.

**12  Trod 'A' Tween**      18m   VS 4b
R Kenyon - 31 Oct 1984

Delicately climb the slab with a necky start.

**13  Trod Tan**            16m   D        ★
B Beetham - 4 Sep 1944

Follow the leftward-slanting crack for 3m then go rightwards to the top.

**14  Trod Yan**            18m   M
B Beetham - 4 Sep 1944

An amble up easy rock and a shallow scoop, finishing rightwards.

**15  Trod On Their Toes**  25m   VS 4c    ☆☆ †
A Phizacklea, JE Holden - 5 Jul 2015

A rising girdle. From *Trod 'A' Tween* head left to the blocky pinnacle on the edge. Cross to gain a descending crack, with little for the feet, until you reach the very edge of the buttress; move up to the belay. The latter section is well-protected and delicate.

**FAVOURITE ROUTES** ⑤ *Paul Ross*

From my first new route in 1954, The *Super Direct* on Black Crag, I have never been very interested in known climbs so my choices are mostly of my first ascents that have given me the most satisfaction and pleasure.

The original **Adam** - I have climbed this many times and always found it fun. Up into my 50's I soloed it both up and down.

**Troutdale Pinnacle Super Direct** - My first new route climbed in 1954 aged 17. My most resent ascent was with my son Andrew in 2014 - 60 years later!

**Post Mortem** - Climbed with my friend Peter Lockey in 1956. I have only climbed this twice. The second time I found it much easier than the first and had thoughts it was perhaps only HVS. I guess we were a bit ahead of our time as it's now graded E4, the first at this grade in the Lake District.

**The Bludgeon** - First Ascent 1957, again with Peter Lockey. Named after the large leaning block which we thought may cut loose, so the only protection I had on the second pitch was a piton below and right of the block, as we thought a sling on the block would pull it off if I took a fall on the upper wall. Peter did fall seconding on the last few feet when a hold broke.

My last two favorites are not my first ascents but superb climbs of modest difficulty - **Little Chamonix** and **Troutdale Pinnacle**. I soloed Little Chamonix at 15 on the very first day that I started rock climbing.

The above first ascents were all climbed on-sight ground-up as was the tradition in those early days.

Derwentwater

Watendlath

Grange

Stonethwaite

Combe Gill

Seathwaite

# Glaciated Slab

Trod Pimp MS (page 231) - Ben Clarke   Richard Tolley

## Glaciated Slab - Upper Buttress

### 16 Bentley's Rib    18m   S    ★
B Beetham - 5 Sep 1937

Takes the prominent attractive rib at the left-hand end of the buttress. Climb the rib on excellent rock, trending left at the bulge.

### 17 Rowan Tree Wall    22m   S    ★
P Latimer, R Tolley - 18 Sep 2008

A good line with pleasant climbing. Climb on good holds to the rowan sapling in the middle of the wall. Continue up and left to the arête and follow this to a ledge. Go up and right into a corner with a mass of heather. Step up and right from the heather onto the obvious prow in a fine position. Continue easily up the rib to the top.

### 18 Palais Glide    11m   VD
BJ Clarke - 16 Oct 2006

A rather contrived route looking for exposure. Start at the foot of the blocky corner with a holly tree on its right. Traverse an undercut slab leftwards to the arête, and instant exposure. Follow the ramps up left to a ledge and climb a short zig-zag crack to easy ground.

### 19 Glace Wall    10m   VS 4c
BJ Clarke - 16 Oct 2006

Climb the fine wall to reach an impasse below the steeper upper section. Move up this, slightly on the left, to gain a rounded finish.

### 20 Glace Groove    11m   E2 5b    ★
BJ Clarke, P Foster, T Coates - 14 Apr 2007

Bold exciting climbing with poor protection where it matters. Move up the wall to gain the groove. Climb this, moving awkwardly up and right near the top to reach a large but suspect hold on the arête. Continue to the top.

### 21 Glace Arête    10m   HS 4b
BJ Clarke, T Coates - 14 Apr 2007

The right arête taken on its right side and utilizing the large pinnacle. Take care with the rock near the top.

## Grolley Buttress
**NY 256 127** ⊘ 🔺 **470m** 🚶 **50 mins**

This short buttress is worth a visit after completing *Intake Ridge*. It lies just below the skyline, 200m behind the top of *Intake Ridge*, and has distinctive leftward-sloping ramplines.

| 22 **Trollied** | 24m | S |
|---|---|---|

BJ Clarke – 14 Oct 2006

Climb past the tree and follow a left-slanting slab to a ledge below steeper rock. Climb up right into a large recess then step left to finish up a crack.

| 23 **The Grolley** | 25m | VD | ★ |
|---|---|---|---|

P Shorter, P Mayers, P Shorter - 22 Aug 1972

Nice climbing with good rock that takes the prominent leftward-sloping groove on the right of the buttress. Gain the groove on the right, follow it and finish up a short layback crack.

ent rock in a superb

small buttress 50m left
nmocks, at the top of the
est reached after climbing
a route o..    cks.

**Glaciated Slab Area**

**237**

**Descent:** Well to the left.

---

## 1    Combe Ghyll Flake    41m    S    ★
B Beetham - 22 Apr 1942

A good route on excellent clean rock. The first pitch
is awkward to protect. Start at the lowest point of
the buttress.

1    19m    Climb the attractive light-coloured
pillar to a belay at the base of the pinnacle
flake.

2    22m    Bridge up the wide crack on the left
of the flake, finishing with a pull onto its top.
Step onto the wall and move up to the right
arête. Belay above. Finish up the easy arête
above.

## Twa Hummocks Buttress

Don't be deterred by the heather ledges.

**Descent:** Either side.

---

## 2    The Twa Hummocks North    38m    VD
B Beetham - 25 Aug 1944

A pleasant route. Start near the centre of the buttress at the right-hand end of a mossy slab. Climb
the right edge of the slab on good holds and cross
a heather ledge to the left end of the clean wall.
Climb the wall on good holds on featured light
grey rock, through a heather ledge and then trend
right to arrive at a grassy ledge and nut belays.

## 3    Brace Yourself    40m    S    ★
BJ Clarke - 16 Oct 2007

A good route on excellent and unusual rock with
good holds and protection. From the heather
ledge, climb a groove and thin crack to a junction
with *The Twa Hummocks North*. Traverse 3m right
and ascend the steep headwall.

Twa Hummocks

## 4 Twa Hummocks Central  35m  VD  ★

T Langhorne - 25 Jul 2015

A direct line with a nice finale. Climb the short clean slab, cross the heather ledge, then up the next short wall to a second heather ledge. Follow the left side of the groove above, finishing up an airy scoop in the headwall.

## 5 The Twa Hummocks South  38m  VD  ★★

B Beetham - 25 Aug 1944

A fine route on excellent rock starting up the right arête of the crag. Compact rock makes protection difficult to find in the central section. Climb the arête, moving right after 10m to the ridge and continue on excellent rock in a fine position with occasional delicate moves to its top. Climb easy slabs above to the top of the First Hummock. The pitch can be split halfway with good belays.
Photo page 303.

## 6 Hummocks End  23m  S  ★

P Latimer, R Tolley - 16 Jun 2010

A pleasant route on good rock on the south-facing wall. Start 10m up from *The Twa Hummocks South*, on the left side of of a mossy corner. Climb the left wall of the corner directly, passing a spike. After 10m step across into another groove on the right. Climb this crossing a small bulge to finish just right of the arête.

## 7 Rowan Groove  16m  HS 4a  ★★

R Tolley, P Latimer - 8 Jul 2010

A short delightful climb on excellent rock. Climb past the rowan and follow the groove to the top. Protection is difficult to arrange at the base of the groove.

# Dovenest Crag

NY 253 117     ⊖ West     ▲ 475m     🚶 50 mins

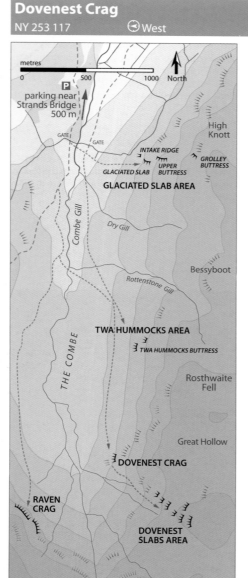

This unusual crag lies on the east side of Combe Gill opposite Raven Crag. The main part of the crag was formed by a great rock face slipping bodily forwards and downwards. It now leans back against the rocks behind, leaving cavities of all sizes between the massive detached blocks and the main face. These passages have made Dovenest Crag well-known. It is worth emphasizing that these passages have been created by rock slippage - take care! The outside routes are generally very good and on excellent rock.

**Descent:** Down either side.

| 1    **Adam's Rib** | 47m | VS 4b |

GB Fisher, G Withington - Aug 1951

Poor protection at the start.
1    16m 4b    Climb the slab and the overlap with difficulty. Move up to a heathery break and belay at the left-hand end near the arête.
2    31m 4a    Move left and continue up steeper rock on the arête, then follow the rib on the right overlooking the slab.

| 2    **Adam's Slab** | 38m | MVS 4b | ★★ |

R Kenyon - 8 Jun 1985.

An excllent pitch; poorly protected at the start. Start as for *Adam's Rib* and take the slab direct, passing a flake block.

| 3    **Meet Your Maker** | 38m | VS 4c | ★ |

D Johnson, E Ostell - 14 May 1997

Good climbing but poorly protected in places. Climb the overlap, starting on the right-hand side of a downward-pointing block. Continue directly and delicately, to the left of the moss and a small tree, to reach the obvious flake block. Climb the right edge of the block, step right from its top and climb straight up to the top of the crag.

| 4    **No Overtaking** | 16m | E1 5c | ★ |

A Hewison, A Davis - 3 May 1999

This takes the slab, featuring two horizontal quartz breaks. Step onto the steep wall and gain a large handhold. Pull onto the slab, cross the double white lines and go straight up to the top, using a friendly flake. Finish up *Face Route* or grovel back down the cave system.

| 1 | Adam's Rib | VS 4b |
| 2 | Adam's Slab | MVS 4b |
| 3 | Meet Your Maker | VS 4c |
| 4 | No Overtaking | E1 5c |
| 5 | Horizontal Pleasure | HVS |
| 6 | The Nose | HVS 4c |
| 7 | Dogs Can't Look Up | VS |

| 8 | Outside or Face Route | VD |
| 9 | Clubfoot | VS |
| 10 | Clubfoot Direct | HVS 4c |
| 11 | South Chimney | VD |
| 12 | Being Done Good To | E1 5b |
| 13 | Crackerjack Groove | MVS 4b |
| 14 | Cab's Arête | MVS 4b |

**⑤ 5   Horizontal Pleasure   80m   HVS 4c   ★★**
SJH Reid, JE Reid - 20 Sep 1995

A very good and worthwhile route, providing an entertaining variety of moves in fine situations. A bold approach is definitely recommended on the final pitch!

1    30m       Climb a mossy scoop, trending right-wards to the large ledge of *Face Route*. Leave the ledge via a short crack on the left and follow the left edge of the buttress, to a belay on the right at the entrance to the left-hand branch of Central Chimney.

2    20m 4c   Enter the chimney and back and foot up it, to gain a jug on the left arête. From a standing position on this, swing across to a jug on the right wall and climb up more easily to a pinnacle stance. Stride across the gap to a good foothold at the base of the long narrow slab that forms the left arête of Central Chimney and climb it, until it is possible to step onto the large chockstone on the right. Go up to a stance on the edge of the Attic Cave.

3    30m 4c   A spectacular pitch, although virtually unprotected and not for the faint-hearted! On the lip of the overhang on the left is a foothold. Make a very awkward move up and around the arête to stand on this.Traverse leftwards along the lip of the overhang on good footholds but poor handholds, until a small ledge on the left can be reached. Breathe a sigh of relief and trend leftwards up easier ground to finish. Photo page 244.

**6   The Nose   25m   HVS 4c**
P Salter, T Rennison - 1906

An incredible achievement and the first HVS in Borrowdale, "with very minute and insecure holds, almost as hazardous for leader as follower. A second ascent is not recommended."
Pull across to the rib and climb the left-hand side directly to easier ground.

**7   Dogs Can't Look Up   67m   VS 4c   ★**
B Barnard, A Godfrey - 9 Sep 2004

This enjoyable climb struggles to maintain its independence, but is a direct way up the crag with a bold and exciting second pitch. Start where a block projects from the wall at head-height.

1    23m 4a   Surmount the block (easier on the left) and continue up and slightly right, crossing *Face Route* to where the slab steepens. Climb the steepening direct to gain the arête. Belay at the top of this beneath North Chimney.

2    25m 4c   Enter the chimney and climb the

right wall to gain the slab above. Move diagonally up and right to the top of the slab, just right of a quartz patch. Make an exciting step across the chasm to an obvious foothold. Move up, crossing *Clubfoot*, and climb directly up the slab to a ledge and belay. Sparse protection on this pitch.

3    19m 4b   Step left from the belay and ascend the slab left of the crack of *Face Route*. Continue just right of a holly tree, then step left onto the arête which is followed to the top.

**8   Outside or Face Route   82m   VD   ★★**
RST Chorley, B Beetham, RW Somervell - May 1944.

A pleasant and varied route which starts 3m right of the lowest point of the crag. Some expertise at traditional techniques is a definite advantage.

1    30m       Climb a crack in the slab, trending left to a large ledge. From the right end of the ledge, climb up the arête to a large ledge, below an obvious chimney (North Chimney). Walk 8m right along the ledge to below the South Chimney. The detour to the right can be avoided by scrambling up North Chimney from the second large ledge on to the gap behind the block.

2    8m        Follow the edge of the large detached block on the left to an interesting belay.

3    16m       Drop down behind the block and disappear up the right chimney (Central Chimney), to emerge in the Attic Cave. Belay on the left on the outside edge of the cave.

4    28m       Step down from the belay and make a stride right across the top of Central Chimney. Move right a few metres and climb a fine crack. Continue up the wide crack above, or up the rock to its right, to a pinnacle on the right. Move left and up to the top.

### The Inside Route 46m VD ⚠

The following subterranean route was formed by the slippage of the rock face with the creation of internal passageways. It is believed that there has been further movement in these passages and the stability of the whole crag is unknown. It should therefore be considered that the use of these passageways is a potentially dangerous activity. It is also not recommended for those of large stature or who suffer from claustrophobia. If you do decide it's a route for you, the use of a torch is recommended but the experience is more interesting without. Start on the right of the crag, then traverse to the base of the South Chimney.

1   6m    Continue traversing across and down over boulders, behind the large detached block to below the North Chimney.

2   20m    Climb the North Chimney for 8m, to a vertical black cleft on the right wall - the Rat Hole. Enter this above the chockstone (easiest done facing in) and squirm up rightwards to an exit at the upper hole, and Central Chimney, which is climbed to the Attic Cave.

3   20m    The Rabbit Hole - start on the right of the Attic Cave and carefully enter the blackness (above or below a chockstone). Assisted by gravity, descend the cleft rightwards to exit at the base of South Chimney. This can also be climbed in reverse to gain the Attic Cave.

### 9 Clubfoot 70m VS ★★
B Evans, S Burns, B Hunt – 1954

A pleasant climb with its sharp crux reserved for the final moves.

1   26m    Climb the easy slab to a short corner. Climb this and step right to easy rock which leads up to belay below the South Chimney.

2   22m 4a   Gain the large slab above by moving left from the foot of South Chimney. Follow the diagonal line of weakness up to the left edge of the slab. Now climb straight up just to the right of Central Chimney, to a stance below a small overhang. An excellent pitch although protection is difficult to arrange.

3   16m    Climb the rib to the right of the crack of *Face Route* and rocks above, to a stance below a steep corner groove.

4   6m 5a   Climb the steep and difficult corner/groove with good protection.

### 10 Clubfoot Direct 61m HVS 4c ★
A Hewison, AC Robinson - 9 Sep 1999

1   26m    Climb the easy slab to a short corner. Climb this and step right to easy rock which leads up to belay below the South Chimney.

2   15m 4c   Gain and climb directly up the slab then traverse left to the stance.

3   20m 4c   Pass the right side of the overhang and continue up easier ground.

### 11 South Chimney 12m VD
M Dalton, A Thompson - 1897

This is the obvious right-hand chimney.

### 12 Being Done Good To 12m E1 5b ★
R Kenyon, C Kenyon - 6 Jun 1999

Climb up just right of the left arête of the buttress, to gain and follow a crackline to the overlap. Continue up the wall above on immaculate rock.

### 13 Crackerjack Groove 18m MVS 4b ★
A German, IT Sharples, G Baxter - 23 May 1987

Climb up into the groove passing a dubious flake. Jam your way to an easy slab and spike belays.

### 14 Cab's Arête 18m MVS 4b
B Clarke, J Hibbert - 29 May 2005

The arête right of and close to *Crackerjack Groove*.

Derwentwater

Watendlath

Grange

Stonethwaite

Combe Gill

Seathwaite

Horizontal Pleasure HVS (page 242) - Andy Dunhill  📷 Richard Tolley

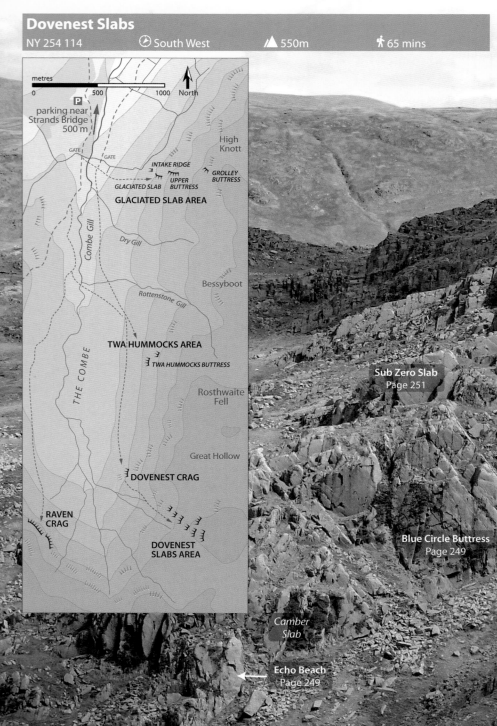

# Dovenest Slabs

NY 254 114    South West    550m    65 mins

metres

0    500    1000   North

P

parking near
Strands Bridge
500 m

GATE    GATE

High
Knott

INTAKE RIDGE

GROLLEY
BUTTRESS

GLACIATED SLAB   UPPER
BUTTRESS

**GLACIATED SLAB AREA**

Combe Gill

Dry Gill

Bessyboot

Rottenstone Gill

**TWA HUMMOCKS AREA**

TWA HUMMOCKS BUTTRESS

THE COMBE

Rosthwaite
Fell

Great Hollow

**DOVENEST CRAG**

**RAVEN
CRAG**

**DOVENEST
SLABS AREA**

Sub Zero Slab
Page 251

Blue Circle Buttress
Page 249

Camber
Slab

Echo Beach
Page 249

This complex area of slabs high above and right of Dovenest Crag offers short routes on excellent rock in a fantastic setting. Exploration reveals many route combinations with the obvious lines recorded.

**Approach:** From the floor of Combe Gill, which might include a route on Dovenest. Alternatively, take in the excellent scramble of Cam Crag Ridge from the Langstrath Valley.

The different areas are described starting by a large pointed boulder embedded in the scree on the ramp rising from to the right of Dovenest Crag.

Stucco SLab
Page 252

Mordent in A Slab
Page 251

Twist

Concrete Slab
Page 251

Thin End
Page 249

248

**Echo Beach**

**Blue Circle Buttress**

## Echo Beach

Situated by the large boulder.

| 1 | **Echo Beach** | 9m | HVS 4c |
|---|---|---|---|

BJ Clarke - 2 Feb 2006

Delicate and without protection.

| 2 | **Camber Slab** | 14m | HVS 4c | ★ |
|---|---|---|---|---|

BJ Clarke - 16 Oct 2006

Fine padding; unprotected.

## Blue Circle Buttress

Contains the longest routes on the slabs; unfortunately many of the cracks hold vegetation.

| 3 | **Precarious Block** | 25m | VS 4c |
|---|---|---|---|

J Moore, D Harris - 4 Sep 1999

Sparsely protected.

| 4 | **Badger Parade on Red Square** | 26m | VS 4c | ★ |
|---|---|---|---|---|

D Harris, J Moore - 4 Sep 1999; BJ Clarke - 16 Oct 2006

Climb the right-hand groove, step left and move up to an overlap. Pull over and traverse diagonally leftwards to reach and climb an obvious crack then the knobbly wall to the top. High in the grade.

## Thin End

| 5 | **Thin End** | 9m | HS 4a |
|---|---|---|---|

BJ Clarke - 18 Feb 2006

The arête and ramp.

| 6 | **In Trutina** | 11m | HVS 5a | ★ |
|---|---|---|---|---|

BJ Clarke - 18 Feb 2006

The slab direct; excellent delicate climbing

## Thin End

# Sub Zero Slab

# Concrete Slab Area

Mordent in A

## Sub Zero Slab

A compelling slab of superb rock.

**7  Silent Partner**      15m   VS 4b      ★
J Roberts, D Harris - 1 May 2000

**8  Seam Stress**         14m   HVS 5a     ★
B J Clarke - 14 Oct 2006

**9  Same Stress**         13m   HVS 5a     ★
B J Clarke - 14 Oct 2006

**10  Lock, Stock and Two**   13m   HS 4b    ★★
**Smoking Barrels**
D Harris, G Moore, G Pattinson - 20 Nov 1999

**11  Tantle Eyes**        12m   HS 4b      ★
T Langhorne - 2 Jul 2006

## Concrete Slab Area

**12  Twister**            9m    S          ★
T Langhorne - 25 Jul 2015

Down and left from *Twist*. Direct up the highest part of the slab on very rough rock.

**13  Twist**              9m    S          ★
BJ Clarke - 30 Jul 2006

Located at the top of the grassy rake rising leftwards from the main slab. Climb the amazingly contorted rock with pleasure.

**14  Yakka**              13m   MVS 4b
J Moore, D Harris - 4 Sep 1999

The right side of the vertical break into a crack.

**15  Jackson Pollock No 5**   14m   HS 4a    ★
D Harris, J Moore - 4 Sep 1999

The right-hand side of the slab to a sentry box then follow the crack leftwards. Scramble to the top.

## 'Mordent in A' Slab

**16  Mordent in A**       10m   VS 5a      ★
BJ Clarke - 30 Jul 2007

Great climbing! Straight up the centre of the slab to a step left at a horizontal crack. Follow the thin crack rightwards to finish.

**17  Vox Trot Direct**    10m   S 4b       ★
T Langhorne - 25 Jul 2015

Lay away up the pebbly rib to reach the easier finishing groove. Nice!

## 'Mordent in A' Slab

## Stucco Slab

**18  Artex Amble**          14m   S
BJ Clarke - 29 Apr 2006

**19  Twinkletoes**          11m   MVS 4c   ★
BJ Clarke - 29 Apr 2006
Delicate climbing up the faint crack

**20  Calypso**          12m   HS 4a   ★
BJ Clarke - 10 Apr 2006
The pleasant crack through the overlap.

**21  Polka Dot**          13m   VS 4c   ★
BJ Clarke, P Foster - 19 Apr 2007
The hanging slab keeping left of the arête.

**22  Stucco Slab**          14m   MVS 4b   ★
BJ Clarke - 2 Feb 2006
The groove under the overlap; poorly protected.

**23  Nippy Sweeties**          20m   VS 4c   ★
BJ Clarke - 1 Mar 2006
The delicate slab trending left to join *Stucco Slab*
under the overlap. Poorly protected.

## Stucco Slab

Raven Crag Gully VD (page 260) - Steve Venabales  📷 Stephen Reid

# Raven Crag

**NY 284 114**    ⊘ North East    ⚠ 360m    🚶 50 mins

This large historic crag provides atmospheric long mountaineering climbs and a selection of shorter ones.

**Approach:** Take the well-marked path on the west side of the beck.

Raven Crag Gully is in the centre with the shallower Tyro's Gully to its left. *Corvus*, the best route of its standard in the valley, takes the buttress on the left of Tyro's Gully.

**Descent:** ⚠.For climbs to the left of Raven Crag Gully go to the left. For climbs to the right of Raven Crag Gully follow the ridge until steep grassy slopes lead underneath the crag. Care is needed on both descents, especially in the wet.

## The Pedestal Wall

This small buttress offers a selection of good quality single pitch climbs.

**Descent:** Scramble easily on the left.

| 1   **B2B** | 25m   VS 4c |
|---|---|

BJ Clarke – 22 Aug 2007

A pleasant but sparsely protected rising traverse. Climb diagonally rightwards to the V-overlap. Step down slightly and make delicate moves right to reach a series of right-slanting cracks. Follow these around the arête (without much height gain), to finish up the short flake/crack of *Just a Quickie*.

| 2   **Pedestal Wall** | 13m   S | ★★ |
|---|---|---|

B Beetham - 6 Aug 1940

An enjoyable little climb starting at the small flake pedestal at the foot of the centre of the buttress. Climb the centre of the face, trending right up a crack near the top.

# Raven Crag

**13m HVS 4c** ★
...y 1984

...he climb starting just right of the pedestal.
...o the wall direct, keeping left of the V-shaped
...verlap; sketchy protection.

| 4 | **Cock It** | 13m | HVS 5a | ★ |

T Langhorne – 14 Jun 1987

Climb past the overlap on its right. Spaced protection.

| 5 | **For the Record** | 22m | VS 4c | ★ |

T Langhorne – 14 Jun 1987

Climb the arête left of the obvious overhung corner to some cracks. Finish on the right-hand side of the nose above. Photo page 227.

| 6 | **Just A Quickie** | 13m | VS 4c | ★ |

R Kenyon - 6 May 1984

Start 3m right of the overhanging corner and climb the wall and cracks above.

| 7 | **Raven's Slab** | 17m | S 4a | |

T Langhorne – 17 Aug 2002

Climb a scooped slab to the right of a dirty crack-line, pulling out right onto the rib at the steepening, just below the top. Poor protection.

| 8 | **Cock's Comb** | 150m | M | |

B Beetham - 15 Apr 1942

This scramble starts up the right edge of The Pedestal Wall then follows the broad broken ridge to the left of *Crystal Slab*, keeping left of the upper Cock's Comb Wall.

## Cock's Comb Wall

This wall offers four good quality single pitch climbs. The abseil approach is rigged from hidden cracks below the top.

| 9 | **Nevermore** | 25m | E1 5b | ★★ |

J Fotheringham, T Bell - Sep 2003

A sustained climb. Takes a line of cracks up the front of the buttress and is best approached by traversing in from the normal descent, starting at an obvious tree. Follow the grassy ramp, down initially, then scramble up leftwards to a short slab leading left to the grass bay below the wall. Alternatively, the same point can be reached by climbing *Cock's Comb*. From the grass bay pull up to gain a rightward-slanting ramp and a ledge. Climb cracks above, move right to gain a ramp, then up this and the continuation cracks to the top.

| 10 | **Cock's Comb Crack** | 25m | E1 5b | ★♂ |

E Rogers, M Biden - 1989

The superb thin crack line up the left side the wall.

| 11 | **Comb Wall Crack** | 18m | HVS 5b | ★♂ |

A Dunhill, C Thistlethwaite – 10 Sep 2014

The left-slanting crack.

| 12 | **Crystal Crack** | 15m | VS 5a | ♂ |

A Dunhill, C Thistlethwaite – 10 Sep 2014

The right-hand crack.

## The Pedestal Wall

| 1 | B2B | VS 4c |
| 2 | Pedestal Wall | S |
| 3 | Wrinkle | HVS 4c |
| 4 | Cock It | HVS 5a |
| 5 | For the Record | VS 4c |
| 6 | Just A Quickie | VS 4c |
| 7 | Raven's Slab | S 4a |

## Crystal Slab Area

### 13  Crystal Slab               94m    MVS 4c    ★★
P Hirst, E Hirst – 1 Jun 1985

This excellent route takes the light-coloured slabby rock to the left of the dark overhung recess. Start at a groove below the slab.

1    45m 4c   Climb a spiky groove and continue up a shallow scoop onto a light-coloured slab, below a wall. Step up at the right-hand side of the wall and traverse left to a jug. Move up and continue more easily to the right end of the ledges, below the overhang at the top of the slab above. Nut and cam belays. Alternatively, continue left along the ledge to a block belay. There are three ways to finish:

2    16m      Go left on ledges for about 5m, then climb the left facing overhung slab above, to a grass ledge below a wide crack with a chockstone. Small nut belays to the right of the crack.

3    33m      Climb the wide crack and the groove above.

### 13a  Cock's Comb Wall finishes

*Cock's Comb Crack*, *Comb Wall Crack* or *Crystal Crack* all make fine finishes. Then use the belay to rig an abseil to climb the others…

### 13b  Birds of Prey Finish    40m    E1 5b
R McHaffie, P Hirst – 31 May 1985

From the right end of the ledges under the overhang, move up into a left-facing corner and swing out right onto a sloping ledge. Climb the overhang above on good holds. Follow the crack and slab to a grass ledge and continue heading up left, avoiding the steep wall above, to the top. A fine position but likely to be dirty.

## The Main Crag - Raven Crag Buttress

Crystal Slab Area is bounded on its right by an impressively steep but dirty wall, above a gully groove, capped by a large and obvious overhang. To the right of this, the main part of the cliff, Raven Crag Buttress, is bounded on its right by a shallow gully, Tyro's Gully.

### 14  Midge Ridge           120m   VS 4b     ★★
SJH Reid, CAJ Reid, SA Baxendale - 24 Jul 2006

The fine left arête of Raven Crag Buttress. Start at a short semi-detached pinnacle.

1    18m 4a   Climb the pillar and pull right onto the arête. Go up this to a narrow ledge, then climb a short wall leading to a scoop and short groove. Belay on a large bilberry ledge.

2    30m 4b   Pull out left and climb slightly rightwards up the wall above to the belay at the top of p1 of *Raven Crag Buttress*. Move left and climb leftwards up a slab and round the arête, where bold climbing leads up a narrowing ramp, until it is possible to step onto some dubious spikes on the left, to gain a short dirty chimney and wide bilberry ramp. Follow the ramp to its end and belay below a short wide slab.

3    19m 4b   Climb the short wide slab until it is possible to step left and make a delicate traverse leftwards, across a scoop to a spike. Pull up into the scoop above and emerge onto *Raven Crag Buttress*. Follow it for 7m to its belay ledge.

4    30m 4b   Climb the leftward-slanting crack system, passing beneath a large flake/crack, then up the wall above. Step airily leftwards to a block and bilberries. Avoid the short blank arête above on the left. Climb up to, and stand on, the protruding block above and finish to the right, as for *Raven Crag Buttress*.

5    23m      Climb the easy rocks above, as for p4 *Raven Crag Buttress*.

### 15  Crystal Clear          35m    E1 5a      ★
T Wood, T Place – 2 Jul 2011

The leftward-slanting spiky groove on the buttress left of *Raven Crag Buttress*, is climbed to a grass ledge. Make bold moves up the wall, heading rightwards, to gain the arête which is followed to a grass ledge. Continue up the centre of the wall above, then move right to belay as for *Raven Crag Buttress* p1. Finish up *Midge Ridge*.

Derwentwater

Watendlath

Grange

Stonethwaite

Combe Gill

Seathwaite

| | | | |
|---|---|---|---|
| 2 | Pedestal Wall | S | ★★ |
| 5 | For the Record | VS 4c | ★ |
| 6 | Just A Quickie | VS 4c | ★ |
| 7 | Raven's Slab | S 4a | |
| 8 | Cock's Comb | M | |
| 9 | Nevermore | E1 5b | ★★ |
| 10 | Cock's Comb Crack | E1 5b | |

| | | | |
|---|---|---|---|
| 11 | Comb Wall Crack | HVS 5b | ★ |
| 12 | Crystal Crack | VS 5a | |
| 13 | Crystal Slab | MVS 4c | ★★ |
| 13a | Cock's Comb Wall Finishes | | |
| 13b | Birds of Prey finish | E1 5b | |
| 14 | Midge Ridge | VS 4b | |
| 15 | Crystal Clear | E1 5a | |

| 16 Raven Crag Buttress | VD | ★★★ |
| 17 Green Cormorant | VS 5a | ★ |
| 18 Raven Crag Grooves | HVS 5a | |
| 19 Ibis | VS 4c | ★ |
| 20 Corax | HS 4a | ★★ |
| 21 Corvus | D | ★★★ |
| 22 The Rib | VS 4c | |
| 23 Tyro's Gully | M | |

**16  Raven Crag Buttress**   112m  VD   ★★★
B Beetham and members of the Goldsborough Club – 6 Sep 1939

This classic and continuously interesting route starts 5m from the left end of the grassy shelf. A worthy companion to *Corvus*; some consider it to be the finer route.
1   33m   Climb the open chimney/groove and ledges above to a good ledge.
2   26m   Bear slightly left and climb up to a ledge overlooking the gully on the left. Continue past a projecting flake to a ledge.
3   30m   Climb up a groove and either continue up the groove above, or move left and climb the groove overlooking the gully, until exposed moves up a short corner lead up to a large bilberry ledge.
4   23m   Climb the easy rocks above.

**17  Green Cormorant**   123m  VS 5a   ★
R McHaffie, B Sutton, T Poole – 12 Sep 1970; FFA A Grieg, R McHaffie

Start at the crack 3m right of *Raven Crag Buttress*.
1   40m 4c   Climb the short crack to a ledge. The crack widens and forms a pinnacle. Gain the top of the pinnacle and move rightwards up a slab. Surmount a bulge and climb the groove above to a grass ledge and then a tree belay on a higher ledge.
2   30m 5a   Climb the crack just left of the tree until an awkward move right leads to a ledge. Move right and up to a grass ledge.
3   53m   As for p3 & p4 *Raven Crag Buttress*.

**18  Raven Crag Grooves**   126m  HVS 5a
R McHaffie, JJ Allison – 25 Jan 1970

Start 5m right of *Raven Crag Buttress* and slightly right of a dirty groove.
1   40m 5a   Climb the crack and the short left-facing corner above (bold), to reach an overhang just below the traverse of *Corvus*. Move up leftwards staying underneath the overhang and follow a dirty groove to a grassy recess below a chimney/crack.
2   16m 4b   Climb the chimney/crack and move right to belay by an open scoop.
3   30m 4c   Climb a slab onto a block. Continue up on good holds to the recess at the left end of the hand-traverse on *Corvus*.
4   40m   P5 of *Corvus*.

### 19  Ibis                          149m  VS 4c        ★
R McHaffie, J Glen, P Denning – 11 Apr 1971

An interesting direct variant on *Corvus*.
1   12m 4b   Surmount the short wall to a big grass ledge below a wall.
2   20m 4c   Climb up the wall to twin cracks which are climbed to the right-hand of two grooves. Move into the left-hand groove and climb this to the left end of the traverse ledge on *Corvus*.
3   16m 4c   Move up right to gain the wall above the traverse on *Corvus*. Ascend this awkwardly to gain a ledge.
4   16m      Climb vegetated rock on the left to gain the belay on *Corvus* at the end of p2.
5-7  85m      Follow *Corvus* to the top.

### 20  Corax                       145m  HS 4a      ★★
B Beetham – 1 Jul 1950

An enjoyable climb starting as for *Corvus*.
1   30m 4a   Climb up and follow the twin cracks left of *The Rib*, leading directly to a large block belay at the top of p1 of *Corvus*.
2   30m 4a   Climb past the block and follow a crackline up the exposed buttress above; slabby rock leads to a belay just right of *The Rib*.
3-5  85m      Move easily left to join *Corvus* at the top of p2 and follow it to the top.

### ⑤ 21  Corvus                   147m  D         ★★★
B Beetham – 10 Jun 1950

'A route for all seasons'. An extremely popular climb starting just left of Tyro's Gully.
1   26m      Start up the slabs and move right at the top to a ledge in the gully. Climb the first V-cleft in the left wall of the gully to a ledge and large block belay.
2   36m      Traverse left along a series of ledges to below a corner. Climb the corner, which deepens into a chimney and a slabby scoop above to a good stance.
3   35m      Move right for 5m to the foot of a rib, which is climbed to gain a steep slabby wall. Belay on the right.
4   10m      Move up right to gain a line of flake handholds (The Hand-Traverse) and follow these left across the wall to a recess.
5   40m      Climb up to a large ledge and continue up a rib to below a scoop. Gain the scoop via a large flake and continue to the top.

### 22  The Rib                     145m  VS 4c        ★
R McHaffie, C Bashforth – 24 Jun 1978

Start at the rib to the right of *Corvus*.
1   30m 4c   Climb the rib to below the crack of *Corax*. Move back just right of the rib and go boldly up to belay at a large block.
2   30m 4a   Climb to the base of a crack, then move left to climb the rib on the right of the dirty groove line. At the top of the rib move right into a groove and up to a block belay.
3-5  85m      Move easily left to join *Corvus* at the top of p2 and follow it to the top.

## The Central Section

### 23  Tyro's Gully               110m  M
B Beetham, H Westmorland – 20 Oct 1945

This is the gully immediately right of Raven Crag Buttress. Initially well-defined, the climbing deteriorates above. Not recommended.

### ⑤ 24  Raven Crag Gully        178m  VD      ★★★
WA Wilson, JW Robinson, CN Williamson – 1 Sep 1893

This is the obvious gully in the centre of the crag; a classic. Start with easy scrambling for 25m to a cave formed by a chockstone.
1   23m      Climb the groove on the right side of the gully. Traverse into the gully bed to a belay.
2   30m      Climb the groove on the right. Avoid a cave by easy climbing on the left.
3   15m      Scramble up the gully.
4   23m      Climb the rib on the right and turn a cave at 12m on the right.
5   60m      Continue up the gully bed to where it steepens.
6   16m      Climb up the right side of the gully past a chockstone and move right to a belay.
7   11m      Move up a short way and traverse across the gully below the capstone which is passed on the left. Photo page 253.

### Wet Weather Finish          10m  S
OG Jones, CW Patchell, HC Bowen - 28 Apr 1897

7a  Climb the steep rocks above.

24 Raven Crag Gully          VD
25 Summit Route              S
   Variation Finish          S
27 Raven Bastion             MS

Summit Route S (page 264) - Andy Dunhill 📷 Richard Tolley

## The Right Hand Section

To the right again, the cliff continues for some distance, gradually losing height. Although generally broken, there are a few good shorter climbs towards the right, together with *Summit Route* and *Raven Bastion*; both worthwhile multi-pitch Severes.

### 25 Summit Route 197m S ★
B Beetham, J Foyle - 13 May 1951

This pleasant mountaineering route initially follows the right edge of Raven Crag Gully, then trends right to gain the large ledge below the final buttress. Start just right of the gully at a grass ledge, below a short wall.

1   16m   Move left and climb a shallow corner to a ledge and block belay.
2   26m   Move up left and climb a short steep wall. Continue up slabby rock to reach a belay on the right.
3   36m   Move left to gain and climb a slabby groove overlooking the gully. Finish either up a short chimney or its left wall. Belay on a grass ledge below a corner/crack.
4   20m   Climb the crack to a ledge on the right. Go diagonally left and up to a tree belay.
5   23m   Move up a crack on the right. Climb a V-groove and crack up to the left, to a belay below a slabby corner.
6   13m   Climb the corner and easy rock above to gain the right-hand end of the large terrace.
7   20m   Walk left to a cairn below a square scoop in the final buttress.
8   8m    Climb the scoop awkwardly, to a sloping ledge on the left. Thread belay.
9   10m   Traverse left along the sloping ledge and continue at the same level to a belay.
10  25m   Climb up to a small overhang on the right. Climb an obvious crack on its left to a rock crevasse. Continue to the top up a short awkward corner, in the same line.
Photo page 262.

### 26 Variation Finish 22m S
D Murray, DA Crawford - 3 Oct 1959

7a  Climb the groove on the front of the buttress and continue up to a saddle. Step down and right to the foot of a groove. Climb the crack in the slab on the left to the top.

### 27 Raven Bastion 184m MS
B Beetham - 31 May 1951

1   16m   P1 of *Summit Route*.
2   35m   Climb broken ribs above which lead slightly right to a ledge. Continue up rounded ribs, on excellent holds, to a ledge.
3   23m   Climb the shallow scoop just to the right, stepping left at its top to a ledge. An awkward short wall leads to a ledge with a flake belay on the right.
4   26m   The break above leads to a short chimney/crack which finishes on a ledge. Good holds on the left lead to another ledge.
5   16m   Climb towards the corner above to reach and stand on a good spike. Move up and then step up right to a ledge. The chimney on the right leads to easier ground.
6   42m   A series of walls and ledges trending diagonally left to a ledge below a V-scoop.
7   16m   Climb into the scoop, move right and climb the rib above to a stance.
8   10m   Climb a short chimney/crack past a projecting block to the top.

### 28 Little Stint 25m S
P Hirst, J Wood – 23 Apr 1987

The short steep arête is climbed on pocket holds. Descend by scrambling right down steep grass.

### 29 Angela 40m HVS 5a
A Dunhill, C Barbier – 14 Jun 2014

Start below a ramp.
1   20m 4c   Climb the ramp and continue straight up to a belay below a slab.
2   20m 5a   Start up the crack, as for *Merkland Street*, then traverse left and step up into a scoop then up to the left arête of the slab which is followed to the top.

### 30 Merkland Street 45m HS 4a
BJ Clarke - 31 Jul 2007

A pleasant, interesting route up the buttress just left of the small gully, leading up to *Easy Street*. Start at a short wall on the left below where the gully narrows.
1   25m 4a   Climb the wall with interest, making a step left then up to the grass ledge. Go up this to the slab which is followed to a ledge. Continue in the same line until moves left lead to a belay on a ledge below a slab.
2   20m 4a   On the right of the slab, move up a rising crack and follow the pleasant arête leftwards to the top.

### 31 Easy Street 56m VS 4c ★★
P Hirst, G Spensley, R McHaffie - 26 Jun 1988

1   28m 4b   From the bed of the gully, climb leftwards to the obvious left-slanting ramp. Follow the ramp then move right over a small overlap on good holds, to below a slab and belay.
2   28m 4c   Climb the slab boldly on incuts passing an overhang on its left. Continue on good holds past a precarious flake to the top groove and finish up the rib above to gain a ledge.

**32 Geometer**    50m    HVS 5a
P Hirst, G Spensley - 28 May 1988

Climb to a rowan tree. Continue up a groove above to an obvious rock boss. Pull up left onto a steep wall on good holds and climb up directly to gain a blunt arête which is followed to the top.

**33 Roller Coaster**    27m    VS 4b
BJ Clarke - 31 Jul 2007

This route offers better climbing than its appearance would suggest! Start at the toe of the rib just right of a small narrow gully.

1    15m 4a    Climb the rib and short walls to a platform below a slab.

2    12m 4b    Climb the slab by a leftwards ascending traverse to reach a gangway below the final slab. Follow good holds up the right side of this slab before escaping left to avoid the cornice. Move up to a tree belay.

# Seathwaite

Robinson S (page273) - Trevor Langhorne  📷 Richard Tolley

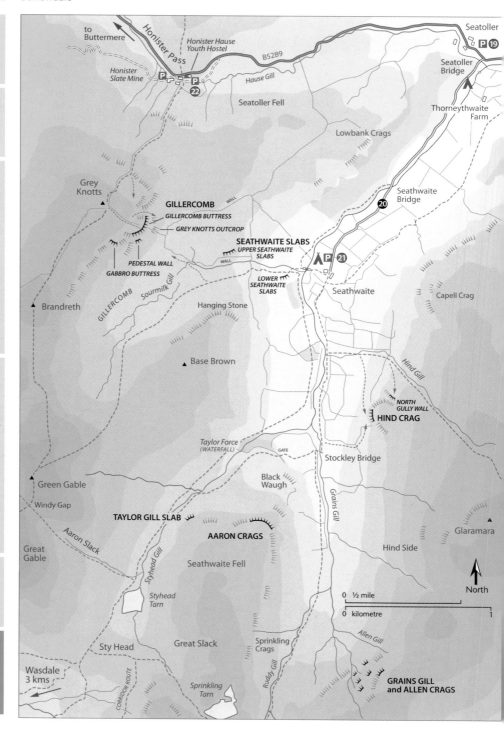

to Buttermere
Honister Pass
Honister Hause Youth Hostel
B5289
Seatoller
P 19
Honister Slate Mine
P P 22
Hause Gill
Seatoller Bridge
Seatoller Fell
Thorneythwaite Farm
Lowbank Crags
Grey Knotts
Seathwaite Bridge
20
GILLERCOMB
GILLERCOMB BUTTRESS
GREY KNOTTS OUTCROP
SEATHWAITE SLABS
UPPER SEATHWAITE SLABS
WALL
WALL
P 21
PEDESTAL WALL
GABBRO BUTTRESS
LOWER SEATHWAITE SLABS
Seathwaite
Capell Crag
Brandreth
GILLERCOMB
Sourmilk Gill
Hanging Stone
Base Brown
Hind Gill
NORTH GULLY WALL
HIND CRAG
Taylor Force
(WATERFALL)
GATE
Stockley Bridge
Green Gable
Black Waugh
Windy Gap
Grains Gill
TAYLOR GILL SLAB
AARON CRAGS
Glaramara
Great Gable
Aaron Slack
Styhead Gill
Seathwaite Fell
Hind Side
North
Styhead Tarn
0   ½ mile
0   kilometre   1
Wasdale 3 kms
Sty Head
Great Slack
Sprinkling Crags
Allen Gill
Ruddy Gill
CORRIDOR ROUTE
Sprinkling Tarn
GRAINS GILL and ALLEN CRAGS

Side tabs: Derwentwater · Watendlath · Grange · Stonethwaite · Combe Gill · Seathwaite

# Hind Crag

NY 238 112          West and South West          350m          45 mins

With two long and entertaining mountaineering routes and two additional areas giving very good climbs on excellent rock, this crag on the west side of Glaramara, above the path from Seathwaite to Stockley Bridge, is worth a visit. The crag even has a route pioneered by the legendary alpine guide, Angelo Dibona. Much of the crag is broken and vegetated. The first area of good climbing lies high on the south-facing wall of the North Gully. The second area is known as Central Slabs, a slab of clean immaculate rock, about 120m right of the toe of the crag and 80m left of a dry-stone wall which runs up to join the crag.

**Approach:** From the roadside parking near Seathwaite Farm.

For North Gully Wall, follow a steep path up the hillside just right of Hind Gill. When the path becomes less steep, just above the 500m contour, turn southwest across the hillside to the top of the routes: NY240 112; alt. 475m.

The Central Slabs are reached most easily by following the same approach; shortly after crossing the stream head diagonally up the hillside to pass below the toe of the buttress to the slabs.

For *Southern Buttress* take the Stockley Bridge path, just before the bridge follow a wall that leads up to the crag

North Gully
Wall
Page 272

Central Slabs
Page 273

The Borrowdale Stare VS (page 272) - Trevor Langhorne ● Richard Tolley

## North Gully Wall

The excellent routes on the gully wall can enjoy summer sun, midday until nightfall. The rock is amazingly rough ignimbrite, although there are a few large blocks that should be avoided. The routes follow naturally clean lines with very little drainage or greenery; they are well-protected and quick-drying.

**Descent:** Retrace the approach or down the steep but grassy North Gully.

The start of *The Borrowdale Stare* can be reached by a 65m abseil from a large block or by descending the upper part of the gully. A rigging rope allows the abseil to be made with 50m ropes.

### 1    The Borrowdale Stare    45m    VS 4b    ★★★
D Bodecott, D Absalom - 26 July 2014

A superb pitch. From a large wedged block (avoid this), at the foot of the rib, follow the right edge all the way to a large rocky boss/pinnacle at the top. Photo page 271.

### 2    Altherrenpartie    35m    VS 4c    ★★
D Bodecott, D Absalom - 26 July 2014

Climb the steep corner with difficulty then follow the slab and obvious crack to the top. Belay at wedged blocks up right.

### 3    Soda Pop    35m    VS 4c    ★★
G Widdowson, D Bodecott - 9 August 2014

Start up the corner as for *Altherrenpartie*, then after 15m move right onto the rib above the large heather ledge. Step right into the slabby groove and follow the right wall to the top on amazing rough rock.

## Central Slabs

The easy-angled slabs at the base rise to a steep clean buttress of excellent rock. There is a shallow vegetated gully to the right of the slabs.

**Descent:** Walk to the top of the buttress and descend North Gully or continue to join the Glaramara – Seathwaite path.

---

**4   Hind Crag Buttress**      188m  HS 4a      ★
A Dibona, AR Thompson 1924;
p2 Direct variation R Tolley, P Latimer - 3 May 2012

An enjoyable mountaineering expedition giving two sections of good clean climbing on excellent rock, separated by 50m of scrambling up easy rock and heather. Pitches can be split if necessary. On p2 the original route has been straightened out to follow the obvious line on the left-hand side of the buttress. This crux is bold and poorly protected. Start below the left side of the prominent slabs.

1   26m      Climb the left-hand edge of the pleasant easy slab to a small ledge. Continue up the steepening slab; step left and use the heather to reach a good ledge and nut belays.

2   24m 4a   Climb the scoop above then move up right onto a slabby rib with superb rock. Up this to the next break. Move left to the edge of the buttress and climb up boldly, slightly rightwards (crux), to a heather ledge. Pull steeply up the block above to a rock ledge and belays.

3   50m      Scramble through heather and easy rocks to belay below a prominent rib.

4   41m      The broken rib leads to a good ledge; the ledge above can be reached by either a sloping crack on the left, or directly, or by a broken crack on the right. Easier climbing leads to a corner.

5   31m      An easy slab is climbed to a grassy terrace. More difficult climbing leads to a rock ledge; then follow easier rock to a ledge below the final steep rib.

6   16m      Make delicate moves up and right to gain the rib which gives a fine and exposed finish.

---

Descent from the next routes is by abseil. The abseil can be avoided by finishing up *Hind Crag Buttress*.

**5   Robinson**      45m  HS      ★★
P Latimer, R Tolley - 5 Sep 2010

An excellent route on superb rock. Climb the slab just right of an indistinct shallow rib to the left-hand end of the overhang. Climb the obvious crack onto the hanging slab and a good ledge, taking care to avoid loose blocks. Climb up leftwards for 5m to gain a crack. Move up, then traverse right below small roofs to easier gound and a good ledge. Belay behind the big block.
Photo page 266.

**6   Crusoe**      45m  S      ★★
R Tolley, P Latimer - 5 Sep 2010

An enjoyable route on superb rock. The route is at times quite close to the bed of the shallow gully, but the quality of the climbing compensates for this. Climb the right-hand edge of the slabs to a small ledge at 13m. Move left and climb clean slabs to the right-hand end of the overhang. Step up right and pull delicately left to gain the hanging slab and continue to a good ledge. Move right onto the facet overlooking the gully and keep right to gain an obvious small pillar of detached blocks. Step up and at a small quartz vein make a strenuous move left on superb rock to good holds. Continue straight up to the good ledge on *Robinson*. Belay behind the big block.

## Hind Crag - Central Slabs

| 4 | Hind Crag Buttress | HS 4a | ★ | 6 | Crusoe | S | ★★ |
| 5 | Robinson | HS | ★★ |

100m right of the Central Slabs is the start of:

## 7    Southern Buttress         175m  S
DN Greenop, JP Greenop, E Brown - 20 Feb 1959

Takes the retaining rib of the crag overlooking South Gully. Rather neglected and with its fair share of vegetation, it gives a worthwhile and challenging expedition. Several variations are possible for most pitches. Start below a shallow corner, 6m left of the foot of South Gully.

1    15m    Climb the corner until it is possible to step left to a mantelshelf. Traverse left and climb up to a large flake and ledge.
2    26m    A short wall leads to a mossy slab. Steep rocks above are climbed from left to right to heathery rocks. Continue up these for about 12m. Traverse round a rib on the right into an open chimney which leads to a ledge.
3    28m    Go up left over much easier rock to the foot of a vertical ill-defined chimney which is followed to a little gully and grassy platform.
4    34m    Climb a short wall and the arête above. Climb the buttress above with an awkward finish.
5    26m    A short wall leads to sterner rock which can be climbed directly using a crack or groove. Easy-angled slabs lead to a belay.
6    12m    Climb the right edge of the slabs overlooking the gully.
7    34m    Keep to the right, over slabs and a broad cracked ridge, to finish up a short steep wall.

One of the many special things about the Lake District is the way each valley has it's own unique character and beauty, but my favourite must be Borrowdale. It's wonderful for late afternoon or evening climbing with so many good crags that are easily accessible. Sitting on a belay ledge, if your leader is taking an awful long time, that view across Derwentwater with stately Skiddaw towering at its end is one of the best in the Lakes.

**Corvus** (D) - When I was Chancellor of Lancaster University one of the fun things I did was to go out with the Lancaster University Mountaineering Club once a year. All too often it was raining and we'd go up to Raven Crag and climb *Corvus*. The rock is clean, the line excellent and it really is a superb route.

**Troutdale Pinnacle Super Direct** (HVS) - Black Crag is magnificent, standing out at the head of Troutdale, with a fine variety of routes. *Troutdale Pinnacle Superdirect* is a superb direct line with a series of brilliant pitches, the crux being a daunting finger traverse where little fingers are a definite advantage. You can always take easier options by sticking to the old classic meandering *Troutdale Pinnacle* or *Troutdale Pinnacle Direct*, which take the slabby buttress up to where it sneaks off to the right .

**FAVOURITE ROUTES** Chris Bonington ⑤

**Mandrake** (HVS) - Quayfoot Buttress is the ultimate road side crag, just 10 minutes from the National Trust car park, and great clean cut rock when you get there. The little, superbly protected, roof overhang on the crux is a delight and one that I've failed on when feeling weak and off form.

**Gillercombe Buttress** (S) - It's a delightful direct airy route up the crag with a few awkward moves on the penultimate pitch. I had an epic on it when taking my 10 year old son up it and our dog traversed in when we were half way up. I only had a couple of slings which I needed to make a harness for the dog, before making a diagonal scramble over heather clad rock, to bring up Daniel and dog, who would have had a huge pendulum if he had come off.

**Athanor** (E3) - I couldn't resist putting this in because it's the hardest route I have ever led, with my old mate, David Absalom. I'd tried it a couple of times and on the third attempt screwed up the courage to make the moves. It's also a cracking good route.

# Allen Crags

The western slopes of Allen Crags overlooking Grains Gill contain a number of worthwhile crags of good rock. The walk is rewarded with no crowds and some good climbs with tremendous views. The crags are found around two ravines that form a prominent V shape and can be seen from Stockley Bridge.

**Approach:** Follow the path up Grains Gill until you reach a footbridge at NY 235 099; cross the bridge and head directly up to the crags.

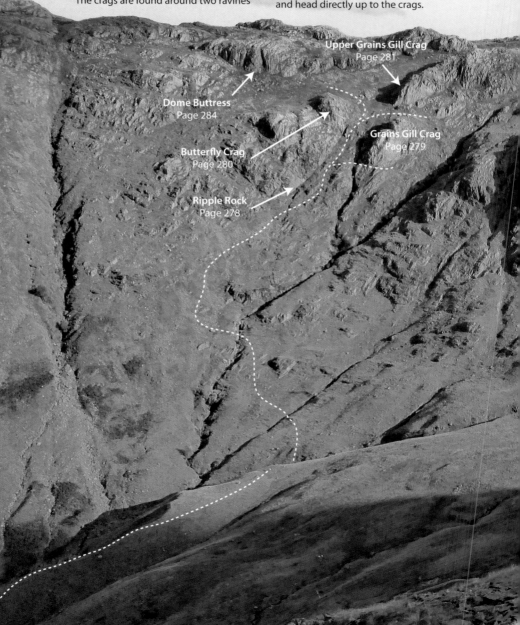

Upper Grains Gill Crag
Page 281

Dome Buttress
Page 284

Grains Gill Crag
Page 279

Butterfly Crag
Page 280

Ripple Rock
Page 278

Rouge Wall
Page 286

of Cracks
e 284

Pink Wall
Page 287

Hanging Stone

Hind Gill

▲ Base Brown

P Seathwaite
600 m

NORTH GULLY WALL

HIND CRAG

Taylorgill Force
(WATERFALL)

GATE

Stockley Bridge

Styhead Gill

Black Waugh

Grains Gill

TAYLOR GILL SLAB

AARON CRAGS

Seathwaite Fell

FOOTBRIDGE

metres

North    0          500         1000

Great Slack

Sprinkling Crags

Allen Gill

FORD

Sprinkling Tarn

Ruddy Gill

RIPPLE ROCK

BUTTERFLY CRAG

GRAINS GILL CRAG

DOME BUTTRESS

UPPER GRAINS GILL CRAG

WALL OF CRACKS

GRAINS GILL
and ALLEN CRAGS

ROUGE WALL

FORDS

PINK WALL

Great End

FORDS

Allen Crags ▲

## Ripple Rock
NY 237 094  ⊝  △ 550m  ⚲ 70 mins

This is the lowest buttress on the hillside, situated just up and left of the bottom of the V formed by the ravines. It is characterised by a series of white water-washed slabs on the left and a fine grey slab on the right.

**Descent:** Move right (looking in) and follow a hidden ramp down to the base (usually wet, care required).

### 1　Placchos Blanco　　26m　VS 4c
BJ Clarke - 19 Jul 2006

Although only the start is technical, this route has a serious feel and is slow to dry. Start at the foot of the water-washed slabs. Climb leftwards to reach a sloping ledge below a steeper section. Overcome the steep wall, step right and move up left into a small sentry box in an overlap. Climb through this and trend right up the final slabs to the top. Small nut belays in the nose above.

### 2　Ripple Shadow　　18m　MVS 4b
BJ Clarke - 19 Jul 2006

A route up the nose just left of the grey slab. Climb carefully up the right side of the hollow flake. Move left and follow the nose to a rock ledge below mossy bulges. Avoid these on the right and finish up easier slabs.

### 3　Ripple Rave　　19m　VS 4c　　★
BJ Clarke - 19 Jul 2006

Quality climbing up the grey slab. Climb the entry wall to reach flat holds. Continue up slightly rightwards to a small ledge system. Follow the diagonal crack on the left, before crossing a shelf rightwards. Pull up the blunt arête and finish up easier slabs.

### 4　Ripple　　18m　VS 4c　　★
T Langhorne - 12 May 2008

More fun. Climb the right side of the grey slab to a blunt flake and ledges. Pull up and right into a niche and finish directly passing an obvious wedged flake.

## Ripple Rock

## Grains Gill Crag
**NY 236 094**   ⊘   ◭ **570m**   ⵌ **75 mins**

This is the lowest crag between the streams that form the V. The first routes start from a grass ledge below the left side of the crag. The rock is excellent and often provides good incut holds.

### 5   Whit's Ridge          50m   D
CR Wilson, TP Loftus – 25 May 1958

Start on a grass ledge under the nose of the left-hand ridge.
1   18m      Make an ascending traverse right, then left to ridge. Continue to a corner and large block belay.
2   22m      Follow the ridge to a large grass terrace and block belay.
3   10m      Ascend the wall above the belay.

### 6   Gable End          30m   VD   ★★
H Beanland, R Smithson – 27 Aug 1987

Start near the left end of the grass ledge. Climb straight up joining a shallow crack at 6m. Continue up in the same line, crossing a slight gangway. At the top of the wall, walk straight across the heathery scoop and ascend the short wall ahead by a narrow crack.

### 7   Low Flyer          30m   MVS 4b   ★
H Beanland, R Smithson – 10 Jul 1987

Bold with well-spaced protection. Climb the slab, past three narrow ledges, and continue up a slight corner until a sloping shelf leads up to the right (marked by a quartz vein). Follow the shelf and traverse right onto a corner ledge. Step left onto the wall above and finish up the slab.

## Grains Gill Crag

| 5 | Whit's Ridge | D | |
|---|---|---|---|
| 6 | Gable End | VD | ★★ |
| 7 | Low Flyer | MVS 4b | ★ |
| 8 | Slow Learner | MVS 4b | ★★ |
| 9 | Late Developer | HVS 5a | ★★ |

### 8   Slow Learner          30m    MVS 4b    ★★
H Beanland, R Smithson – 10 Jul 1987

A fine route with considerable exposure. Bold
with well-spaced protection. Start where a sloping
grassy rake meets the horizontal ledge. Follow a
gangway steeply up to the right until forced onto
the wall on the right. Climb the wall steeply until
a step left leads to the corner ledge of *Low Flyer*.
Finish as for that route.

### 9   Late Developer          30m    HVS 5a    ★★
H Beanland, R Smithson – 14 Aug 1987

The obvious rightward-slanting crack just right
of the centre of the crag. Steep climbing on good
holds, with occasional steps onto its right wall.
When the angle eases and the rough rock near the
top of the crag is reached, climb a short delicate
wall then pull left on small holds to gain access to
the scoop. Finish up the slab bounding the scoop
on the right.

### Butterfly Crag
### NY 238 094  ⊕  ⚠ 600m  🏃 75 mins

Forty five metres left of Grains Gill Crag, and at the
same level, is a crag characterised by a rib on its
right with a butterfly-shaped roof at 1/3 height.
The crag currently holds some suspect blocks.

### 10   Butterfly          18m    HS 4a
BJ Clarke - 12 Sep 2005

A pleasant route that is poorly protected; take care
with some of the blocks. Start from the grass terrace on the left. Traverse right to the rib and follow
it to a sloping ledge below the roof. Avoid the roof
on the left, return to the rib and follow it to the top.

**Butterfly Crag**

10

## Upper Grains Gill Crag
**NY 237 093**   ⊙   ▲ 600m   ⋏ 80 mins

Lying a mere 40m above Grains Gill Crag is a fine-looking buttress of excellent rock with a central groove line (*Gee-Gee*) and slabby ramps on the right.

### 11  Ygrain                16m   HS          ★
BJ Clarke - 17 Jul 2005

Takes the left-hand arête of the buttress with an interesting finish. Follow the arête via a groove to a steep rounded exit.

### 12  Gee-Gee              16m   HS 4b
BJ Clarke - 17 Jul 2005

Start at the shallow corner below the upper open groove. Steep moves up the corner lead to the stacked blocks; move left onto the nose of the buttress from where easy rock leads to the top.

### 13  Whole Grain          20m   HVS 5b     ★★★
P Clarke, T Langhorne, R Tolley, A Dunhill - 9 Sep 2015

An excellent route on superb rock. Start 5m right of *Gee-Gee*. Climb slabby rock trending leftwards before using a good handhold to swing left into a narrow groove. Almost immediately, swing left again into another groove and follow this with difficulty to the top. Photo page 282.

### 14  Ugg                  20m   MVS 4b      ★
BJ Clarke - 17 Jul 2005

A line across and up the rightward trending slabby ramps. Climb the right-hand ramp-line to a steepening. Move up and swing left into a groove and a slab finish.

⚠ A route has been climbed between *Ugg* and *La Kalinda* – **Gilgamesh** (25m HVS 4c). This takes the conspicuous line although it crosses large and suspect cracked blocks and is not recommended.

### 15  La Kalinda           23m   S 4a
BJ Clarke - 19 Jul 2005

Towards the right side of the crag, a corner leads up to mossy overhangs. To its right, a thin crack splits a short steep wall. The climbing is better than it looks. Climb the thin crack (crux) then follow the undercut slab leftwards to its end, where a few moves up a groove lead to a juniper ledge. Follow the slanting ramp on the left, before stepping right and finishing up a slab.

## Upper Grains Gill Crag

Whole Grain HVS (page 281) - Paul Clarke 📷 Richard Tolley

## Dome Buttress
NY 238 093   ⊘   ⚠ 630m   ⚡ 85 mins

Dome Buttress is characterised by a vegetated gully in the centre, flanked by a slabby wall on its left and a deeply-cut chimney a further 15m left. Some loose rock in places

### 16  Marimba Rib     21m   MVS 4b   ★★
BJ Clarke - 19 Aug 2005

Takes the fine rib a few metres left of the deep-cut chimney. Climb the front of the rib (hollow blocks), to reach a good spike at 10m. Make a committing move right onto the arête and finish up the slab above.

### 17  The Dome     23m   VS 4c
BJ Clarke - 19 Aug 2005

A route up the main nose of the buttress. Serious with poor protection. Climb the delicate slab and rib above to reach a steep little wall. Overcome this with a strenuous pull and continue up easier rocks, eventually finishing up the slab of *Gricer's Grooves*.

### 18  Gricer's Grooves     23m   VD   ★★
BJ Clarke - 15 Aug 2005

Nice climbing on rough clean rock. Start 3m left of the vegetated gully at a prominent boulder. Climb a series of ribs and shallow grooves directly, keeping just right of the main nose, to finish up a pleasant slab.

### 19  Locomotion     21m   VD
BJ Clarke - 19 Aug 2005

A pleasant climb up the slabs left of the vegetated gully. Start as for *Gricer's Grooves*. Move up and right past a sapling to reach a shallow groove. Climb this, avoiding the overhang on its left, before stepping back right and following a ramp rightwards. Meander up the slab above to the top.

### 20  Rhythm Stick     18m   S
BJ Clarke - 19 Aug 2005

Two metres right of the vegetated gully is a jagged loose arête. Start one metre further right at a slabby rib. Climb the slabby rib, moving right near the top to avoid a loose overhang.

### 21  Triple Time     20m   HS 4b   ★
BJ Clarke - 19 Jul 2005

Start one metre right of *Rhythm Stick*, below a small V-chimney. Climb the wall and chimney, to finish up a series of delicate slabs and grooves.

## Wall of Cracks
NY 237 092   ⊘   ⚠ 630m   ⚡ 85 mins

About 150m south east (up and right) of Upper Grains Gill Crag there is a steep clean wall split by many cracks.

### 22  Cork Wall     11m   S 4a
BJ Clarke - 16 Jun 2006

Shelving rock followed by cracks through an overlap.

### 23  Champagne Cracks     17m   S 4a   ★
BJ Clarke - 8 Jun 2006

Elegant climbing up the fine wall keeping left of an alcove then a line of thin cracks on the right.

### 24  Wall of Cracks     14m   VD
BJ Clarke - 8 Jun 2006

The crack system just left of the arête.

Derwentwater · Watendlath · Grange · Stonethwaite · Combe Gill · Seathwaite

**Dome Buttress**

**Wall of Cracks**

## Rouge Wall
### NY 237 090 ⊕ ▲ 675m ⚡ 90 mins

This fine little wall of wonderful rough rock lies about 150m south east of Wall of Cracks from which it is clearly visible. All these short routes are worthwhile.

### 25 Lipstick  12m  MVS 4c  ★
BJ Clarke - 2 Aug 2006

Delicate climbing up the rib at the left end of the wall.

### 26 Penwithian Crystal  22m  HVS 5a  ★
BJ Clarke - 8 Aug 2006

A delightful traverse. Follow *Lipstick* to a quartz vein then make a slightly rising traverse rightwards to *Rouge Groove*. Continue to the sloping ledge of *Vin Rouge*; finish up this route.

### 27 Rougemont  9m  E1 5b  ★★
BJ Clarke - 19 Jul 2006

Climb the slab leftwards, cross the small overlap (bold and serious) and finish up the thin seam.

### 28 Rouge Wall  11m  HVS 5a  ★
BJ Clarke - Jul 2006

Bold climbing up the wall past a clean cut ledge to finish on the left.

### 29 Rouge Groove  12m  MVS 4b  ★
BJ Clarke - 17 Jul 2005

Climb the groove past stepped overlaps, cross the top roof and finish up the groove on the right.

### 30 Vin Rouge  10m  HVS 5a  ★
BJ Clarke - 2 Aug 2008

The overlap and thin crack left of the black moss finishing up cracks leading to the right

### 31 Red Mystique  8m  MVS 4b  ★
BJ Clarke - 15 Aug 2005

Short but appealing; delicate moves just right of the arête to finish up small right-slanting ramps.

## Rouge Wall

## Pink Wall
### NY 234 087 ⊖ ▲ 700m ⫷ 100 mins

Three hundred metres north west of the summit of Allen Crags and just before the fellside descends steeply to Grains Gill, lies a slabby reddish-coloured buttress of excellent rough rock, characterised by square-cut roofs at its base. It is about 500m south east of Rouge Wall and plainly visible from the Esk Hause footpath. The buttress can also be approached by Grains Gill then Ruddy Gill path to below Great End.

## Enchainments
### MVS

**Ripple Rock** – *Ripple Rave* (or *Ripple Shadow*); **Grains Gill Crag** - *Slow Learner*; **Upper Gains Gill** – *Ugg* (or *Gee-Gee*); **Wall of Cracks** – *Champagne Cracks*; **Rouge Wall** – *Rouge Groove*.

### All of the VSs
### HVS

**Ripple Rock** – *Ripple Rave*; **Grains Gill Crag** – *Late Developer*; **Upper Gains Gill** – *Whole Grain*; **Rouge Wall** – *Penwithian Crystal*.

| 1 | **Pink Hinterland** | 19m | VS 4c | ★★ |

BJ Clarke - 17 Jul 2005

Offers fine friction climbing on superb rock with spaced protection. Start directly below the lowest roof. Move up and avoid the roof by using the flakes on the right. Move left again and up round the end of the overhang. Continue up the slabby grooves to finish up the quartz-studded arête.

| 2 | **Pink Mischief** | 19m | S 4a | ★ |

BJ Clarke - 17 Jul 2005

Pull over a slight nose using a flake and move up to the corner right of the roofs. Follow this for 3m then step left onto the wall using the prominent handhold. Continue to finish up the quartz-studded arête of *Pink Hinterland*.

Pink Wall

# Aaron Crags

NY 232 105          North and North East    ▲ 500m          🚶 45 mins

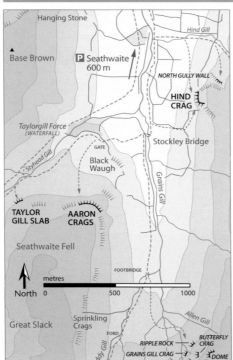

These crags overlook Stockley Bridge from the northern slopes of Seathwaite Fell, offering some good climbing with a remote feel, but without a difficult walk.

**Approach:** From Seathwaite by following the Sty Head Pass path to the hole-in-the-wall gate; shortly after this strike diagonally up left to the crag.

**Descent:** Either by scrambling down to the left, or by continuing up to the top and then down the easy grassy gully on the right.

| 1 | **The Rasp** | 40m | VS 4c | ★★ |
|---|---|---|---|---|

G Oliver, C Mitchell – 16 Jun 1988

Superb friction climbing. On the left side of the crag is an obvious narrow slab bounded by heather.
1    30m 4c   Climb the slab in four sections broken by horizontal cracks. Follow a crack through a bulge to a belay on the left, below the final wall.
2    10m 4b   Climb the wall above.

| 2 | **Maginot Line** | 50m | HVS 5a | ★ |
|---|---|---|---|---|

G Oliver, D Craig – 26 Jun 1989

Well-protected. On the right-hand side of the crag, 20m to the right of the central gully, are two obvious cracks.
1    25m 5a   Climb the right-hand crack. Block belay on the ledge above.
2    25m 4b   Climb the groove on its left then continue up pleasant ribs above.

# Taylor Gill Slab

NY 226 105          North West          450m          45 mins

Easy-angled and superb rock makes it a good place
to take a beginner. This short but pleasant slab
stands 50m above the Sty Head footpath on the
north west flank of Seathwaite Fell, soon after the
path levels out. It is possible to climb anywhere,
with the best lines shown.

| 1 | Side Saddle | 15m | S | |
|---|---|---|---|---|
| 2 | Tracking | 17m | S | ★ |
| 3 | Smear at Sunset | 16m | VD | ★ |
| 4 | Bullet Hole Slab | 16m | VD | |
| 5 | Taylor Made | 15m | VD | ★ |

All the routes - BJ Clarke - 30 Jun 2008.

# Gillercomb

NY 223 124    ⊙ South East    ▲ 480m    ⚹ 45 to 60 mins

Borrowdale's sunny mountain crag towers above the hanging valley of Gillercomb and offers excellent climbing on marvellous rock. It has an easy approach, dries quickly and can be a good choice on a windless and sunny winter's day.

**Approach:** From the top of Honister Pass.

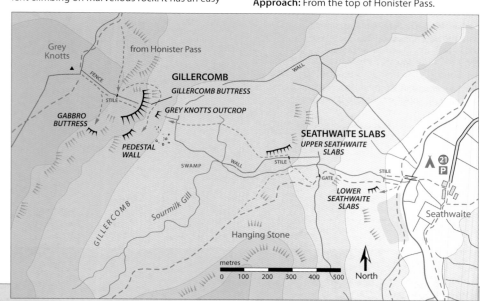

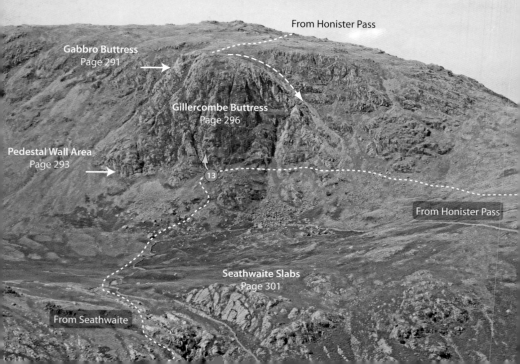

## Gabbro Buttress

This buttress is most easily reached from the top of the crag and provides good climbing on incredibly rough rock; a good place to climb after completing one of the main buttress routes.

**1    Gabbro                47m    VD    ★★**
B Beetham – 14 Apr 1941

Pleasant climbing on brilliant rough rock. Start just left of the toe of the buttress.
1    27m      Gain the top of the pinnacle on the right and go right into a small V-corner; continue up another corner to belay under a large flake on the right.
2    20m      Swing round the flake on the right and continue up the slab.

The next three routes start fro[m] reached by scrambling 8m righ[t] slabby grassy ramp that starts at ded boulder in the scree gully. Alt grassy gully on the right of the but[tress] descended to the same point.

**2    Rough Magic            38m    HS**    ★★
BJ Clarke - 7 Jun 2005

Some bold climbing on flawless rock. Start at some blocks on the grassy ledges.
1    18m      Pull up the steep wall and follow the exposed rib to join *Gabbro* and follow this to the belay at the top of pitch 1.
2    20m 4a   Up the corner then swing right onto the front of the buttress; the bold edge gives good moves. When the angle eases, climb the centre of the buttress to the top.
Photo page 292.

| 1 | Gabbro | VD |
| 2 | Rough Magic | HS 4a |
| 3 | Rough Stuff | MVS 4b |
| 4 | Just Say Non | MVS 4b |

Rough Magic HS (page 291) - Trevor Langhorne 📷 Richard Tolley

| 3 | **Rough Stuff** | 32m | MVS 4b | ★★ |
|---|---|---|---|---|

W Hurford, SJH Reid - 30 May 2005

This excellent pitch starts at a small juniper below a short clean slab. Climb to a small cave and reach the slab above, either by stepping off the block on the left side of the cave, or by the right rib. The former is better but the latter harder at 4c. Continue up the fine slab, move a few metres left and follow clean rock to the top

| 4 | **Just Say Non** | 35m | MVS 4b | ★ |
|---|---|---|---|---|

SJH Reid, W Hurford – 30 May 2005

Takes the slab/groove right of *Rough Stuff*. Climb to below the slab/groove, gain the slab from the right and pad up to a ledge. Climb the wall right of a thin crack and continue up the slab and rib above.

## Pedestal Wall Area

A short steep wall composed of excellent rock giving some very good short steep climbs. Well worth visiting. About 200m left of *Gillercombe Buttress* the wall does suffer from moss growth so some cleaning may be needed. There is a belay block 6m back from the top.

| 5 | **Pedestal Nose** | 25m | MVS 4b | ★ ♂ |
|---|---|---|---|---|

A Dunhill, P Clarke - 29 Sep 2015

Climb the thin crack in the slab then step left onto the nose. Move up and left to a grass ledge from where steep juggy climbing leads past an obvious block to the ledge on the right.

| 6 | **Clara Bow** | 25m | EI 5b | ★★ ♂ |
|---|---|---|---|---|

T Walkington, S Hubball – 11 Jun 1988

Climb the steep right-facing shallow corner and then reach up left to gain another similar corner. Above this, a couple of thin moves lead to easier but still steep climbing to the top.

| 7 | **The Third Man** | 20m | E3 6a | ★★ ♂ |
|---|---|---|---|---|

T Walkington, S Hubball - 10 Jun 1988

Gain a crack just left of *Citizen Kane*. Difficult climbing leads straight up to a large hold at 10m. Move rightwards for 3m, then back left to the top.

| 8 | **Citizen Kane** | 20m | E4 6a | ★★ ♂ |
|---|---|---|---|---|

T Walkington, S Hubball - 8 Jun 1988

A great climb with some good but hidden protection. Climb the right-hand of two short grooves in the centre of the wall (peg on left) and pull over the right side of a small overhang to good holds. Move up to more good holds and step left above the roof (hidden runner slots down and left). Continue up a groove (hidden runner slots down and right), with a pull onto its right rib and a steep finish over the final overhang.

| 9 | **The Wizard of Oz** | 20m | E6 6b F7b | ★★ ♂ |
|---|---|---|---|---|

T Walkington - 20 May 1988

Bold, intricate and lacking substantial gear. Climb the initial bulges onto a ledge and follow a crack on the right. Steady climbing leads to an overlap passed by a hard sequence leading to the obvious vertical slot and a reasonable hold on the left. More hard moves lead up (peg on the right). Step right and up again to a side-pull and salvation.

| 10 | **Andy Warhol** | 20m | HVS 5a | ♂ |
|---|---|---|---|---|

T Walkington, A Cammack - 20 May 1988

Climb the obvious deep groove on the right of the wall to an awkward exit.

294

# Gilercombe Buttress

Gabbro Buttress
Page 291

A

Pedestal Wall

Top of
hidden descent

18
19

Letterbox

5  16

17

Grey Knotts
Outcrop

## Gillercombe Buttress

200m right of Pedestal Wall there is a large gully (**Gillercombe Gully** VD 1913) between steep buttresses; the next route climbs the steep clean rib to the left of the gully.

### 11 Gillercombe Bastion 134m VS 4c
P1 W Peascod, DG Conner, SB Beck, JH Conner - 19 May 1940
P2 & p3 B Beetham – 15 Sep 1938

Delicate and bold climbing up the clean buttress to the left of *Gillercombe Gully*. The first pitch is very good but the upper half gives steep, insecure and thoroughly unpleasant climbing directly above the first belay. With care it is possible to traverse off to the left from the top of p1.

1   54m 4c   Climb into a V-opening at 3m, exit left, then continue rightwards and follow a slab slanting up to the left to a sloping ledge, beside a large block. Gain the slab on the left by bold and difficult moves and continue to a niche high up. Move right and up a short rib to ledges.

2&3 80m   Follow ledges up to the left and around the broad buttress before following stepped walls to the top.

Photo page 299.

### 12 Mad Dogs and Englishmen   195m HVS 5a   ★
SJH Reid, W Hurford - 30 May 2005

Enjoyable climbing up hanging ramps and grooves between *Gillercombe Gully* and *Gillercombe Buttress*; low in the grade. Start just right of Gillercombe Gully at the lowest point of the buttress.

1   30m 4a   Climb slabby rock and move left to below a square recess (as for *Gillercombe Buttress*); follow a ramp-line leftwards to a stance almost in the gully at the point where the ramp-line steepens into a wall.

2   45m 5a   Gain a short corner/crack with difficulty and climb it to the top of a huge flake; pull out right to follow a crack to a slabby recess. Climb out of the recess and up leftwards across slabs and then a clean nose to more slabs. Go up these to a good ledge below a steep corner/crack.

3   40m 4b   Traverse left across a juniper ledge and around the arête. Climb up steeply just left of the arête; when it eases, step right and follow a crack to easier ground. Climb left towards a platform below a slim groove. Belay on another platform just down and right.

4   30m 5a   Climb a clean rib from the top platform to just below the slim groove (good side runner above a juniper bush on the right).

Traverse left under the groove and make a steep and committing pull onto its left rib. Climb up right to regain the groove and follow it to a narrow ledge and block belay.

5   50m   Bold but not difficult. From the block, climb leftwards to a clean buttress, go straight up this and another above on the right. Continue in the same line to finish up a short groove.

### ⑤ 13 Gillercombe Buttress   195 m S   ★★★
HB Lyon, W Woodsend - 28 May 1912
Upper part J Ray, H Harland, GA Solly, G Wilson - 17 May 1921

A justly popular classic on superb quick-drying rock; it has a lovely sunny aspect. Start just right of *Gillercombe Gully* at the lowest point of the buttress.

1   30m   Slabby rock leads to a steepening; move left and pull into a square recess on the right wall of the gully. Climb the recess, then move right past a flake to an upper ramp which leads right to a stance.

2   40m   Move up right and awkwardly traverse left for 7m. Climb easy rock to a steep wall; traverse left across ledges to a platform below an imposing corner/crack

3   20m   Climb the crack then move up right to a stance.

4   40m   Climb a short steep scoop/corner on the right to a large ledge. Scramble up an open corner to a large ledge and wedged flake belay

5   40m   Step left from the flake and climb a difficult groove to a ledge. Continue up slabs, passing a V-groove on the right, to easier ground.

6   25m   Scramble to the top.

### 14 String of Pearls   149m E2 5c   ★★
C Read, G Swainbank - 22 Jul 1996

Good interesting climbing on a direct line up the steepest sections of the main buttress to the right of *Gillercombe Buttress*; the first pitch is rather pokey! Start 8m to the right of *Gillercombe Buttress* at a grass ledge and block thread belay.

1   23m 5c   Enter the short slabby groove above the belay and step left to a rightwards-slanting ramp beneath a steep shallow groove. Climb the groove; pull over the small overlap onto the wall above. Move up, then left to gain and climb a slab, passing a ledge. Continue up the wall above on the left, before moving right to a small ledge below a prominent corner beside an overhang.

2   25m 5a   Climb up onto the corner and ascend it until it is possible to pull up left and continue

directly to a belay below a steep wall.
3    25m 4c   Climb straight up the wall to a notch
and short corner in a darker area of rock. Pull
up the corner then move left and up onto a
ledge. Climb the short steep wall above then
follow a crack in the slab above to a good
ledge and a block belay.
4    27m 4c   Climb the wall behind the belay and
then the easier shallow rib to the final headwall. Move left 3m to belay below a prominent
steep groove, 2m right of the start of p5 of
*Gillercombe Buttress*.
5    24m 5a   Ascend the groove directly and exit
right at the top. Trend right and up the crest
of the buttress on good rough rock to a ledge
and belay.
6    25m        Scramble to the top.

### 15  Moss Wall                      161m E1 5b    ★★
P1 R McHaffie, D Durkin - Aug 1973; FFA A Dunhill - 19 Sep 2015

Climbs the light-coloured clean slab right of the
lower part of *String of Pearls* giving a fine alternative start and making a route of more consistent
grade. Start at the obvious corner 8m left of the
fence.
1    35m 5b   Climb the groove then pull over the
steepening to gain the slab (bold); climb to
a good but hollow flake/jug below a small
overlap. Traverse left using undercuts until it is
possible to climb the wall to a belay at a large
block below some overhangs.
2    25m        Mount the block and move leftwards
to easy ground which is followed to belay below the next steep clean buttress joining *String
of Pearls* at its second belay.

### ⑤ 16  Grey Knotts Face              131m VD     ★★
B Beetham - 18 Jun 1939; p2a A Marr, M Tooke - 1 May 2007;
p2b T Langhorne, J Bradley - 29 May 2007

A character-building mountaineering route with a
traditional squeeeeze; stout climbers will probably
choose one of the two harder options. Start just
left of the fence at the base of the crag.
1    13m        Scramble to a large grass ledge.
2    25m        Climb diagonally right into a corner
and follow it past a square ledge to arrive at
the Letter Box; post yourself through the slot
and wriggle up the cleft to gain the top of the
block. Having regained your composure, move
left and ascend to a large ledge. The Letter
Box can be avoided by either a) climbing the
corner directly above the slot or b) by moving
right from below the slot and then pulling up
a crack on the front face using a wedged flake;
both of these options are harder than the slot
at Severe, but if you don't fit, what choice do

you have?
3    13m        Climb the chimney/crack at the left
of the ledge.
4    20m        Continue up the chimney with a
chockstone to a grass ledge.
5    60m        The continuation of the chimney is
a shallow gully; follow its right rib belaying as
needed.

The easy buttress below the start of *Grey Knotts
Face* is Grey Knotts Outcrop; it provides a nice
grade 2 scramble.

### 17  Rabbit's Trod                   230m M      ★★★
B Beetham – 9 Sep 1943

The longest route on the crag straddles the bound-
ary between scrambling and climbing; either way
it is very enjoyable. Start at the bottom of a long
tongue of easy slabs leading to the right side of an
impressive grey wall. Climb the slabs to a notch in
the arête, below and right of the grey wall. Move
right around the rib and climb the well-marked
break in the short steep wall. Continue up well-
scratched walls, slabs and corners; any difficulties
can normally be avoided. There is an attractive
looking crack near the top which is much harder
than the rest of the route (VD), with a committing
entry and an awkward exit; it is best avoided on
the right. Don't forget to visit the summit!

String of Pearls E2 - Peter Sterling
📷 Laetitia Sterling

Gillercombe Buttress S (page 296) - Richard Tolley    Andy Dunhill

## The Right Wall

High on the right side of the crag there is a stunning steep grey wall which currently offers two outstanding test pieces. Sadly the rest of the right side of the crag, although steep, is coated in an impressive mantle of moss.

### 18 Caution          E8 6c F8a ★★★
D Birkett - 2 Jul 1992

Brilliant fingery climbing. Follow an easy crack on the left-hand side of the crag for 7m, move right along a break (2 pegs; the first is poor) and then climb directly to the top with hard moves to finish.

### 19 Prudence          25m  E7 6b F7a+★★★
P Deady, J McHaffie – 13 Sep 2007

The excellent steep and bold groove and diagonal crack 4m right of *Caution*. The start is more easily approached by abseil allowing a sneak preview, in which case E6 is probably more applicable. Go up the slab to a bilberry ledge. Climb directly (peg) and continue strenuously up the groove, using a large undercut, to a rest (peg). Pull out leftwards onto a flake on the steep headwall and gain the diagonal crack via a hard move into an undercut. Follow the continuously difficult crack to the top; protection is difficult to find and strenuous to place.

### The Seathwaite –          500m  M ★★★
### Gillercomb Enchainment
B Beetham - 1943 - 1952

This great combination of scrambling and very easy climbing links together a series of easy routes to give an expedition from the valley floor to a summit. Many variations are possible; the grade given is for the easiest line.

From Seathwaite Farm head to Lower Seathwaite Slab and climb your chosen route, then walk right to enter the lower section of Sourmilk Gill. Follow the gill keeping clear of the water; in general any slippery or difficult sections can be passed on the right. It is safest to avoid the final cascade of the gill by slabs on the right as the rock is poor. A short walk leads to Upper Seathwaite Slabs and a choice of routes. From the top of the slabs, contour leftwards above the boggy floor of the combe, before walking up to the base of the easy buttress below Gillercomb Crag: Grey Knotts Outcrop. Climb this outcrop and then walk right to below continuous clean slabs, leading up to a prominent grey wall: *Rabbit's Trod*. Climb the slabs to below the right end of the wall; traverse right around the ridge and follow the well-marked line up short walls, slabs and corners. There is a nice-looking crack near the top; this should be avoided on the right as it is much harder than the rest of the scramble, with a committing entry move and difficult moves thereafter. The summit of Brandreth (715m) is a short walk from the end of the scrambling.

# Seathwaite Slabs

These sunny slabs of excellent rock are a great place for introducing newcomers, especially children, to climbing; they are also good venues for a picnic. The classic stream scramble/climb of *Sourmilk Gill* can be used to link the two areas of slabs.

## Lower Seathwaite Slabs
### NY 232 122   ⓨ   ▲ 150m   ⭧ 5 mins

The lower slabs lie just above the valley floor and are composed of clean cut, smooth and compact rock, split by cracks and short corners; the routes are about 8m long. The observant will find some good belay bolts at the top (hint - look low down).

About 30m to the South there are two very easy slabs, which are ideal for very young children.

A further 200m south (left) and 100m higher, there is another rib of superb rock with a short south-facing slab; the routes are 10-12m in length.

| | | |
|---|---|---|
| 7 | Slides | D |
| 8 | Swings | D |
| 9 | Playground | D |

**Lower Seathwaite Slabs**

| | | |
|---|---|---|
| 1 | | VD |
| 2 | | S 4a |
| 3 | | S 4a |
| 4 | | D |
| 5 | | D |
| 6 | Tiny Tot's Ridge | M |

### Sourmilk Gill 270m M ★★

The stream draining Gillercomb forms a series of cascades which give a fun expedition; most children will enjoy the opportunity to get wet (take spare clothes)! All difficulties can be reduced to easy scrambling or increased to D by avoiding or accepting the various challenges. The lower part of the gill forms a series of short steps which lead to an open area below the very prominent waterslide slab. Scramble up the right side of the slabs keeping off the wet black rock which can be slippery. Continue up the line of the stream avoiding difficulties on the right until a cross wall is reached. Above this a series of steps lead to an amphitheatre below the final waterfall which is definitely not scrambling terrain. The rock deteriorates here and it is best to escape either left along a path or, better, right by pleasant grey slabs. The Upper Slabs are visible after a further 100m.

### Upper Seathwaite Slabs
NY 228 123 ⓨ ◮ 375m ⭧ 30 mins

In contrast to the Lower Slabs, these quick-drying slabs of superb rough rock are set at a gentle angle and are covered in small holds, so a lack of reach is not a handicap. The smooth slabs between the easy cracklines give the best climbing; the routes are about 20-25m long with good belays.

## Upper Seathwaite Slabs

| 1 | Yan | D |
| 2 | Tan | D |
| 3 | Tethera | D |
| 4 | Smooth Lethera | M |
| 5 | Pimp | D |

| 6 | Smoot Sethera | M |
| 7 | Lethera | D |
| 8 | Hovera | D |
| 9 | Dovera | D |

The Twa Hummocks South VD (page 239) - Chris Shiels   Richard Tolley

# Borrowdale Bouldering

Borrowdale is home to the most famous boulder in the Lakes – the Bowderstone. Throughout the valley there are a number of fine bouldering venues, the best source for details and downloads is the Lakes Bloc website - www.lakesbloc.com

Here is a taste:

| Jopplety How |||
|---|---|---|
| NY 264 163    ▲ 400m    🏃 20 mins |||
| Problems: 4 | Grades: Font 6c+ – 7a+ ||

A highball wall in a beautiful location. Must do *The Secret Garden* 7a.

**Approach:** From Watendlath follow the path west across the beck and uphill towards Rosthwaite, the wall is on the northern flank of Brund Fell.

http://www.lakesbloc.com/news/news-2011/298-the-secret-garden-a-private-press.html

| The Bowderstone |||
|---|---|---|
| NY 254 164    ▲ 90m    🏃 10 mins |||
| Problems: 50+ | Grades: 6b – 8a ||

The harder you work, the more you'll get out of this amazing venue. The 'Stone' is a popular tourist attraction, so don't be shy! 2000 tons of bouldering perfection with access to the top by a ladder. The East / Ladder Face stays dry in most weather conditions

**Approach:**  From the NT car park follow the well-worn path south to the boulder.

www.lakesbloc.com/guides/bowderstone-guide.pdf

The Secret Garden, Jopplety How - Pete Gunn    📷 Davina Mouat

## Langstrath Boulders

Huge amounts of rock can be found in the valley these being the most well-documented venues.

www.lakesbloc.com/guides/langstrath-guide.pdf

## Blea or Gash Rock
**NY 267 115** 🔺 190m 🚶 35 mins

**Problems: 24**          **Grades: 4 – 7b**

The bouldering circuit near Gash Rock incorporates two small sectors of solid rhyolite blocks and has numerous easier and some very good mid-grade problems. Must do *The Fury* 7b+.

**Approach:** From Stonethwaite follow the track into Langstrath, take the east side of the river to a prominent large boulder, Gash Rock, directly below Sergeant's Crag Slabs.

## Blackmoss Pot (DWS)
**NY 266 113** 🔺 190m 🚶 35 mins

Blackmoss Pot is a popular swimming location with problems taking the wall out of the pot.

**Approach:** From Stonethwaite follow the track into Langstrath and along the east side of the river to Gash Rock. Blackmoss Pot is in a small gorge in the river nearby.

## Cam Crag Boulders or Woof Stones
**NY 263 111** 🔺 300m 🚶 45 mins

**Problems: 15**          **Grades: 4 – 7c**

A lovely spot set on a high platform overlooking Langstrath. An obvious huge boulder, The Pyramid, dominates the scene with three good lines up its south face. Not many problems here so combine with the lower boulders. Must do *Goldfinger* 7c.

**Approach:** From Stonethwaite follow the path into Langstrath, stay on the west side of the river to the start of Cam Crag Ridge.

www.lakesbloc.com/guides/camcrag-guide.pdf

## Sourmilk Boulders
**NY 233 122** 🔺 150m 🚶 10 mins

**Problems: 28+**          **Grades: 5 – 8a+**

Very accessible high-quality area with a large circuit of problems Mark's Boulder. A great location when time is limited. Must do *The Cloud Chamber* 7b+.

**Approach:** From Seathwaite take the path west, over the bridge. The boulders are at the bottom of the path by Sourmilk Gill.

www.lakesbloc.com/crags/north-west/198-giller-combe-a-sour-milk-ghyll.html

## Gillercomb Boulders
**NY 223 124** 🔺 420m 🚶 45 mins

**Problems: 41**          **Grades: 3+ – 7b**

Situated just below Gillercomb Crag, on the finest mountain rhyolite and in a fabulous situation. The problems are spread between the easy to mid-grades, with a limited number of classics offered at the harder end of the spectrum. Must do *Awesome Arête* 6c.

**Approach:** From top of Honister or slog up from Seathwaite by Sourmilk Gill.

www.lakesbloc.com/crags/north-west/198-giller-combe-a-sour-milk-ghyll.html

Gillercomb 📷 Richard Tolley

# Graded List

**E9**
Caution

**E8**
The Ego Has Landed
Bleed in Hell

**E7**
Grievous Bodily Arm
Burn at the Stake
Campaign
The Whipping Post
The Torture Board
Mesrine
Genocide in Cambodia (Extension)
The Codebreaker
Disorderly Conduct
Prudence
The Gymnast
Hock Clock
Inferno
Camouflage
Satan's Little Helper
Alter-Ego
Cambodia
De Quincy

**E6**
Hell's Wall
Footless Horse
The Machinist
Campagnolo
Daylight Robbery
Camikaze
Borrowdale Volcanic

**E5**
Penal Servitude
The Mastercraftsman
Mirage
Professional Direct
The Restraint of Beasts
The Technician
The Bulger
Squashed Racquet
Lucifer
Inclination

**E4**
Cam Crag Crack
Nagasaki Grooves
Wheels of Fire
Inquisition
Dry Gasp
Bitter Oasis
Post Mortem
Grand Alliance
Free Falling

**E3**
The Voyage
Terminal Velocity
Joke
Porcupine
Heaven's Gate
Crime and Punishment
Paint it Black
White Noise
Daedalus
Fear of Flying
Falcon Crag Buttress Route 1
Guillotine
Athanor
Prana
Battering Ram
The Cleft Direct
Not with a Bang
Thumbscrew
Stranger to the Ground
Vertigo

**E2**
Fuel Crisis
Kidnapped
The Niche - Falcon
Tumbleweed By-Pass
The Sting
Traverse of the Frogs
Tumbleweed Connection
Big Foot
Little Nose
Wild Sheep
The Dangler
Cellulite
The Rack - Finger Flake Finish
Bilberry Topping
Pussy Galore
Slab Happy
Widdowmaker
M.G.C.
Loss Adjuster
Ricochet
Plagiarism
True North
Where Eagles Dare
Aphasia
The Grasp
The Go Between
String of Pearls
Boris in Wonderland
The Question
Rack Direct
Bleak How Buttress

**E1**
The Bludgeon
Funeral Way
Supermodel
Aaros
Route 2
Zoar
Interloper
Vortigern
Devil's Wedge
Flaming Fandango
Brown Crag Grooves
Banzai Pipeline
North Buttress
The Crypt Direct
Usurper
Crunchy Frog
Autopsy
Quicksilver
Jaws
Dedication Direct
The Black Icicle
Dedication
Meandering Maggot
Alone in Space
Raindrop
Between the Lines
Praying Mantis
Jubilee Grooves
The Niche - Goat
Mort
City of Love and Ashes
1993
Cholesterol Corner
Holly Tree Crack
Conclusion
D.D.T.
Munich Agreement
PS
Greatend Corner

## HVS
Finale
The Mortician
Brush Off
The Rack
Creeping Jesus
Whole Grain
Illusion
Troutdale Pinnacle Superdirect
Point Blank
Kransic Crack Direct
Delight Maker
The Crypt
Fuel Economy
Lamplighter
The Reiver
Mandrake
Emma Line
Endurance
The Lost Boys
Irony
Bits 'n' Pieces
Evil Kneivel
Lost in Space
Alka Salsa
Terminator 2
Tottering Tortoise
Horizontal Pleasure
Monolith Crack
The Noose
Falconer's Crack
Gemma
Obituary Grooves
Lakeland Cragsman

## VS
Adam
The Coffin
Spinup
Woden's Crack
True Cross
The Shroud
Kransic Crack
Eve
Midge Ridge
Hedera Grooves
Aberration
Clubfoot
Shepherd's Chimney
Brown Slabs Crack
C.D.M.
Fool's Paradise/ Kaleidoscope
Fisher's Folly
Brown Crag Wall
Revelation
Troutdale Pinnacle Direct
Borrowdale Stare
Holly Tree Corner
Pink Hinterland

## MVS
Derision Groove
Crystal Slab
Rough Stuff
Ardus
Woden's Cheek
Ambling Ant
Woden's Face
Adam's Slab

## HS
Rowan Groove
Evening Wall
Chamonix
Rough Magic
Scratch
Son of Oz
Donkey's Ears
Corax
Brown Slabs Scoop
Trod Too Far

## S
Robinson
Woden's Needle
Troutdale Pinnacle
Sergeant Crag Gully
Gillercombe Buttress
Pedestal Wall
Trod Methera
Wimpey Way
Woden Face Direct

## MS
Trod Pimp
Brown Slabs Face

## VD
Brown Slabs Direct
Little Chamonix
Twa Hummocks South
Outside or Face Route
Quayfoot Buttress
Raven Crag Buttress
Grey Knotts Face
Gabbro
Ashness Gill
Raven Crag Gully
Bowderstone Pinnacle
Ullscarf Edge
Trod Tethera

## D
Brown Slabs Arete
Corvus
Brown Slabs
Jackdaw Ridge

## M
Cam Crag Ridge
Seathwaite - Gillercomb Enchainment
Rabbit's Trod

# Chronology

In the late 1800s Borrowdale was seen as a backwater of Lakeland climbing with the main action being based around Wasdale Head, Pillar Rock and in Coniston. The first recorded rock climb was *Walla Crag Gully* (VD -1892) by local explorers the Abraham Brothers who were mainly involved with the lesser crags near Keswick - an interesting book from this period is "Hound and Crag" by Benson which details climbing on Castlehead, just outside Keswick. From this period came three gully climbs: *Mouse Ghyll* (D 1897) above Grange, *Raven Crag Gully* (VD 1893) on Glaramara, and *Sergeant Crag Gully* (S 1893), climbed by C Slingsby, WA Wilson, and OG Jones respectively. There was nothing noteworthy till the years just before The Great War when HB Lyon climbed *Gillercombe Buttress* (S 1912), and F Mallinson and R Mayson of Keswick climbed *Bowderstone Pinnacle* (VD 1914) and *Black Crag Buttress*, better known as *Troutdale Pinnacle*, (S 1914). The photograph of the first ascent of *Troutdale Pinnacle* shows a pronounced pinnacle which has since fallen away.

In the early 1920s B Beetham and CD Frankland made a number of short climbs in the valley, including *Brown Slabs Arête* (D 1922) on Shepherd's Crag. In 1924 AR Thomson of Portinscale, with the Dolomite guide A Dibona, added some pleasant moderates to the list.

### 1925 Great Gable and Borrowdale
HS Gross, AR Thompson

1930 saw H Cooper with J Cameron discover the possibilities of Lining Crag.

### Bentley Beetham

Beetham was a teacher at Barnard Castle School, with a notable interest in natural history and had been on the 1924 expedition to Everest. The school formed The Goldsborough Club, named after a local outcrop, and through this, boys from the school went out to climb and learn about the outdoors with Beetham. In 1926 the Club acquired a lease on a property near Rosthwaite and this became a base for the next 25 years to explore the valley. Beetham surveyed every sizeable crag in the valley, working out well over a hundred routes with a wide range of difficulty and interest. Many pupils were involved in first ascents and more about this fascinating chap is available in the book "Lure of the Mountains" by Michael D Lowes. This exploration continued through the Second World War until,

in 1946, he turned his attention to the hitherto neglected Shepherd's Crag. The close proximity to the road (and the hotels), the quality of the climbs and the beauty of the surroundings made this a favourite climbing location and so it remains.

### 1937 Great Gable, Borrowdale and Buttermere
CJ Astley Cooper, E Wood-Johnson, LH Pollitt

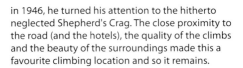

W Peascod and SB Beck broached the formidable defences of Eagle Crag with *Falconer's Crack* (HVS 1946) and *The Great Stair* (MVS 1946). More routes followed such as *Ardus* (HS 1946), *Kransic Crack* (VS 1952) as well as *Eve* (VS 1951) with Peascod accompanied by the likes of V Veevers, GB Fisher and D Oliver.

### 1953 Borrowdale
Bentley Beetham

### Paul Ross

P Greenwood and P Ross entered the scene and started to notch up the grades with *North Buttress* (E1 1954) and *Troutdale Pinnacle Superdirect* (HVS 1954). Greenwood had an enviable collection of first ascents around the Lakes and elsewhere but decided suddenly in 1956 to hang up his climbing shoes and rope. Ross's route - *Post Mortem* (E4 1956) – was a tour de force climbed with P Lockey, who later was one of the founders of Berghaus. Again with Lockey, he climbed *The Bludgeon* (E1 1957) a remarkable and bold achievement as the only protection was a peg at the base of the pinnacle. Ross thought the pinnacle would break away if he put a sling round its top and then were to fall onto it! Ross energetically continued to develop new routes and new crags (Falcon Crags, Eagle Crag, Walla Crag etc.) - always looking out for adventure. He moved to North America and returned in the 1990s and managed more new routes including *Prodigal Son* (E3 1988) on Glaciated Slab and even managed to entice Greenwood out of retirement to climb some new routes before going back to North America for more rock. In 2014 he returned to Keswick still keen to get out onto the rock - he has shunned climbing walls as he is leaving these until he gets "old".

### The Iron Men of Keswick

The style of climbing in the 1950s and 1960s was

generally ground up with no prior inspection or cleaning. Climbing equipment was basic post-war surplus and the nature of the crags, overgrown with vegetation and containing loose rock, often necessitated the use of aid. Critics suggested that excessive aid was being used as direct aid was often reduced on subsequent ascents when the offending nails were reassuringly in place for runners and the routes were much cleaner.

### Mac

In the early 1960s R McHaffie did the first of his many, many routes in the area. *The Niche* (E2 1962) and *Interloper* (E1 1962) with A Liddell were a taste of what was to come. His enthusiasm to develop some crags and routes sometimes got the better of him. Mac was a prolific explorer and source of knowledge and inspiration. Realising he couldn't always climb his finds he would often rope in more proficient climbers to lead him up the routes.

L Brown and S Bradshaw investigated the potential of Goat Crag and climbed the classic *Praying Mantis* (E1 1965). This opened what became "the crag" of the year and signalled the development of arguably the most significant crag in the valley.

**1960 Borrowdale (reprint)**
Bentley Beetham

**1966 Borrowdale**
P Ross, M Thompson

**1968 Borrowdale**
P Nunn, O Woolcock

In the 1970s there was a sea-change in climbing - improved protection, the advent of indoor climbing walls, which played a large part in developing the 'steel claw' necessary for today's top performers, but also routine pre-cleaning and checking of routes by abseil. This led to more climbers being active at the highest standard. One climber took this further, approaching his climbing as a professional athlete would, his legacy is in Borrowdale.

### Pete Livesey

P Livesey appeared in Borrowdale climbing *Raindrop* (E1) with J Sheard in 1973. 1974 was a vintage year when Livesey's free ascents of *Footless Crow*

(E6 1974), *Bitter Oasis* (E4 1974), *Nagasaki Grooves* (E4 1974) and *Dry Gasp* (E4 1974). These routes immediately gained a reputation for excellence and extreme difficulty leaving all gasping in his wake – but not for long...

Local climbers, with fingers stiffened on Armathwaite sandstone, had been steadily eliminating aid from old routes and indulging in new ones. Notable amongst these were J Lamb, S Clegg, P Botterill and P Whillance. The profile of Eagle Crag throws out an adventurous challenge. Botterill and Clegg free climbed *The Cleft Direct* (E3 1974) then added *Autopsy* (E1 1974). August saw a summer heat wave continue, and taking advantage of a bone dry Eagle Crag, Whillance and Clegg climbed *Where Eagles Dare* (E2 1974) and shortly after Clegg with Botterill climbed *Verdict* (E4 1974) - both excellent routes on the very steep central section of the crag.

April 1975 saw the grand unveiling of Greatend Crag after a winter of secret activity unearthing routes: *Greatend Grooves* (E1 1975), *Earthstrip* (HVS 1975) *Greatend Corner* (E1 1975) - and later *Banzai Pipeline* (E1 1977) and *No Holds Barred* (E2 1982) - from D Nicol, C Downer, I Conway, D Hellier and R Wilson. Routes that proved to be very popular at the time that sadly nature has now reclaimed.

On Goat Crag the creation of *Tumbleweed Connection* (E2 1976) by P Botterill and D Rawcliffe was seen as a 'last problem' on the crag where Clegg and Botterill also completed *The Voyage* (E3 1976), a rising traverse of Great Buttress. Meanwhile, across the valley on Black Crag, R Matheson and E Cleasby were cementing the bold *Grand Alliance* (E4 1976); P Gomersall worked out a route to its right *Prana* (E3 1977) and to the left of *Vertigo* Livesey was busy putting up *Tristar* (E4 1977).

Watendlath Valley is a quiet backwater however J Lamb realised the potential with a trio of excellent routes on Reecastle Crag - *White Noise* (E3 1978), a reminder of the verbal banter from the second - Ray MacHaffie, *Thumbscrew* (E3 1978) and *Guillotine* (E3 1978).

**1978 Borrowdale**
S Clark

Spectacular routes often come from free climbing old aid climbs - the formidable *Hell's Wall* (E6 1979) on Bowder Crag eventually fell to R Fawcett after a concerted effort and *Exclamation* (E6 1979), a ridiculously steep route on Shepherd's Crag, was free-climbed by R and M Berzins. The South Lakes team of R Graham and D Lyle added a first pitch to *The Mirage Finish* of *Bitter Oasis*, which when combined gave *Mirage* (E5 1981) an excellent route and a fitting companion to the adjacent *Footless Crow*.

Action continued with the difficult, and potentially dangerous, *Devil's Alternative* (E6 1981) on Shepherd's Crag by Lamb and Whillance, the excellent *Penal Servitude* (E5 1981) on Reecastle Crag by D Armstrong and Whillance and three good hard routes being added to Bowder Crag – *Lucifer* (E5 1981), *Heaven's Gate* (E3 1981) and *The Bulger* (E5 1981)

July and August saw nine new lines added to Eagle Crag by Whillance and Armstrong, updating the development of 1975 and transforming it into a 'modern' crag, with some fine and difficult routes. The roofs at the left end of Shepherd's Crag also received some attention - these included *Parting Shot* (E5 1981) by Lamb immediately prior to his departure for Australia, where a climbing accident robbed us of a great guy and the Lakes of one of its most active climbers.

P Kirton, living in the adjacent climbing hut, set to work cleaning the Bowder Stone and together with J Moffatt produced a number of extremely difficult boulder problems on the steep north side of this block. On a day off, Moffatt snatched the soaring arête to the left of *Hell's Wall* to produce the bold and technical *De Quincy* (E7 1981).

During the closing months of 1982 a development started which was to dominate 1984 – the excavation of Bleak How Buttress and Grange Crags. D Hellier sparked off interest in Bleak How while the Keswick team of C Downer, C Bacon, the irrepressible R McHaffie and P Taylor led the enterprise on Grange Crags. They then also turned their attention to Bleak How and unearthed yet more hidden gems of all grades. An Eden Valley group, with R Kenyon, C Dale, C King and R Curley keen to get in on the action, were banished to the nearby Upper Heron Crag and produced several good climbs. The development of these crags resulted in the largest number of new routes being climbed in Borrowdale in any single year. Many proved worthwhile, with a number of easier grade routes. The development of Grange Crag created a national furore regarding the amount of gardening undertaken; many of the routes have reverted back to nature. At the top end Chris Sowden and Martin Berzins stole the impressive line on Reecastle to the right of *Executioner*, then to 'rub salt in the wounds' called it *Daylight Robbery* (E6 1984).

## 1986 Borrowdale
D Armstrong, RJ Kenyon

The new guide included 250 new climbs and in the previous eight years ethics and protection had changed radically. Yo-yoing had become an almost accepted method of ascending the hardest routes together with top-roping and 'dogging' becoming more widespread. 'Micro nuts', 'Rocks' and 'Friends', together with the latest Fire 'sticky boots' became the norm, thus helping to make routes safer and, coupled with the increase in training, made the ascent of more difficult and sustained routes possible.

Strength and above all stamina were becoming essential for one to succeed on the hardest routes and training programmes to increase fitness were being extended and improved every year by the leading activists in an attempt to stay ahead. Alas, virgin rock is a finite material which is becoming more and more scarce each year, particularly on the lower crags. Eliminates and variations continued to be added and walking was an accepted part of the climbing day with the more remote crags being inspected. The acceptable route length had reduced over the years however the quality and sustained nature of the climb became more important than footage.

P Ingham was to be found battling up a previously top roped problem on Shepherd's Crag to give the desperate *Geronimo* (E7 1986). The dedication, preparation and skill required to produce new routes of this period were typified by routes climbed by Ingham and P Cornforth on Reecastle Crag - including *Breach of the Peace* (E7 1987) and *The Torture Board* (E7 1987) - as walls previously thought unclimbable eventually fell to those with the 'eye of faith' and the necessary talent. A Jones was active, finding two hard routes on the neglected Long Band Crag with *Mastercraftsman* (E5 1987) and *The Apprentice* (E4 1987) then Ingham, with I Cummins, pushed up the grades in the valley with *Inferno* (E7 1988) on Hell's Wall.

The development of smaller crags continued and in particular T Walkington accepted the hint given in the 1986 guide and blitzed the steep Pedestal Wall area of Gillercombe Buttress to produce several excellent short routes. At about the same time R Smith and J Earl climbed three short but hard routes on the left-hand side of Greatend Crag.

On Goat Crag N Foster and M Berzins climbed *Trojan Horse* (E6 1990) up the centre of Great Buttress – a stunning, impressive line! D Booth launched out right from Hell's Wall to produce the rarely repeated *Mesrine* (E7 1990) and A Jones and R Graham seduced *Vicky* (E5 1990).

## 1990 Borrowdale
### RJ Kenyon

D Booth climbed *Bodycount* (E6 1991) on the easily accessible Car Park Crag and M Lowerson and team developed the area on the right of Walla Crag. However these were never popular and now, like so much else, have become buried under grass and ivy.

During the summer of 1991 the indefatigable McHaffie developed Sergeant's Crag Slabs in Langstrath destined to become arguably the best slab climbing venue in the district, particularly for the middle grade climber, with delightful climbing on perfect rock. Not one to miss out on the action C Downer paid a visit with McHaffie and produced the now uber-classic *Aphasia* (E2 1992).

Young D Birkett made his mark on the valley with a series of outstanding hard routes – *The Whipping Post* (E7 1992), *Bleed in Hell* (E8 1992), *Hellish* (E8 1992) and *Caution* (E9 1992) - some of the most difficult routes in Britain and taking some years to be repeated. At Reecastle Crag, P Cornforth was also responsible for the powerful and technical *Burn at the Stake* (E7 1992) and with his brother G Cornforth - *Camikaze* (E6 1994) at Cam Crag.

Local lad A Hocking, after honing his skills on the recently opened Keswick Climbing Wall, added the Direct Start to *Penal Servitude* (E5 1994). P Cornforth and M Greenbank climbed the bold and difficult *Rock Lobster* (E7 1996) and *Borrowdale Volcanic* (E6 1996) on Long Crag, or should it be Long Walk Crag?

The poor summers of 1997 and 1998 saw less activity and only a few worthwhile routes. Amongst these were Hocking's *Disorderly Conduct* (E7 1997) at Reecastle Crag; D Booth and I Turnbull's *Satan's Little Helper* (E7 1998) on Black Wall Langstrath (another long walk) and Martin Dale's *Camouflage* (E7 1998) on Cam Crags. Hocking (then aged only 17) astounded some by his solo of *Ker Plunk* (E5 6a).

During the late 90s Keswick was home to talented young climbers. Adam Hocking made the long awaited second ascent of *Bleed in Hell* (E8) in 1999, and, his schoolmate and son of Mac, James McHaffie, on-sighted *Camouflage* (E7) the following year. At that time the near future surely looked healthy for climbing in the valley.

## 2000 Borrowdale
### GR Baum, AP Hewison

"There are undoubtedly good lines still unclimbed but who can really predict what developments the next few years will bring? Whatever happens, the valley will always continue to offer the climber first class routes at all grades in the unique and beautiful setting that is Borrowdale."

Eagle Crag came once again to the forefront. Guns of *Navarone* (E6 2000), involving 6c climbing protected by a skyhook runner, was the work of A Hocking and A Wilson, accompanied by Borrowdale veteran C Downer. *The Ego Has Landed* (E8 2000), pioneered by J McHaffie and S Wood was possibly the most outrageous ascent in the valley at that time, with total commitment being required to tackle unprotected and sustained 6b climbing. C Downer enlisted W Hunter to lead *The Restraint of Beasts* (E5 2000) a climb that attracted several repeats. At that time Hocking, Hunter and McHaffie were all still in their teens!

The new century came in with the "young guns" ready for action. A Hocking and J McHaffie unlocked Black Wall and climbed *The Codebreaker* (E7 2001). Foot and mouth descended on the area which had a devastating effect on the livestock and farmers but also tourism and rock climbing during 2001. Once unleashed however Caf and Hock made the long walk to Long Crag to climb *Hock Clock* (E7 2002).

Eagle Crag has a dramatic profile which used to attract a fair number of climbers however with a scary approach, bird restrictions, changes in fashion and spreading vegetation it rarely sees visitors – J McHaffie with A Hocking and A Wilson weren't put off and raised the difficulty and seriousness levels with *Alter-Ego* (E7 2003) a brilliant bold pitch and *Awkward Logistics* (E8 2003) which tackles the awesome overhanging wall right of *Post Mortem*.

A crucial undercut had disappeared and *Footless Crow* became harder and more serious. C Hope linked the lower section with *Trojan Horse* to produce the superb *Footless Horse* (E6 2003).

Steel Knotts is often overlooked, despite facing south-east with good clean rock, but drew interest with a number of new routes in particular *Samurai Jack* (E4 2004) by T Suddaby and C Reid. Long Band Crag faces west and throws out challenges with its hard lines. C Hope and A Wilson forced *The Machinist* (E6 2003) then D Booth and J Robertson enjoyed some mutual pleasure seeking with *Sado-Masochist* (E6 2004) as well as *Professional Direct* (E5 2004).

BJ Clarke tends to make guidebook writers quake. He has moved to various parts of Britain and given the area the "Barry Clarke Treatment," hoovering all crags, some rarely visited by other climbers, to produce masses of new routes. 2005 to 2008 was Borrowdale's turn with development of crags such as Grains Gill; Allen Crag; Dove's Nest Slabs; Taylor Gill Slabs, Dessert Crag and many more; there are some real crackers in his tally of new routes. R Graham and P Graham climbed *Prana Right-Hand* (E2 2007) a straightened out version of the old Ross route *The Lastest*, on Black Crag. Upping the ante somewhat, on Gillercomb, P Deady and J McHaffie climbed *Prudence* (E7 2007) about the same time as D McLeod completed the second ascent of the adjacent *Caution* (E8) fifteen years after its first ascent.

M Przygrodzki was a quiet chap finding and painstakingly creating new hard lines around the valley, often close to existing routes, but still dramatic – with in particular *Islands in a Deep Blue Ocean* (E5 2011) and *Edge of Trust* (E7 2012) both at Shepherd's Crag – sadly Mike died in October 2012. Langstrath still held secrets – C Fisher and J Surman climbed the short but sustained *Frozen in Exile* (E5 2008) on Apex Buttress at Cam Crag - but more was to follow on the Lower Crag with *Cam-pagnolo* (E6 2009) from cycling fit K Phizacklea and C Matheson and *Campaign* (E7 2011), *Cambodia* (E7 2012) and *The Genocide Extension* (E7 2012) from A Hocking (and friends) making Cam Crag into one of the best hard crags in the Lakes.

Back down the valley at Long Band Crag, Hock went space walking with M Norbury to produce *The Gymnast* (E7 2012). New, and often good, routes are still to be found in the valley and not always at the harder grades – D Bodecott and D Absalom climbed the superb *The Borrowdale Stare* (VS 2014) by the North Gully Wall of Hind Crag and at Steel Knotts *Loss Adjustor* (E2 2013) and *Terminal Velocity* (E3 2013) from the Grahams and *Lost in Space* (HVS 2014) from the Kenyons are worthy additions - but you have to look for them and need some imagination.

Today there is a dedicated local gang of climbers – the King Kong Wall was opened in October 2014 and there is a special bouldering wall for Hock and Co. Caff has moved away but Paul Ross is still about in the valley. As new climbers appear will they continue to push the grades at trad, will they have fun and boulder, or be content clipping bolts at Bramcrag Quarry – there will probably be a mix and climbers will continue to develop and enjoy climbing in Borrowdale at whatever grade or style.

Ron Kenyon
February 2016

Combe Gill & Seathwaite from Watendlath    Richard Tolley

# Archived Crags

Many of the crags that have been explored in the past have not become enduringly popular. The clean valley air and warm humid climate of the Lakes ensures that, with no passage of feet, these crags quickly become vegetated. Here is a list of those crags that have recorded routes yet are not included in this edition.

| | GR | ⊕ | ▲ | 🏃 min | Grades | Routes | Height | Notes |
|---|---|---|---|---|---|---|---|---|
| Castle Head Outcrops | 369 227 | SW | 130 | 10 | VD - E2 | 7 | 15m | Short walk and short climbs. Dolerite. Great viewpoint. |
| Castle Head Quarry | 272 227 | E | 100 | 10 | E1 - E5 | 3 | 20m | Serious, intimidating, unstable and not recommended. |
| Rakefoot Buttress | 277 236 | W | 300 | 20 | VS - E2 | 16 | 20m | Fractured appearance. Difficult belays. Great views. |
| Walla Crag | 274 212 | NW | 250 | 20 | VD - E5 | 33 | 40m | Airy and vegetated - a clutch of harder climbs and a ** HVS. |
| Powterhowe Buttress | 274 178 | W | 300 | 15 | E4 | 1 | 15m | Very small. One route. |
| Caffell Side Crag | 269 175 | E | 260 | 5 | HVS - E2 | 8 | 25m | Slaty with some dubious holds. Difficult protection. |
| Torquemada Buttress | 268 177 | E | 300 | 10 | VS - HVS | 2 | 35m | Small dirty crag. |
| Brown Dodd | 268 178 | E/NE | 300 | 15 | S - E1 | 10 | 40m | Overhanging wall. Dirty and lichenous. |
| Cat Ghyll Bluffs | 268 196 | W | 170 | 5 | VD - E4 | 23 | 70m | Short upper tier, longer lower; suspect rock. |
| Surprise View Buttress | 268 192 | W | 170 | 10 | VS - E2 | 10 | 40m | Unstable with poor loose rock. |
| Lodore Crag | 265 187 | E | 120 | 10 | HVS - E3 | 3 | 80m | Extremely vegetated. |
| Ladder Brow Crag | 262 181 | W | 140 | 10 | VD - E3 | 14 | 20m | Clean looking wall but loose rock. Ants! |
| Green Bank Crag | 262 181 | W | 140 | 15 | S - E2 | 8 | 30m | N and S crags. S crag can be sheltered. |
| Aard Crag | 261 169 | E | 250 | 20 | VS - E5 | 6 | 10m | Small and clean. |
| Grange Crags | 258 177 | NW | 150 | 5 | S - E3 | 40 | 35m | Mostly poor routes. Three good E2s. Access problems. |
| King's How | 257 168 | NW | 270 | 15 | HVS - E2 | 3 | 40m | Generally broken crag. |
| Bowderstone Quarry | 253 167 | Var | 110 | 5 | S - E3 | 6 | 15m | Unstable quarry, some bolts. |
| Cave Quarry | 254 168 | SW | 120 | 10 | F6a - F6c+ | 2 | 15m | Insignificant. |
| Yew Crag | 264 153 | W | 250 | 15 | M - E1 | 7 | 45m | Mossy slab. |
| How's Crag | 250 160 | E | 195 | 25 | VD - E6 | 10 | 40m | Generally vegetated. |
| Mac's Wall | 249 163 | NW | 150 | 25 | S - E3 | 11 | 15m | Short wall. |
| Waterslide Slab | 254 158 | SE | 150 | 25 | S-VS | 4 | 10m | Not worth the effort. |
| Millican's Buttress | 252 159 | NE | 160 | 25 | MVS - E6 | 17 | 25m | Steep. Near Millican Dalton's Cave. |
| Knitting Needle Gully Wall | 245 165 | NNE | 325 | 30 | VS - HVS | 10 | 80m | Neglected and vegetated. Some good routes if clean. |
| Nitting Haws | 247 168 | NE-SE | 160 | 15+ | S-E6 | 11 | 25m | Broken and generally unappealing. |
| Blea Crag | 238 172 | NE | 420 | 45 | D - MVS | 5 | 45m | Dank. |
| Cat Bells Quarry | 248 197 | N | 150 | 1 | | | 10m | A few top rope problems. |
| Plum Buttress | 267 141 | W | 360 | 25 | S - VS | 2 | 30m | Broken. |
| Heron Crag | 263 143 | SW | 200 | 20 | S - VS | 6 | 25m | Poor climbing. |
| Alisongrass Crag | 265 129 | NE | 340 | 25 | HS - HVS | 3 | 20m | Vegetated. |
| Stanger Gill Crag | 265 128 | NE | 310 | 25 | VS | 2 | 30m | Vegetated and best avoided. |
| Bull Crag | 266 131 | W | 170 | 35 | VS | 2 | 35m | Low lying slab handy for Stonethwaite campers. |
| Paper Crag | 260 136 | NE | 220 | 30 | E1 - E6 | 6 | 30m | Obvious and steep but overgrown. |
| Buck How Outcrops | 257 132 | W | 170 | 15 | D 0 HVS | 18 | 30m | Easy access. Apparently superb rock under the vegetation. |
| Coombe Door Crag | 252 109 | NE-N | 650 | 80 | D - VS | 17 | 20m | Broken and gloomy. |
| Thornythwaite Knotts | 248 119 | E | 330 | 30 | VS - E3 | 3 | 40m | Very vegetated. |
| Capell Crag | 242 122 | W | 360 | 10 | D | 1 | 140m | Broken and vegetated. |
| Dessert Crag | 227 094 | SW | 610 | 75 | S - HVS | 9 | 15m | Good rock broken by ledges. |
| Strawberry Buttress & Base Brown Tors | 228 112 / 227 113 | S | 450 | 45 - 60 | VD - HVS | 32 | < 20m | Awful approach, short above steep broken ground. |
| Upper Seathwaite Walls | 234 123 | E | 310 | 30 | VD - E2 | 12 | 8m | Very short, some suspect rock. |
| Dub Crag | 229 113 | SE | 390 | 40 | S - VS | 3 | 9m | Not worth the walk. |
| Black Waugh Crag | 233 107 | NE | 200 | 35 | VD - E2 | 4 | 35m | Often damp. |
| Hanging Stone | 228 119 | NE | 470 | 35 | VS - E2 | 6 | 25m | Slaty and loose. |

# Mountain Accidents

### Basic First-Aid

Safety First - Are you safe? Check – then make the Casualty safe... this may mean moving them.

**A**irway – open

**B**reathing – look, feel and listen. Only start basic support if, the casualty is unconscious; you know what you are doing; and you can continue until help arrives.

**C**irculation – stop any bleeding; elevate and direct pressure help.

**D**isabled – due to head or spinal injuries.
Check responsiveness.
Don't move them, unless in danger.
Immobilise fractured limbs.

**H**ypothermia – keep them warm and dry.

Wear a helmet; carry a map, compass, torch and whistle.

Keswick Mountain Rescue Team above Force Crag    Rob Grange

# Index